Celebrating Women in American History

Volume V
Modern Feminist Movement and Contemporary Issues
1961 to the Present

Celebrating Women in American History

Volume V
Modern Feminist Movement and Contemporary Issues
1961 to the Present

Elizabeth Rholetter Purdy
GENERAL EDITOR

Facts On File
An imprint of Infobase Publishing

Celebrating Women in American History: Volume V: Modern Feminist
Movement and Contemporary Issues 1961 to the Present
Copyright © 2011 by Infobase Publishing

All rights reserved. No part of this book may be reproduced or utilized in any form or by
any means, electronic or mechanical, including photocopying,
recording, or by any information storage or retrieval systems, without
permission in writing from the publisher. For information contact:

Facts On File, Inc.
An Imprint of Infobase Publishing
132 West 31st Street
New York NY 10001

Library of Congress Cataloging-in-Publication Data

Celebrating women in American history / Elizabeth Rholetter Purdy,
general editor. — 1st ed.
   v. ; cm.
  Includes bibliographical references and index.
  Contents: v. 1. Colonization, revolution, and the New Republic
beginnings to 1860 — v. 2. Industrialization and political activism,
1861 to 1899 — v. 3. The Progressive Era and Great Depression
1900 to 1937 — v. 4. Expanding social roles and
postwar activism 1938 to 1960 — v. 5. Modern Feminist
Movement and contemporary issues 1961-Present.
  ISBN 978-0-8160-7879-0 (v. 1 : hc : alk. paper) — ISBN
978-0-8160-7880-6 (v. 2 : hc : alk. paper) — ISBN 978-0-8160-7881-3 (v.
3 : hc : alk. paper) —ISBN 978-0-8160-7882-0 (v. 4 : hc : alk. paper)
— ISBN 978-0-8160-7883-7 (v. 5 : hc : alk. paper) — ISBN
 978-0-8160-7878-3 (5-volume set) 1. Women—United
States—History—Juvenile literature. 2. Women—United
States—Biography—Juvenile literature. 3. Women—United States--Social
life and customs—Juvenile literature. I. Purdy, Elizabeth Rholetter.
  HQ1410.C45 2010
  305.40973—dc22
                            2010012695

Facts On File books are available at special discounts when purchased in bulk quantities
for businesses, associations, institutions, or sales promotions. Please call our Special Sales
Department at (212) 967-8800 or (800) 322-8755.

You can find Facts On File on the World Wide Web at
http://www.factsonfile.com

Excerpts included herewith have been reprinted by permission of the copyright holders;
the author has made every effort to contact copyright holders. The publishers will be glad
to rectify, in future editions, any errors or ommissions brought to their notice.

Text Design and Composition by Golson Media
Cover printed by Sheridan Books, Ann Arbor, Mich.
Book printed and bound by Sheridan Books, Ann Arbor, Mich.
Date printed: January 2011
Printed in the United States of America

11 10 9 8 7 6 5 4 3 2 1   This book is printed on acid-free paper.

CONTENTS

Volume V

Modern Feminist Movement and Contemporary Issues

1961 to the Present

PREFACE	vii
1 INTRODUCTION	1
2 WOMEN IN SOCIETY	21
3 WOMEN'S HEALTH	41
4 WOMEN'S EDUCATION	59
5 WOMEN IN POLITICS	77
6 WOMEN IN SCIENCE AND MEDICINE	97
7 WOMEN IN THE ARTS AND LITERATURE	115
8 WOMEN IN BUSINESS	133
9 WOMEN IN ENTERTAINMENT AND SPORTS	151
10 WOMEN AND FAMILY	169
INDEX	187

PREFACE

FOR CENTURIES, AMERICAN women were assigned only a minor role in chronicling and participating in the history of life in the United States. Because it operated on the fringes of scholarly society, women's history was constantly undervalued. The history of women was generally told within the context of domesticity even though many women were involved in the same pursuits as males. From a practical perspective, women's history was perceived only as being preserved in letters and diaries, and through feminine arts such as quilting and needlework.

By the mid-19th century, a handful of women had launched a campaign to ensure that women be made aware of their own history, demanding that society recognize the contributions of women at all stages of historical development. Elizabeth Cady Stanton and Susan B. Anthony, leaders of the battle for woman suffrage, placed themselves at the forefront of this campaign by beginning work on a history of the woman suffrage movement. Published between 1881 and 1922 by Stanton, Anthony, Matilda Joslyn Gage, and Ida Husted Harper, the six volumes of *History of Woman Suffrage* became a standing testimony to the significance of women's history and activism and to the impact of women on American politics and society.

Despite these efforts of female scholars and activists, male historians continued to ignore women's history, propagating the notion that women's contributions were insignificant by excluding any mention of women from standard textbooks on American history. Education of females became one of the most significant factors in calling scholarly and public attention to the importance of women's lives. Literacy rates had been low for both sexes during colonial times, but the years leading up to the American Revolution called for a more politically aware citizenry. In the past, girls had been educated at home or in "dame schools" where they were taught the basics of reading and writing along with deportment and other "feminine skills" such as dancing and needlework. Some wealthy families had sent their daughters to British-inspired boarding schools that were designed to fit their students to take up the roles assigned to women of good breeding. During the late 18th century, however, in response to the necessity of expanding the rhetoric of the American Revolution and promoting the tenets of democracy, goals for educating females were redefined. Female seminaries opened up around the United States. There were also limited opportunities for women in higher education. Mount Holyoke opened in Massachusetts in 1837, and Vassar College was founded in New York in 1861. These expanded educational opportunities for women created an environment in which women's lives and history began to be reexamined.

In Europe, salons were transforming expectations of the roles of women in society by gathering the wealthy, political, literary, and philosophical together at the homes of noted women who exercised considerable influence over decision makers and those engaged in the various arts. In the United States, salons were distinctly political. Writers such as Anne Bradstreet, Mercy Otis Warren, Abigail Adams, and Elizabeth Graeme invited the notables of American society to their homes for heated discussions on the issues of the day. During her husband's years as president of the United States, Martha Washington held regular Friday evening drawing rooms for the nation's political elite. Throughout the 19th century, life experiences for women of all classes underwent massive changes. As early as 1830, women's publications began calling public attention to women's contributions to history. Godey's *Lady's Book* regularly offered profiles of significant women. In 1848 Elizabeth Fries Lummis Ellet published *The Women of the American Revolution* in two volumes. Three years later Harriet Beecher Stowe declared a war of her own with the publication of *Uncle Tom's Cabin*, which resulted in an upsurge in abolitionist sentiment outside the South.

The 20th century proved to be a watershed for American women. When women answered the call to service during World War I, it proved that females were capable of breaking down gender barriers to participate in the public sphere while continuing to care for their families. After the war, the government issued a public thank you to those women who had served "beyond their capabilities" and encouraged women to return to hearth and home. In response to their efforts during the war, the long battle for woman suffrage culminated with ratification of the Nineteenth Amendment in 1920. Many female activists believed the battle for women's rights had been won, and the surge of activism dwindled. However, some women, including birth control pioneer Margaret Sanger, continued to call attention to the need for a well-articulated women's rights agenda. In 1933 historian Mary Beard edited *America through Women's Eyes*, offering documentary proof of the significance of women's history. During the 1940s World War II forever changed the ways in which women's roles were perceived, and the history of women began to be considered more germane to the chronicle of American history as a whole. In 1949 in *The Second Sex*, French existentialist writer Simone de Beauvoir suggested that the cause of women's omission from history had been a result of the fact that throughout history women had been defined entirely in reference to man, causing man to be considered the "absolute" and woman to be defined as "the Other."

In the 1960s American society experienced major social upheavals that served to redefine the fabric of the lives of women, resulting in a constantly expanding body of scholarship on the ways in which American women had participated in history in both the public and private spheres, simultaneously opening up a new dialogue about how women's experiences of history are distinctly different than those of males. Women's history of the 1970s focused on what feminist historian Gerda Lerner identifies as "compensatory history," the conscious effort of historians to include women in American history by identifying the impact of particular women and their activities. In response to charges that both activists and historians had focused only on the experiences and contributions of white, middle-class women, historians of the following decades began examining women's lives and history across boundaries of race, class, ethnicity, and sexual orientation.

The National Women's History Project (NWHP) was founded in 1980 in Santa Rosa, California, through the efforts of Molly Murphy MacGregor, Mary Ruthsdotter, Maria Cuevas, Paula Hammett, and Bette Morgan to call public attention to the history of American women. That same year, NWHP was instrumental in President Jimmy Carter's recognition of March as Women's History Month. The first women's studies program was established at Sarah Lawrence College in 1974, precipitating a rush to rectify the omission of women's history and issues from college and university curricula. As a result, by the 1980s, women's history courses were being taught throughout the United States. Both female and male scholars began publishing a plethora of biographies of American women from all walks of life, offering new explanations of the ways in which lives of ordinary women at work and at home had been instrumental in shaping America.

The *Celebrating Women in American History* series is intended as a supplement to the existing body of research on women's history. The series is divided into five volumes that reflect the historical development of American history according to major events, trends, and movements. By examining women's rights and roles within the context of the domestic realm and through female participation in the fields of health, education, politics, science, the arts, business, and entertainment, the series demonstrates how ordinary women lived out their lives from the beginning of American history to the present day and recognizes particular women who paved the way for the transformation of women's roles and lives through political and social activism, military and community service, and employment in jobs that varied from the mundane to the exotic.

VOLUME V: MODERN FEMINIST MOVEMENT AND CONTEMPORARY ISSUES: 1961 TO THE PRESENT

John F. Kennedy entered the White House in January 1961, as the second youngest president in American history. Accompanied by his beautiful wife Jacqueline and daughter Caroline, and later by his son "John John," Kennedy introduced Americans to a more youthful, vigorous style of politics. That same year, he created the President's Commission on the Status of Women to examine the position of women in American society and to make recommendations for improving their status. Following the release of *To Kill a Mockingbird* in 1961, Harper Lee became the first American female writer to win a Pulitzer Prize for Literature in 19 years and opened a new debate on issues of race. The following year, Rachel Carson's *Silent Spring* gave new life to the environmentalist movement. In 1962 Martha Griffiths (D-MI) became the first woman ever to serve on the powerful Ways and Means Committee in the House of Representatives. As the civil rights movement gained momentum, African-American women, including Daisy Bates and Fannie Lou Hamer, were at the forefront of the battle.

Betty Friedan published *The Feminine Mystique* in 1963, and Americans began discussing "the problem that has no name." Feminists responded to the debate by launching the contemporary women's movement under the leadership of Friedan, Gloria Steinem, and Robin Morgan and establishing the National Organization for Women. Reproductive rights took center stage in the 1960s. At mid-decade, in *Griswold v. Connecticut*, the Supreme Court determined that the right of married couples to obtain birth control was grounded in a right to privacy. A surge in incidences of babies born with birth defects as the result of a German measles outbreak and of mothers' being exposed to the European tranquilizer thalidomide led to a reexamination of laws governing access to abortion. Feminists held consciousness-raising meetings throughout the United States to teach women about themselves, their bodies, and their rights. When sex was included as a protected class in Title VII of the Civil Rights Act of 1964, it provided legitimacy for the feminist agenda that included equal pay for equal work, control over reproduction, and increased access to child care, education, health care, and job opportunities.

In 1970, the publication of Kate Millett's *Sexual Politics* reframed the debate on women's rights. Feminists of the 1970s continued the battle for women's rights, and more women were elected to political office at all levels, including African-American Congresswomen Shirley Chisholm (D-NY) and Barbara

Jordan (D-TX). The National Women's Political Caucus was founded in 1971, and the Congresswomen's Caucus was established in 1977. On the sports scene, Billie Jean King became the first female tennis player to earn more than $100,000 in a single year. On September 23, 1973, King became an American legend when she defeated male tennis champion Bobby Riggs in three televised matches. Title X of the Women's Education Act opened up new avenues for females by stating that all schools receiving federal funds were required to provide equal access to sports activities, vocational studies, and math and science. The most acrimonious debate of the decade centered on the abortion issue after the Supreme Court determined in *Roe v. Wade* (1973) that access to abortions was a constitutional right based on a right to privacy. Despite the swing toward conservatism with the election of Ronald Reagan, feminists continued to push for reforms in the 1980s, and EMILY's List was founded in 1985 as a means of providing funding for pro-choice candidates. The Congresswomen's Caucus changed its name to the Congressional Caucus for Women's Issues and invited men into its ranks. The U.S. Post Office launched a campaign to recognize women's contributions to history, issuing a series of stamps depicting noted American women. Sandra Day O'Connor became the first woman to serve on the Supreme Court, and Geraldine Ferraro became the first woman to run for vice president on a major party ticket.

The 1990s ushered in what feminist writer Susan Faludi called a "backlash" against the gains American women had made during the previous decades. The issues of abortion, violence against women, sexual harassment, and the glass ceiling dominated the feminist agenda. During the Gulf War, women answered the call to service in staggering numbers. The dawn of the 21st century brought even more changes to women's lives as females continued to break down barriers in all fields, and Nancy Pelosi (D-CA) became the first female speaker of the House of Representatives. The election of 2008 further shattered centuries-old traditions when African-American Barack Obama was elected president. During the presidential campaign, former First Lady Hillary Clinton had become the first female to be considered a major contender for the White House, and Sarah Palin had become the first Republican woman to run for vice president on a major ticket.

ELIZABETH RHOLETTER PURDY
GENERAL EDITOR

CHAPTER 1

Introduction

THE 1960s AND 1970s ushered in a period of shifting social mores in the United States, and the lives of women were forever changed as a rejuvenated civil rights movement and the birth of the second wave of the women's movement redefined what it meant to be an American. Various minority groups began to demand a voice, and such diverse groups as students, Native Americans, Chicanos, gays, environmentalists, animal rights activists, and pro-life activists joined the protest movement. With the election of Ronald Reagan in 1980, the United States pulled to the right politically, but neither Reagan nor his successor George H.W. Bush were able to undo all of the liberal reforms of the 1960s and 1970s.

The latter part of the 20th century was also characterized in large part by technological advances that included the home computer, the internet, cell phones, cable and satellite television, video gaming, digital video recorders, mp3 players, and home theater systems that made the world smaller and changed the way Americans lived their daily lives. Unprecedented advances in medical technology expanded life spans, even as lifestyles made Americans more susceptible to certain medical conditions such as heart disease.

Because the second wave of the women's movement had helped to break so many barriers for women, females of the late 20th and early 21st centuries were able to take advantage of unprecedented opportunities in the vari-

The day the Florida House of Representatives was to take up the equal rights amendment resolution in 1973, a woman and her daughter were up early to wave a sign at passing motorists.

ous fields of technology and advance them further. The number of women attending graduate schools surpassed that of males, and diverse student bodies on all college campuses became more representative of the general population than they had in the past. Older women began returning to school to pursue new degrees or to complete degrees they had set aside during marriage and motherhood. Women also earned degrees in fields that had once been closed to them. The gap in wages between males and females was narrowed, but not closed, and women continued the difficult task of trying to balance their lives as career women with their roles as wives and mothers.

THE KENNEDY AND JOHNSON ADMINISTRATIONS

In the 1960s, the women's movement, which had begun with the Seneca Falls Convention in 1848, finally came to fruition as part of a massive social revolution. Although many changes occurred only incrementally over the following decades, they did serve to bring the country closer to emphasizing that all people were assumed to have been created equal. As the first year of the decade drew to a close, Democrat John F. Kennedy won one of the closest presidential elections in American history to become the second-youngest American president. Kennedy and his wife Jacqueline (Jackie) brought youth and vigor to the White House and were extremely popular. John Kennedy began his presidency with a call to action, advising Americans to "ask not what your country can do for you—ask what you can do for your country." Because of Kennedy's youth and idealism and the mood of hope and rejuvenation that swept the country, his administration was nicknamed Camelot. It was only later that the public learned about Kennedy's chronic medical issues and rumors of extramarital affairs.

Kennedy aided developing third world countries through programs such as the Peace Corps and the Alliance for Progress. He continued the arms race and challenged the Soviet Union to a space race to land a man on the moon. He also traveled to Berlin to protest Soviet construction of the Berlin Wall, which prevented East German refugees from escaping into non-communist West Berlin. The Kennedy Administration was defined by two key cold war crises involving Cuba: the 1961 Bay of Pigs Invasion and the 1962 Cuban Missile Crisis. The Bay of Pigs Invasion had been planned by the Eisenhower Administration, but Kennedy chose not to provide air cover for the U.S.-trained Cuban exiles who conducted the invasion. When the Cuban people did not rise up to join them, the exiles were quickly killed or captured. The failure was a major public embarrassment for Kennedy, but he accepted responsibility for the fiasco.

The following year, Kennedy learned that the Soviet Union was building missile sites on the island and transferring ballistic missiles there, aiming them at the United States. Kennedy instituted a naval blockade around Cuba. The crisis was ultimately resolved when the United States agreed not to invade Cuba, and secretly pledged to remove nuclear weapons from Turkey in exchange for the Soviets permanently removing nuclear weapons from Cuba.

By the fall of 1963, Kennedy had helped to raise public consciousness about issues of both gender and race. On the morning of November 22, he was assassinated while riding on a motorcade through downtown Dallas, Texas. Officially, assassin Lee Harvey Oswald shot Kennedy by firing from the fifth floor window of the Texas School Book Depository. Various conspiracy theories raged for decades, and many people refused to accept the official explanation. The assassination led to a sense of lost innocence among Americans that was never regained, and many Americans forever remembered where they were when they heard the news of the president's death. Some historians designate the Kennedy assassination as the symbolic point at which the relative peace of the 1950s and early 1960s came to an abrupt end.

President Kennedy inspects missiles at the Boca Chica Station in Florida in November 1962, shortly after the Cuban Missile Crisis had ended.

When Vice President Lyndon Johnson assumed the presidency after Kennedy's assassination, he

Lawrence E. Spivak and Secretary of Housing and Urban Development Patricia Roberts Harris take to the microphones on NBC's Meet the Press *television program in 1971. Jimmy Carter appointed Harris and three other women to cabinet positions, the most of any president up to that time.*

pledged to enact the programs Kennedy had left unfinished. Johnson's implementation of the Great Society and his War on Poverty created the biggest expansion of federal government authority since Franklin Roosevelt's New Deal of the 1930s. Johnson's programs included increased federal funding of education, job training, and housing; the Head Start program to prepare preschoolers from poor families for school; urban renewal; conservation; and federally-funded health care for the poor and the elderly through Medicaid and Medicare.

The grassroots civil rights movement that became a national phenomenon in the 1950s continued into the 1960s as African Americans battled ongoing discrimination, segregation, poverty, and the loss of civil rights. Although African Americans were guaranteed the right to vote in the Fifteenth Amendment, many southern states blocked them from voting. Without that political voice, African Americans were limited in their ability to precipitate change. Under the leadership of Dr. Martin Luther King Jr. and groups such as the Southern Christian Leadership Conference, African-American women such as Rosa Parks, Daisy Bates, and Fannie Lou Hamer joined in protest marches and demonstrations. Civil rights activists included both black and white women, as did the Freedom Riders and participants in sit-ins who challenged segregation and pushed for an end to Jim Crow laws in the south. King electrified the country when he delivered his *I Have A Dream* speech to a crowd

Women in Presidential Cabinets

Before 1972, only two women had ever served in a presidential cabinet. The first was Democrat Frances Perkins, who was appointed by Franklin D. Roosevelt as the secretary of Labor in 1933. Two decades later, Republican Dwight D. Eisenhower chose Oveta Culp Hobby to head the newly created Department of Health, Education, and Welfare. Between 1933 and 2009, 40 women—23 Democrats and 17 Republicans—served in 45 cabinet-level positions in 10 separate presidential administrations.

Appointments of women to cabinet-level positions began to increase in the 1960s and 1970s. Anne Armstrong served as presidential counsel to both Richard Nixon and Gerald Ford in the 1970s. Ford appointed Carla Anderson Hills as his secretary of Housing and Urban Development. Jimmy Carter appointed four women to cabinet positions: Patricia Harris, secretary of Housing and Urban Development; Juanita Kreps, secretary of Commerce; Shirley Hufstedler, secretary of Education; and Patricia Harris, secretary of Health and Human Services. Ronald Reagan also appointed four: Jeane Kirkpatrick, United Nations ambassador; Margaret Heckler, secretary of Health and Human Services; Elizabeth Dole, secretary of Transportation; and Ann Dore McLaughlin, secretary of Labor. Dole also served as secretary of Labor under George H.W. Bush. She was succeeded by Lynn Martin in 1991. Barbara H. Franklin served as secretary of Commerce under Bush.

Democrat Bill Clinton chose 14 women in his cabinet: Janet Reno, the first female attorney general; Madeleine Albright, the first female secretary of State; Hazel O'Leary, secretary of Energy; Donna Shalala, secretary of Health and Human Services; Alexis Herman, secretary of Labor; Carol Browner, Environmental Protection Agency; Alice Rivlin, Office of Management and Budget; Laura D'Andrea Tyson, Council of Economic Advisors (1993–95) and National Economic Council (1995–96); Janet Yellen, Council of Economic Advisors; Ada Alvarez, Small Business Administration; Charlene Barshefsky, U.S. trade representative; and Janice Lachance, director of Personnel Management.

Republican George W. Bush appointed eight women to key positions. Condoleezza Rice became the second female secretary of State in 2005. Other Bush appointees included Elaine Chao, secretary of Labor; Ann Veneman, secretary of Agriculture; Gale Norton, secretary of Interior; Mary Peters, secretary of Transportation; Margaret Spellings, secretary of Education; Christine Todd Whitman, Environmental Protection Agency; and Susan Schwab, U.S. trade representative. Initially, Democrat Barack Obama chose seven women to serve in cabinet-level positions: former First Lady Hillary Clinton, secretary of State; Hilda Solis, secretary of Labor; Kathleen Sebelius, secretary of Health and Human Services; Janet A. Napolitano, secretary of Homeland Security; Christina Romer, chair of the Council of Economic Advisors; Lisa P. Jackson, Environmental Protection Agency; and Susan Rice, United Nations ambassador.

of hundreds of thousands of people in Washington, D.C., on August 28, 1963. The Johnson Administration passed several key pieces of legislation, including the Civil Rights Act of 1964, which ended many forms of legal discrimination and created the Equal Employment Opportunity Commission (EEOC); and the Voting Rights Act of 1965, which allowed the federal government to oversee voters registration in areas with historic patterns of discrimination.

NEW FORMS OF ACTIVISM

In response to the publication of several books, ranging from Betty Friedan's *The Feminine Mystique* (1963) to Erica Jong's *Fear of Flying* (1973), women continued their long struggle for equality during the 1960s and 1970s, and the second wave of the women's liberation movement gave new meaning to the word feminism. In the workplace, women sought equal pay for equal work, access to traditionally male occupations, and an end to the glass ceiling, an informal practice that prevented women from rising to the top tiers of professions. Legally, women sought more equitable divorce laws, more stringent rape laws, an end to violence against women, and control over their own reproduction. They also sought to overcome the traditional feminine ideal of beauty and the belief that happiness could only be achieved through marriage and family. Some feminists wore pants and comfortable clothing, shunned makeup, did not shave, protested beauty pageants, kept their maiden names, and used the title Ms. rather than Mrs. or Miss. Activists such as Gloria Steinem and Betty Friedan formed the National Organization for Women (NOW) to serve as a focal point of the movement.

Other minorities, such as Native Americans and Mexican Americans, also fought for equality during the turbulent 1960s. Native Americans, both on and off reservations, faced poverty, high unemployment, high alcoholism and suicide rates, and discrimination. Native-American activists battled to improve these conditions while seeking the return of lost tribal lands, more control of tribal governments, the reburial of remains exhibited in museums, and fishing and timber rights. The militant group American Indian Movement (AIM) staged sieges of symbolic sites such as Alcatraz Island off the coast of San Francisco, California, and Wounded Knee, South Dakota, site of a U.S. Army massacre of women and children in 1890. Activists such as Wilma Mankiller fought the discrimination of women within the Native-American community and mistreatment of Native Americans in the greater society. By 1985, Mankiller had become the principal chief of the Cherokee Nation. The Chicano Movement sought to instill Mexican-American cultural pride and precipitate an end to poverty, discrimination, and segregation. Cesar Chavez gained national attention by founding the National Farm Workers Association to improve migrant farm worker rights. Chicano women decided to create the Comisión Femenil Mexicana Nacional because they felt that males within the movement were not addressing their particular needs. Gays and lesbians also fought for their rights

The march during the Poor People's Campaign event in Washington, D.C., on June 18, 1968, wrapped up a three-week event run by the nation's poor as well as by Ralph Abernathy, who led the movement in the wake of Martin Luther King's death.

in the 1970s and later. Phyllis Lyon and Del Martin, for instance, were instrumental in forcing NOW to add lesbian rights to the feminist agenda.

The tumultuous 1960s were also characterized by the rise of the youth-driven counterculture and growing activism on college campuses. The counterculture came mainly from young, middle-class Americans who warned, "Don't trust anyone over 30." Former Harvard professor Timothy Leary used LSD and encouraged his followers to "turn on, tune in, and drop out." Folk and rock music became forms of protest, and a sexual revolution encouraged free love and an end to sexual repression. The most famous element of the counterculture were the hippies, who protested mainstream society through their appearance, including jeans, long hair and beards, flowers, beads, peace symbols, and bright clothing.

THE VIETNAM ERA

Arguably the most protracted protests of the period were those surrounding the Vietnam War. The United States had become involved in events in Southeast Asia and Vietnam in the post–World War II period in order to help activists who were fighting for independence from colonial rule. The country was divided into North and South Vietnam in 1954, and when communist leader Ho Chi Minh of North Vietnam allied himself with the Soviet Union, the United States began providing aid to South Vietnam to ensure that it did not

Family and Medical Leave Act

In 1993, with the full support of President Bill Clinton, the Congressional Caucus for Women's Issues promoted the passage of the Family and Medical Leave Act (FMLA), which recognized that mothers perform dual roles in society and encouraged fathers to share parenting responsibilities. The act provided for up to 12 weeks of unpaid leave for eligible employees without threatening job security to care for newborns and newly adopted children, or a seriously ill family member, and in cases of personal ill health:

The Family and Medical Leave Act (FMLA) provides a means for employees to balance their work and family responsibilities by taking unpaid leave for certain reasons. The Act is intended to promote the stability and economic security of families as well as the nation's interest in preserving the integrity of families. The FMLA applies to any employer in the private sector who engages in commerce, or in any industry or activity affecting commerce, and who has 50 or more employees each working day during at least 20 calendar weeks in the current or preceding calendar year. The law covers all public agencies (state and local governments) and local education agencies (schools, whether public or private). These employers do not need to meet the 50-employee test. Title II of FMLA covers most federal employees who are subject to regulations issued by the Office of Personnel Management. To be eligible for FMLA, an individual must be employed by a covered employer and work at a site within 75 miles of which that employer employs at least 50 people; have worked at least 12 months (which do not have to be consecutive) for the employer; and have worked at least 1,250 hours during the 12 months immediately before the date FMLA leave begins. The FMLA provides an entitlement of up to 12 weeks of job-protected, unpaid leave during any 12-month period.

The authors of the bill identified six major factors that had provided the impetus for FMLA:

Section 2601, Congress finds that:

The number of single-parent households and two-parent households in which the single parent or both parents work is increasing significantly.

It is important for the development of children and the family unit that fathers and mothers be able to participate in early childrearing and the care of family members who have serious health conditions.

The lack of employment policies to accommodate working parents can force individuals to choose between job security and parenting.

There is inadequate job security for employees who have serious health conditions that prevent them from working for temporary periods.

Due to the nature of the roles of men and women in our society, the primary responsibility for family caretaking often falls on women, and such responsibility affects the working lives of women more than it affects the working lives of men.

fall to communism. A 1964 incident in the Gulf of Tonkin provided President Johnson with the impetus he needed to escalate the war. Although Americans initially supported U.S. involvement in Vietnam, it came to be viewed as a politician's war that gave no thought to human costs. As cover-ups and atrocities came to light, support for the war declined, and activists demanded that it end. On March 31, 1968, President Johnson gave a televised speech in which he proclaimed that he would not seek or accept the Democratic Party's nomination heading into the 1968 presidential election.

As the United States approached the presidential election, more and more Americans were alarmed at the direction in which the country was headed, feeling that society had become an out-of-control chaos of protest movements and violent incidents. The 1968 assassination of Martin Luther King Jr. only added to the turmoil, sparking race riots in over 100 cities, including Washington, D.C. Republican presidential candidate Richard Nixon and his running mate, Spiro Agnew, campaigned on a theme of restoring America to law and order and engineering peace with honor in Vietnam. Nixon claimed he spoke for the "great quiet forgotten majority" of the American people. The campaign was marred by a nationally televised violent clash between antiwar protesters and police outside the Democratic Party convention in Chicago and the assassination of Democratic frontrunner Robert Kennedy in June. The Republicans won the election with the help of southern Democrats who were still smarting over the success of the civil rights movement.

One of Nixon's first priorities was the gradual withdrawal of U.S. involvement in Vietnam, a process known as Vietnamization. Nixon was unwilling to simply abandon South Vietnam. Instead, he escalated the war by launching bombing raids on neighboring Cambodia and Laos. His actions accelerated antiwar protests on college campuses, including the 1971 incident at Kent State University in Ohio in which a clash between students and National Guard troops left four students dead. In 1973, Congress withdrew funding for the Vietnam War, and American troops began to withdraw. When North Vietnam took over South Vietnam in 1975, American television

Members of the National Women's Political Caucus demonstrate against the Vietnam War in 1972.

broadcast images of Vietnamese desperately jumping onto the last departing American helicopters.

President Nixon's main interest lay in foreign affairs. In addition to Vietnam, he was concerned with easing the tensions of the cold war, opening Soviet markets to U.S. businesses, and placing limits on the nuclear arms race. Results of détente included a Nuclear Nonproliferation Treaty and the Strategic Arms Limitation Treaty (SALT I). One of Nixon's biggest achievements was his extension of diplomatic recognition to the People's Republic of China for the first time since it had become communist in the late 1940s. Domestically, Nixon was a moderate conservative who sought to decrease the size and authority of the federal government. He had a mixed record on women's rights and civil rights.

Nixon enjoyed high approval ratings and won his reelection bid in 1972. Afterward, *Washington Post* reporters Bob Woodward and Carl Bernstein broke the story of a cover-up involving high administration officials following the break-in of the Democratic National Headquarters at the Watergate Hotel in 1972. As Nixon's role in the cover-up became clear and as the activities of his Committee to Reelect the President (CREP) came to light, Nixon was forced to resign, becoming the first president in American history to do so. Gerald Ford, who had recently been appointed vice president after the forced resignation of Spiro Agnew, assumed the presidency. Ford's credibility was almost immediately damaged by his unpopular pardon of Nixon, who had been named an "unindicted coconspirator" in the Watergate scandal, and by economic problems and ongoing battles with Congress. Georgian Jimmy Carter was elected to the presidency in 1976 as a Washington outsider. Many Americans continued to be cynical about politics as the legacy of the Watergate scandal lingered.

THE POST-WATERGATE ERA
Like Gerald Ford, Jimmy Carter frequently battled with Congress over legislative issues. Carter was also confronted with growing economic troubles, including periodic recessions, growing federal budget deficits, an unfavorable balance of trade, and the development of stagflation, a combination of high interest rates and high inflation. Under Carter's leadership, environmental issues also became a major political issue, with the president supporting research into alternative energy and conservation of existing resources. Partly because of pressure from First Lady Rosalynn Carter and several feminists on his White House staff, and partly because of his own strong belief in human rights, Carter was supportive of women's issues.

The liberal Carter Administration negotiated the controversial Panama Canal Treaty of 1977 wherein the United States agreed to surrender control of the Panama Canal in 2000 as stipulated by a previous agreement. Carter achieved his greatest success with the 1979 negotiation of the Camp David

President Jimmy Carter dances with First Lady Rosalynn Carter at a White House Congressional Ball in Washington, D.C., in 1978. Rosalynn Carter sat in on cabinet meetings, at the invitation of President Carter, and was also a strong supporter of the Equal Rights Amendment.

Accords, a peace agreement between Egypt and Israel. He faced his greatest challenge in 1979 when a revolution in Iran replaced the shah, a strong American ally, with Ayatollah Khomeini, a strong opponent of the United States. When Carter allowed the exiled shah to enter the United States for medical treatment, anti-American forces reacted by seizing the American Embassy in Iran on November 4, 1979. The hostages were held for more than 400 days. As a slap in the face to Carter, they were released only after Ronald Reagan was sworn in as president at noon on January 20, 1981.

The election of Ronald Reagan, a former Hollywood actor and popular governor of California, returned the Republicans to the White House. Reagan's conservative agenda included a reduction in the size of the federal government and deregulation of many businesses. His aggressive budget was characterized by cuts to some social programs as well as tax cuts, where the share for the bottom 50 percent of taxpayers dropped from 7.5 percent in 1981 to 5.7 percent in 1988, while the income tax burden of the wealthiest taxpayers increased from 48 percent to 57.2 percent, with most of the poor exempted from the individual income tax. His power base included the Conservatives and Christians who sought a return to traditional American values. Reaganomics was predicated on four major areas: reducing the growth of government spending, reducing marginal tax rates on income, scaling back government regulations, and reducing inflation by controlling the growth of the money supply. Results were mixed and controversial. The national debt soared, the Iran-Contra scandal proliferated, and the reduction in money growth initiated by the Federal Reserve in 1979 sparked a major recession. However, both the unemployment and inflation rate declined significantly by 1988, and the U.S. economy had experienced the longest peacetime expansion ever. Reagan's personal popularity was largely untouched, earning him the nickname of the Teflon President.

The Reagan Administration experienced the escalation of the Cold War in his first term, when he famously called the Soviet Union the "evil empire," and oversaw the end of the Cold War in his second term in response to the efforts of moderate Soviet leader Mikhail Gorbachev and his policies of *perestroika* (economic restructuring) and *glasnost* (freedom of thought), which led to the collapse of communism. In 1989, the Berlin Wall was torn down and Germany reunified in 1990. The Commonwealth of Independent States replaced the Soviet Union in 1992, leading then President George Bush to proclaim that a New World Order now existed.

The end of Reagan's second term had been marked by the Iran-Contra scandal, which involved the Reagan administration's trading arms to Iran in exchange for hostages and using proceeds from the arms sales to fund the activities of the Sandinistas in Nicaragua, despite congressional bans on such activities. The ensuing coverup finally damaged Reagan's reputation and wrecked havoc among key Reagan political advisers. Despite the realities of the military chain of command, Colonel Oliver North was designated as the engineer of the affair. Many people saw him as a scapegoat, rather than an instigator.

Vice President George Bush was elected in 1988 in what some consider to be a lackluster presidential campaign that saw many voters staying home on Election Day. Significant events of his administration included the 1989 invasion of Panama and capture of General Manuel Noriega as part of an ongoing federal government war on illegal drug smuggling and rising rates of illegal drug use within the country. The United States also played a leading role in the 1991 Persian Gulf War after Iraqi leader Saddam Hussein invaded Kuwait, a strong American ally and an oil-producing nation. United Nations forces, led by U.S. General Norman Schwarzkopf, quickly defeated the Iraqi army and liberated Kuwait, although they did not pursue Hussein as ardently as did the George W. Bush administration after September 11, 2001.

In response to Bush's continued support for overturning certain liberal reforms of the 1960s and 1970s and in view of a number of Supreme Court decisions limiting civil rights, Congress passed the Civil Rights Act of 1991, reaffirming the Civil Rights Act of 1964. Because of an unfulfilled campaign promise not to raise taxes, an ailing economy, and a general lack of approval of his policies, Bush lost the election of 1992 to Bill Clinton, the Democratic governor of Arkansas.

Hillary Rodham Clinton

Hillary Rodham Clinton is unique among women in American history. She is the only former first lady to ever serve in a presidential cabinet, to be elected to the U.S. Senate, or to be a viable candidate for president. Many people know her as the author of *It Takes a Village, and Other Lessons Children Teach Us* (1996). Clinton won a Grammy for her audio recording of the book the following year. Following in the steps of Eleanor Roosevelt and Rosalyn Carter, Hillary Clinton was an activist first lady. She and her husband Bill had attended Yale Law School together in the 1970s, and he was well aware of her intelligence and her drive. Instead of returning to her native Chicago, Hillary Rodham followed Clinton to his home state of Arkansas in 1974 and began teaching at the Arkansas School of Law. She and Clinton were married the following year. In 1977, the same year she joined the Rose Law Firm, President Jimmy Carter appointed her to the board of the Legal Services Corporation. The following year, she became first lady of Arkansas when her husband was elected governor. She dropped the Rodham from her official name because some of her husband's constituents saw it as too modern and too feminist.

Her new position gave Clinton the clout she needed to improve the lives of children, a special passion for her. She chaired the state Education Standards Committee and co-founded the Arkansas Advocates for Children and Families. She also served on the boards of the Arkansas Children's Hospital and the Children's Defense Fund. During Bill Clinton's campaign for president in 1992, his wife was criticized for not being fashionable enough and for spending too much on a haircut. When she received complaints about her husband's oft-repeated claim that the voters would get two for one if they elected him, as well as accusations that Bill Clinton was funneling money through her law firm for state business, she retorted, "I suppose I could have stayed home and baked cookies and had teas, but what I decided to do was to fulfill my profession which I entered before my husband was in public life." Although Clinton went on to say that feminism meant the right to choose work, home, or both, she was accused of making fun of traditional women. After she stood by her husband when he was forced to admit to sexual relations with a White House intern and when he was impeached, she was both admired and criticized.

As first lady, Hillary Clinton unsuccessfully led the aggressive campaign to overhaul the American health care system. She was more successful in promoting children's rights, and became a key figure in the global women's rights movement due to her participation in the Beijing Conference on Women in 1995. In the Senate, Clinton served on the Armed Services Committee; the Education, Labor and Pensions Committee; the Environment and Public Works Committee; the Budget Committee, and the Select Committee on Aging. As first lady, Hillary Clinton traveled to 80 countries and met with scores of world leaders. That experience prepared her well for her role as secretary of State under Barack Obama, to whom she had lost the Democratic primary in 2008.

ENTER THE BABY BOOMERS

When Bill Clinton won the presidency in 1992, he became the third youngest president in American history and the first of the baby boomer generation to attain that office. During his two terms in office, Clinton oversaw the passage of the Family and Medical Leave Act, which provided employees with unpaid leave to care for newborns, newly adopted children, and ailing family members; the Brady Bill, which provided a five-day waiting period for the purchase of handguns; and the 1993 North American Free Trade Agreement (NAFTA), which extended an earlier agreement between the United States and Canada to include Mexico. Despite concentrated effort, Clinton failed to institute a system of universal health care coverage. The widely publicized reports of scandals such as Whitewater and Travelgate, which ended in the suicide of Clinton's personal lawyer in 1993; and long-term affairs and liaisons with women tainted the successes of his presidency. Two Arkansas state troopers claimed to have facilitated affairs with dozens of women, and newspapers publicized accounts of his extramarital relationship with Gennifer Flowers as well as numerous other women. Eventually, Clinton became the target of repeated efforts to force him out of office and was impeached in the House of Representatives, allegedly for lying about his relations with White House intern Monica Lewinsky. The Senate refused to remove him from office, and his popularity was undiminished among the general public.

President Bill Clinton and First Lady Hillary Rodham Clinton during the Presidential Inaugural Parade in 1997. The couple stayed married despite widespread scandal due to President Clinton's extramarital affairs, and he dodged frequent accusations of abuses of power to be elected to a second term.

During the 1996 campaign and at the Democratic Convention, Hillary Clinton addressed the administration's score card on children's and women's issues. Throughout the campaign and as first lady she was a significant political force in her own right, with both positive and negative results. As Ted Koppel commented on ABC News *Nightline*, "perhaps never in a presidential campaign has the candidate's wife become such a strong symbol of the campaign's strength and weakness."

During the 1992 Democratic primaries, former California Governor Jerry Brown implied that as Hillary Clinton's work as an attorney involved state funds, she had unethically profited from her husband's position. Hillary Clinton's sharp response to a journalist that the only way an attorney and wife of a governor could have avoided controversy would have been if she had "stayed home and baked cookies" sparked public debate as to whether she was demeaning the role of stay-at-home mother and underlining family values.

U.S. Secretary of State Condoleezza Rice was the second woman to hold that post (2005–09); Hillary Clinton, appointed in 2009, was the third.

Hillary Clinton had a role in several key policy areas during the Clinton presidency, including health care reform, which was criticized as being too complicated or leading to socialized medicine. However, Hillary Clinton successfully initiated the Children's Health Insurance Program in 1997, which provided state support for children without health coverage. She also advocated for research funding for illnesses resulting from the Gulf War. She was a U.S. senator from New York (2000–09), and later, as secretary of state, she advocated for human rights and progress for women around the globe.

At the beginning of the 21st century, the United States became embattled over the ways in which elections were conducted when Democrat Al Gore carried the popular vote in 2000 with 48.38 percent, but Republican George W. Bush, with 47.87 percent of the popular vote, was declared the winner because the Supreme Court upheld a controversial Florida vote count that gave Bush 271 electoral votes to Gore's 266. The terrorist attack on the United States on September 11, 2001, propelled Bush into a crisis presidency and galvanized the administration's control over intelligence activities, which protestors claimed allowed the administration to override the First Amendment's protections of civil liberties and the Fourth Amendment's protections of rights of the accused.

Army Spc. Janie Reyna, of the 56th Brigade Combat Team from the Texas Army National Guard, holds an Iraqi child she befriended during a civil affairs mission in southern Iraq in 2005. The war in Iraq changed the way battles were fought; women soldiers were increasingly sent to the front lines.

In what has been termed a "faith-based presidency," Bush promoted an agenda of tax cuts, No Child Left Behind, government restructuring, and a war on terrorism with mixed results. Although he initially received a good deal of support for instituting the war on Iraq in the wake of 9/11, including wide House and Senate approval, his critics insist that the war was always based on faulty intelligence. Bush's refusal to address the issues of global warming and alternative sources of energy led to severe criticism from Republicans as well as Democrats. When he left office in January 2009, his approval rating had dropped to only 22 percent.

The election of 2008 was historic in a number of ways. Former First Lady and Senator from New York Hillary Clinton became a major contender for president of the United States, and Republican Sarah Palin, the governor of Alaska, battled blatant media displays of sexism as she ran as a Republican vice presidential candidate. As a mother of five, Palin was subjected to media insinuations that to run for office was to abandon her family. Even Clinton strategist Howard Wolfson was taken aback, commenting, "There's no way those questions would be asked of a male candidate."

The election was ultimately won by Barack Obama, the first African American to ever serve in that office. Obama named Clinton as his secretary of State and selected six other women to serve in cabinet-level positions. Obama's first Supreme Court nomination was Sonia Sotomayor of New York. His immediate major policy efforts were geared toward passage of a massive health care reform package intended to provide universal, government-subsidized health care in the United States. He was successful, but opposition and controversy continued.

CONCLUSIONS

Life for Americans from 1961 to the present has been one of massive changes, and both Democratic and Republican presidents have elevated women to positions of power. The women who filled those positions have proven that there are no limits to what women can do. Within society, women's roles were redefined, as cohabitation before marriage became more socially acceptable. Divorce rates rose, as did the number of single-parent households, particularly those headed by women.

More forms of birth control became available, giving women a wider range of choices, and family size shrunk accordingly. Access to abortion continued to be hotly debated. More women worked outside the home and two-income families became the norm, leading to increases in the number of children in daycare and the phenomenon of "latchkey" children who stayed home by themselves after school.

In additional to the political and social changes that took place, new technologies led to organ transplants, coronary bypass surgery, the development of the pacemaker, the medical use of laser technology, and an increasing reliance on pharmaceuticals. Medical advances aimed at women included a greater understanding of causes and treatments for breast cancer, new technologies for treating infertility, and a greater understanding of how diseases affect women differently than men.

Although it had started among homosexual males, human immunodeficiency virus and acquired immune deficiency syndrome (HIV/AIDS) became a women's issue when it became clear that women and children around the world had become the newest victims of the disease. A major breakthrough for women occurred in 2006 when a vaccination was released for girls and young women to prevent genital human papillomavirus (HPV), the cause of most cases of cancer and genital warts.

Marcella Bush Trevino
Barry University

Further Reading

Berkowitz, Edward D. *Something Happened: A Political and Cultural Overview of the Seventies*. New York: Columbia University Press, 2006.

Bernstein, Carl. *A Woman in Charge: The Life of Hillary Rodham Clinton*. New York: Alfred A. Knopf, 2007.

Braunstein, Peter, and Michael William Doyle. *Imagine Nation: The American Counterculture of the 1960s and '70s*. New York: Routledge, 2002.

CAWP. "Women Appointed to Presidential Cabinets." Available online, URL: http://www.cawp.rutgers.edu/fast_facts/levels_of_office/documents/prescabinet.pdf. Accessed December 2009.

Cole, Johnnetta B., ed. *All American Women: Lines That Divide, Ties That Bind*. New York: The Free Press, 1986.

Cott, Nancy F. *No Small Courage: A History of Women in the United States*. New York: Oxford University Press, 2000.

Daniels, Roger. *Coming to America: A History of Immigration and Ethnicity in American Life*. New York: HarperCollins, 1990.

DeBenedetti, Charles, and Charles Chatfield. *An American Ordeal: The Antiwar Movement of the Vietnam Era*. Syracuse, NY: Syracuse University Press, 1990.

DeGroot, Gerard J. *The Sixties Unplugged: A Kaleidoscopic History of a Disorderly Decade*. Cambridge, MA: Harvard University Press, 2008.

Echols, Alice. *Shaky Ground: The '60s and its Aftershocks*. New York: Columbia University Press, 2002.

Evans, Sara M. *Born for Liberty: A History of Women in America*. New York: Free Press, 1997.

Find Law. "Family and Medical Leave Act-FMLA-29 U.S. Code Chapter 28." Available online, URL: http://finduslaw.com/family_and_medical_leave_act_fmla_29_u_s_code_chapter_28. Accessed December 2009.

Gates, Henry Louis, and Cornel West. *The African-American Century: How Black Americans Have Shaped Our Country*. New York: Free Press, 2000.

Hampton, Henry, and Steve Fayer. *Voices of Freedom: An Oral History of the Civil Rights Movement from the 1950s through the 1980s*. New York: Bantam Books, 1990.

Harris, John F., and Beth Frerking. "Clinton Aides: Palin Treatment Sexist." *Politico* (September 3, 2008). Available online, URL: www.politico.com/news/stories/0908/13129.html. Accessed February 2010.

Herring, George. *America's Longest War: The United States and Vietnam, 1950–1975*. Boston: McGraw-Hill, 2002.

Hewitt, Nancy A., ed. *A Companion to American Women's History*. Malden, MA: Blackwell, 2002.

Jackson, Kenneth A. *Crabgrass Frontier: The Suburbanization of the United States*. New York: Oxford University Press, 1985.

Joint Economic Committee. Congress of the United States. "The Reagan Tax Cuts: Lessons for Tax Reform." (April 1996). Available online, URL: http://www.house.gov/jec/fiscal/tx-grwth/reagtxct/reagtxct.htm. Accessed February 2010.

Kerber, Linda K. and Jane Sherron De Hart. *Women's America: Refocusing the Past.* New York: Oxford University Press, 1991.

National First Ladies Library. "First Lady Biography: Hillary Clinton." Available Online, URL: http://www.firstladies.org/biographies/firstladies.aspx?biography=43. Accessed February 2010.

Nightline. "Making Hillary Clinton an Issue." (March 26, 1992). Available Online, URL: http://www.pbs.org/wgbh/pages/frontline/shows/clinton/etc/03261992.html (accessed February 2010).

Powers, Richard Gid. *Not Without Honor: The History of American Anticommunism.* New York: Free Press, 1995.

Santoli, Al. *Everything We Had: An Oral History of the Vietnam War.* New York: Random House, 1981.

Stetson, Dorothy McBride. *Women's Rights in the U.S.A.: Policy Debates and Gender Roles.* Pacific Grove, CA: Brooks/Cole Publishing, 1991.

Troy, Gil. *Morning in America: How Ronald Reagan Invented the 1980s.* Princeton, NJ: Princeton University Press, 2005.

U.S. Department of State. "Hillary Rodham Clinton." Available online, URL: http://www.state.gov/secretary. Accessed December 2009.

Whitney, Sharon and Tom Raynor. *Women in Politics.* New York: Franklin Watts, 1986.

Young, Andrew. *An Easy Burden: The Civil Rights Movement and the Transformation of America.* New York: HarperCollins, 1996.

CHAPTER 2

Women in Society

SINCE 1961, ROLES have changed dramatically for women in the United States. In 1963 Betty Friedan published *The Feminine Mystique*, in which she outlined the "problem that has no name" and helped to unleash the second wave of women's liberation, a movement that drastically altered women's roles in education, the professions, home and childcare, religion, and politics. Throughout the final decades of the 20th century, the women's liberation movement (WLM) continued to gain momentum, and feminists organized multiple campaigns for women's rights, demanding equal pay, educational and employment rights, an end to sexual discrimination, control over their own reproduction, and access to affordable childcare facilities. They also succeeded in raising the political consciousness of hundreds of thousands of women.

By the 1990s, young feminists (teenagers to 30-somethings) had begun to define their concerns through what Rebecca Walker labeled the "third wave" of feminist activism. Between 1961 and the early 21st century, thousands of laws and court decisions transformed the legal rights of women. Occupational and educational barriers were broken down; and for the first time in American history, one female became a viable candidate for the office of president of the United States, another was named as national security advisor, and another became the Speaker of the House of Representatives.

BIRTH OF SECOND WAVE FEMINISM

One of the classics of the second wave of the women's movement is Simone de Beauvoir's *The Second Sex* (1949), in which she describes woman as "the incidental, the inessential as opposed to the essential," which is man. "He is the Subject, he is the Absolute—she is the Other." During the 1960s Beauvoir's words and ideas helped to spawn a plethora of books about women's roles, in which authors expressed their dissatisfaction with female stereotypes and the traditional roles assigned to women by men. In 1955 Rosa Parks, an African American living in Montgomery, Alabama, refused to give up her bus seat to a white person and provided the spark for a more activist stage of the civil rights movement and, ultimately, for the women's movement. In the 1960s social turmoil, feminist activism through the creation of NOW (National Organization of Women), and feminist dictums provided women with opportunities to reexamine their roles within both the private and public spheres.

Despite the fact that women had been voting since 1920, women's position in society in 1961 when John F. Kennedy took office was drastically unequal to that of men. Established in 1961, the President's Commission on the Status of Women, which reported its findings in 1963, revealed that women's wages were not only lower than men's, but had actually declined in the 1950s. Esther Peter-

Women marchers in Dade County, Florida, vocalize their support for the ERA in 1975. Roxcy Bolton, Florida's leading women's rights activist, led the protests with Representative Gwen Cherry. In 1969 Bolton successfully challenged the practice of "men's only" sections in restaurants.

Race and Women's Rights

African-American feminists were often accused of racial treachery by their communities. After 1967, with the increasing influence of the black power movement within the civil rights movement and growing hostilities between black and white civil rights activists, it became even harder for African-American women to insist that they needed to combat sex discrimination as well as racism, because they did not want to be seen as siding with white women against black men. Nevertheless, by the early 1970s, African-American women were acknowledging that sexism did indeed have a profound impact on their lives and opportunities and became increasingly involved in the women's movement.

Once African-American women did become involved, they quickly made their voices heard, criticizing the "whiteness" of the women's movement. Writers and activists like Alice Walker, Toni Morrison, and Audre Lorde raised the profile of African-American feminists. There was also a great deal of writing by Native-American, Chicano, and Asian-American women who argued that recognition of their differences was crucial. African-American feminists introduced the concept of the "simultaneity of oppression," a feminism that did not comprehend what it was like to be poor and black in America, considering it irrelevant to them. In a 1972 poll, two-thirds of black women, as compared to only one-third of white women, were sympathetic to the women's movement. Furthermore, a 1976 survey of Chicano students showed that many agreed with the goals of feminism.

"The shedding of our differences" is not necessary in order to achieve solidarity, wrote African-American lesbian feminist Audre Lorde. However, it was not long before identity politics began to shatter solidarity between feminists. This was partly due to the changing political climate, which was becoming more conservative, but also to the fact that recognition of one's difference began to be more important than organizing and building the movement. This has generally been attributed to the difficultly inherent in negotiating the questions of gender, class, and race within the women's movement, rather than the fault of any particular group of women.

Audre Lorde, author of The Black Unicorn, *in the 1970s.*

Two Radical Feminists

Radical feminists argued that patriarchy was at the root of women's oppression. Some advocated feminist revolution, but others were less militant, content with advocating separatism and organizing women-only spaces and communities. Robin Morgan and Andrea Dworkin, both radical feminists, chose to express their radicalism in distinct ways.

Robin Morgan, born in 1941, blamed the New Left, which she described as "terminally diseased with sexism and toxic with characteristic U.S. arrogance and impatience," for many of the problems facing women. In the late 1960s, Morgan, who had been both a child actor and a civil rights activist, decided to devote all of her time and energies to the women's liberation movement (WLM). Throughout her career as a writer and poet, Morgan's feminism has dominated her life. She cofounded the Women's Media Center and founded the Sisterhood is Global Institute. From 1990 to 1993, she served as editor of *Ms.* magazine. Denying typical female stereotypes, Morgan has said, "Women are not inherently passive or peaceful. We're not inherently anything but human."

Born five years after Robin Morgan, in 1946, Andrea Dworkin also remembers the extreme sexism exhibited by male activists during the civil rights movement as they joked about sexual conquests and pornography. "What the men said was so vile that I was really wounded by it. I seemed unable to learn the lesson that pornography trumped political principle and honor." Dworkin spent three decades campaigning and writing about violence against women, rape, pornography, and prostitution. Along with many other feminists such as Susan Brownmiller, author of *Against Our Will: Men, Women and Rape* (1975), Dworkin placed the issue of violence against women at the top of the feminist agenda. She joined forces with feminist lawyer and academic Catharine MacKinnon to draft and promote an anti-pornography law in Minnesota that would have defined pornography as a form of sex discrimination and made it a violation of civil rights.

son, a well-known labor organizer and member of the American Federation of Teachers who had asked Kennedy for an investigation into women's position, became the vice chair of the commission. Former First Lady Eleanor Roosevelt, who had pressured Kennedy to create the commission in exchange for her political support, served as advisor. Kennedy has often been criticized for his failure to support the Equal Rights Amendment, which returned to the forefront with the resurgence of the women's movement, but his position was largely due to his dependence on the political support of labor unions, which strongly opposed ERA. With the commission turning the spotlight on women's issues, Congress began considering more than 400 pieces of legislation dealing with women's rights.

In 1970 in Kate Millett's highly touted examination of sexual politics (power-structured relationships whereby men controlled women), *Sexual Politics*, she delineates the "inalienable" predominance of males in all facets of society. Ideologically, "all that is distinctly human is defined by maleness." Millett argues that both women and men were taught that "biology is destiny." Consequently, both women and men believed that women were physically unfit for many jobs that men could do. Most radical feminists believed that since men have always controlled governments, women have consistently been stymied and made vulnerable by patriarchal decision-making.

John F. Kennedy with Eleanor Roosevelt in 1961, whom he appointed chair of the President's Commission on the Status of Women that same year.

REEDUCATING SOCIETY

During the 1960s, women gathered all over the country in "consciousness raising groups" to explore the causes of their suppression and develop strategies for collectively altering women's positions in society. The women's movement benefited enormously from the amount of publicity showered upon it by the media. For instance, mention of the women's movement in the national press increased 10 times in the 10 months from May 1969 to March 1970. The media attention was not always positive, but it certainly helped to recruit many women to the cause.

Despite some similarities, there were different approaches to accomplishing the goals of feminism. Radical feminists wanted to overhaul the whole society, claiming that the problem was patriarchy and contending that change would not come until all institutions were purged of this structure. Two of the most well-known radical groups were the Redstockings, founded by Shulamith Firestone, and WITCH (Women's International Terrorist Conspiracy from Hell) set up by Robin Morgan. These groups were much more militant than the reformist feminists. However, they sometimes joined forces with feminists from NOW for speak-outs outside abortion hearings. Socialist feminists claimed that both male domination and class exploitation were to blame for discrimination of women. Liberal feminists wanted to work within the system to change existing laws and role models. All of these feminists played a role in forcing society to reexamine women's roles. During the 1960s, the United States was confronted with demands to revise attitudes and behaviors that classified women solely as wives and mothers. Feminists of the second wave energetically entered the endless debate over whether nature or nurture was to blame for gender divisions in American society.

The feminist movement became more stridently vocal as it lent itself to more radical subgroups in the 1970s. Vociferous demonstrations garnered more media coverage for feminist causes, but not all of it was positive.

By the 1970s, the impetus to change had led to a reexamination of women's roles in both history and society. In colleges and universities, women's studies courses were introduced. By labeling them "interdisciplinary," such courses were able to focus on women within politics, history, literature, psychology, sociology, and science. Subsequently, many college courses began including women's contributions as part of the standard curriculum. During this same period, the number of women receiving higher education and advanced degrees rose markedly. Over the following decades, hundreds of universities began offering B.A., M.A., and Ph.D. programs in women's studies, and other universities adopted gender studies courses and degrees that focused on the effects of gender in relation to class, race, and ethnicity.

As new attitudes emerged on women's roles in society, girls were allowed, and even encouraged, to take "nontraditional" courses such as woodshop and electronics in middle and high schools. Increasingly, gender-biased courses were eliminated or redesigned, and boys began taking home economics, typing, and shorthand classes. In 1972, Title IX of the Education Amendment stated that "No person in the United States shall on the basis of sex, be denied the benefits of, or be subjected to discrimination under any education program or activity receiving Federal financial assistance." Thus, girls increasingly had more opportunities to be involved in sports at both the high school and college levels.

WOMEN IN THE PUBLIC SPHERE

The dramatic changes in women's roles in the public sphere can best be understood by examining women's participation in the workforce. In the 1870 U.S. census, 15 percent of the total workforce was female. That number had risen to 18 percent by 1900 and to 46.4 percent by 2005, During this time, women had not only taken on a plethora of roles in the workplace, they had also continued to raise families and do most of the housework. In 2004, 70.7 percent of all mothers with children under the age of 18 were in the workforce. Another key indicator of the dramatic change in America's workforce is the rise in the number of two-earner families. In the 1940s, 66 percent of all families claimed only one wage earner, typically the male head-of-household. By 2003, that number had declined to 18 percent.

The vast increase of women in the labor force was due to increased access to education and to the enhanced ability to obtain the capital needed for starting up businesses and engaging in career networking. According to the report by AFL-CIO union coalition Department for Professional Employees, *Professional Women: Vital Statistics,* between 2004 and 2014, men's share of the workforce is expected to decrease in conjunction with an increased number of women in the workforce, including those with small children. Despite these gains, women in the workforce continue to cluster in female-dominated occupations such as nursing and teaching at the K-12 level. While the number of women in technical writing, pharmacy, and chemistry is constantly rising, women are still a minority in fields such as electrical and chemical engineering and airplane piloting.

In the 1960s, women's demands for changes in the workplace resulted in two key pieces of legislation. In 1963, Congress passed the Equal Pay Act (EPA), eliminating pay differentials based on sex. The following year, the Civil Rights Act of 1964 was passed to eliminate racial discrimination in employment, schools, and public places. In a controversial move, Senator Howard W. Smith added the word "sex" as an amendment to Title VII. To the surprise of Smith and many other members of Congress, the amendment passed, banning sexual discrimination in employment and removing many barriers to job opportunities and career advancement for women.

Although women's roles have changed dramatically in the decades since the passage of the Equal Pay Act and Civil Rights Act, the contentious gaps between wages and career advancements remain. By the early 21st century, women were still making less than men, even when they were performing the same jobs. In 2008, for instance, full-time female workers earned only 79.9 percent of the pay of full-time male workers. Women were also more likely than their male cohorts to work part-time and were less likely to have benefits such as health insurance, pensions, and vacation pay.

Another tenacious problem thwarting women's ability to obtain higher positions is what has become known as the glass ceiling, which describes the prevention of women from rising beyond a certain level in their careers. The term, which was coined in the 1980s, is generally perceived to be the result of both conscious and unconscious gender discrimination and the tendency to limit working women's opportunities during child bearing and child rearing.

WOMEN AND RELIGION
One of the most profound changes in women's roles during the post-1961 period occurred within Judaism and Christianity. The efforts of Muslim feminists, however, led to more limited changes within the Islamic community. Although there were changes in Judaism throughout the 19th and 20th centuries, it was not until the beginning of the 1960s that a dramatic shift took place in women's roles in the synagogue. There are three major branches of Judaism: Reform, Conservative, and Orthodox, varying from less strict to more strict interpretations of the Torah, the first five books of the Old Testament. The most liberal movement is Reform, which ordained Sally Pries as the first female rabbi in the 1970s. By the 1980s, Conservative synagogues had begun accepting women. The most conservative branch of Judaism, the Orthodox, continued to believe that women should not be rabbis because it was considered contradictory to Jewish law, which is accepted as divinely inspired.

In 1997, Blu Greenberg, an Orthodox Jewish woman, founded the Jewish Orthodox Feminist Alliance to address some of the most egregious barri-

"Sally," a former Muslim, looks up a favorite Bible passage. She now serves as a translator for multinational forces in Iraq; in turn, her family placed a $5,000 bounty on her head. Muslim women have benefited greatly from the women's movement in America, which has given them the freedom to demand escape from oppression.

Lesbian Rights

The gay liberation movement, ignited by the Stonewall riots of 1969, was not particularly welcoming of lesbians. Lesbian feminists also discovered that they had to struggle for recognition within the women's movement, finding that it was dominated by the heterosexual culture. The leadership of National Organization for Women (NOW), for example, was not sympathetic to the organizing of lesbians. Friedan and other liberal, or "bourgeois" feminists, as they were dubbed by Robin Morgan and others, were concerned that the "Lavender menace" would give feminism a bad name. Friedan argued that the movement had fought hard for mainstream status, and she felt that the inclusion of lesbian rights on the feminist agenda would return the movement to a marginalized status, resulting in feminists being viewed as childless man-haters bent on the destruction of American family values. In 1971 lesbian members of NOW demanded that the organization pass a resolution recognizing their rights. Two years later, a task force on sexuality was finally established within NOW.

Radical feminist women's liberation movement (WLM) groups empowered lesbians to politicize their sexuality. The Radicalesbians, a group of New York feminists formed in 1970, denounced relationships with men and proclaimed lesbianism as a political choice. However, there was a distinction between moderate lesbians who were keen to raise awareness about lesbianism as a mode of love compatible with heterosexuality, and radical feminists who espoused political lesbianism. Nevertheless, as a result of the influence of radical feminism and the emerging power of the gay liberation movement, along with the support of feminist groups, women living outside of marriage and heterosexual relationships became more recognized. While being gay was still not accepted by society at large, acceptance by radical feminists was a key element in paving the way for passage of laws, in some states, that legalized civil partnerships for gay women in America.

ers and requirements for women within traditional Judaism. According to traditional Jewish law as defined in the Torah, women were exempted from time-bound obligations such as praying in the synagogue at a certain time each day because a woman was required to remain available to fulfill the needs of her family. Due to the exemption from time-bound requirements, women were considered secondary members of the synagogue and were not counted as members of the *minyan*, which required a quorum of 10 or more adult males gathered to pray. Women could not function as witnesses in a Jewish court, initiate divorces, or hold positions of leadership within a synagogue.

Perhaps the most egregious of the requirements for Jewish women was the necessity to receive a *get* (divorce document) if she wished to divorce her husband. Husbands could use this document to declare, "I will release and set aside you, my wife, in order that you may have authority over yourself to marry any man you desire ... you are permitted to every man ... this shall be for you a bill of dismissal, letter of release, a *get* of freedom." Without this piece of paper, Jewish women could not obtain a divorce recognized by Jewish law, and any subsequent marriage would not be recognized. Thus, offspring from such marriages would be identified as illegitimate.

Jewish feminists have attempted to recover the history of Jewish women's contributions to the religion by resurrecting women's celebrations and women's symbols and integrating the goddess tradition into Judaism. A particularly effective tactic has been the rewriting of the prayer books to eliminate gendered references to God as always a male figure.

Christian feminists began promoting more gender equality within the church in the 1960s. In Catholicism, the Second Ecumenical Council of the Vatican (Vatican II, which started in 1962 and ended in 1965) increased the freedoms and influence of nuns. Since then, Christian feminism has focused on generating greater egalitarianism within the church by fostering the equality of men and women morally, socially, and spiritually and in increasing the number of women in leadership positions. Christian feminists have also focused on the ordination of women. Nevertheless, Roman Catholicism, Southern Baptists, and the Church of Christ have continued to exclude women from entering the priesthood or pastoral positions. Some Christian feminists also advocated equal roles in marriages, support for homosexual rights, and promotion of the pro-choice stance on abortions.

Elizabeth A. Johnson, a prominent Christian feminist, decries what she sees as the androcentrism of Christianity, in which the traits of men are promoted as the "norm" for all humankind. According to Johnson, this necessarily implies that all religious discussions about human nature, God, sin, and redemption are tempered by the maleness of the language utilized.

She contends that the wisdom literature (The Book of Job, Proverbs, and Ecclesiastes) is consistently female and that Christ is the "incarnation of God imaged in female symbols." Christian feminists, and many Christians in general, insist that Jesus never demanded that women have a subordinate role in the church, nor did God intend for Christianity to be a patriarchal religion.

Muslim women have gradually become aware of their societal roles in comparison to other women around the world. Since the advent of television, and particularly since the widespread use of the Internet, Muslim women have begun to make more demands for change, focusing on marriage, divorce, custody of children, and marital property. They have worked to change unequal treatment concerning inheritance laws, the legal age of marriage and sexual consent, and restrictions on Muslim women marrying non-Muslim men.

Feminist Muslim women such as Canadian Irshad Manji and Iranian Shirin Ebadi have been at the forefront of the effort to educate Muslim women about alternatives to traditional lifestyles. Irshad Manji advocates returning to what she points to as the original message of Islam: justice, equality, unity, and peace. In 2003, Shirin Ebadi became the first Muslim woman to win the Nobel Peace Prize in recognition of her fight for social justice and her use of the legal system to work for change for Islamic women.

THE PERSONAL IS POLITICAL

Sheer numbers alone highlight the change of women's roles in politics from secretaries and assistants to powerful positions as leaders and decision makers. "The personal is political" became a familiar phrase during the 1960s and 1970s as women began to demand that their voices be heard. Feminists called for political solutions to problems associated with personal issues, such as gender discrimination and violence against women.

In 1960, the FDA approved the contraceptive pill for married women only. In 1965 in *Griswold v. Connecticut,* the Supreme Court confirmed the right of married couples to obtain birth control by upholding it as a right of privacy. In 1972 the "age of majority" was reduced from 21 to 18, and the Supreme Court extended that right to unmarried couples. The following year, the landmark decision *Roe v. Wade* legalized access to abortions based on the stages of fetal development, allowing women unprecedented control over their reproduction.

The push to make the personal political was in large part a response to the increasing number of women in politics after 1961. In 1960, the only women serving in the Senate were Margaret Chase Smith (R-ME) and Maurine B. Neuberger (D-OR). There were 18 women in the House of Representatives, 11 Democrats and eight Republicans. By 2009, 260 women had served in the U.S. Congress. The election of 2008 established records for women in both the House and the Senate. Thirteen Democratic and four Republican women sat in the Senate, and 57

Senator Maurine B. Neuberger (D-OR). In 1962 she filled the Senate seat of her deceased husband after a 1960 special election.

The Barbie Doll Syndrome

In 1956, Ruth Handler, an American businesswoman vacationing in Switzerland, saw a Bild Lilli doll, which had long, shapely legs and wore heavy makeup. In actuality, it was based on a German cartoon prostitute. Nevertheless, Handler was inspired to bring the Lilli dolls back to California and create the world's first Barbie doll, which Mattel introduced at the New York City Toy Fair in 1959. While the traditional standard of beauty at the time was inspired by curvaceous celebrities like Marilyn Monroe and Sophia Loren, the image of the Barbie doll eventually became entrenched in American society. In the years that followed there was also a shift in women's body standards toward the slender, somewhat emaciated-looking stars like Sandra Dee, who later admitted to excessive dieting to maintain that idealized, and totally unrealistic, expectation of beauty. By the early 1960s, First Lady Jacqueline Kennedy became the new standard of beauty.

Over the years, the Barbie doll evolved to reflect the times, and even demonstrated changing perceptions of women in modern society by role-playing as, among other things, a flight attendant, paleontologist, doctor, figure skater, gymnast, astronaut, fashion designer, firefighter, and politician. Nevertheless, the Barbie doll continued to be an ageless white female with an improbable waistline who perennially represented an unattainable image of timeless femininity. Based on research by Rader Programs, if Barbie were a real woman, she would be six feet tall, weigh 100 lbs., and wear a size four, with measurements of 39-19-33. According to Size USA, women's measurements in 2004 averaged 40 inches in the bust, 34 inches in the waist, and 43 inches in the hips (40-34-43).

Most little girls growing up in the United States and in many other countries saw Barbie and other skinny media icons as the yardstick by which they measured themselves. When they failed to compare, they often resorted to desperate measures to remold themselves in the Barbie image. In general, those measures included dieting that was sometimes severe enough to lead to anorexia, a disease in which the sufferer literally starves herself to death, or bulimia, a condition in which the sufferer follows binge eating with vomiting or purging. No matter how thin such dieters become, they continue to view themselves as too fat and in need of further dieting. In many cases, these conditions become so severe that they threaten the lives of girls and young women. Studies have consistently shown that girls as young as 10 begin dieting in order to conform to the Barbie-doll style and to popular culture's stringent standards of female beauty.

Democratic and 17 Republican women sat in the House of Representatives. Of the 74 women in the House, 12 were African American, seven were Latinas, and two were Asian American.

In 1974 Ella T. Grasso became the first woman elected as a governor in her own right, rather than being elected as the wife or widow of a previous governor. In 2009, there were eight women serving as governors. In 1981, Sandra Day O'Connor became the first woman appointed to the Supreme Court. She was joined by Ruth Bader Ginsburg in 1993. In the 1990s Janet Reno became the first female U.S. attorney general, and Madeleine Albright became the first female secretary of State. In 2008, for the first time in U.S. history, a female candidate, former First Lady Hillary Clinton, became a serious contender for president. After losing the election to Barack Obama, she became secretary of State. Overall, 40 women have been appointed to presidential cabinets. Twenty-three of those were appointed by Democratic presidents, starting with Franklin D. Roosevelt in 1933, and 17 have been appointed by Republican presidents, starting with Dwight D. Eisenhower in 1953. One of the most important elements in making the personal political concerned the attempt to pass the Equal Rights Amendment (ERA), which stated, "Equality of Rights under the law shall not be denied or abridged by the United States or by any State on account of sex." Although the ERA had been authored by suffragist Alice Paul in 1923, it was not until the second wave of the women's movement that Congress began seriously considering the amendment, partially in response to the intensive lobbying efforts of NOW.

Gloria Steinem at a news conference for Women's Action Alliance in 1972. A prominent feminist, she cofounded the National Women's Political Caucus in 1971, and founded Ms. magazine in 1972.

In the face of disagreement from labor activists, concerned about losing the protection won for female workers in the early 20th century, by 1973 the ERA had gained wide legislative and public support. Opposition came from the public, politicians, and groups such as Phyllis Schlafly's Stop ERA, which argued that equal rights for women was contrary to biblical teachings and would lead to unisex bathrooms, sending women into combat, federal funding for abortion, legalization of homosexuality, and the decline of the American family. Despite an unprecedented extension of the ratification deadline to 1982, opponents were ultimately successful in blocking ratification, and the ERA fell three votes short of the 38 states required to ratify the amendment. Despite this failure, many of the issues that the ERA would have addressed were dealt with in piecemeal fashion through laws, court decisions, and federal regulations.

Reproductive rights continued to generate heated debate, and abortion became a touchstone issue after *Roe v. Wade* (1973). By the end of the 1960s, 12 states had adopted some form of legal changes concerning abortion. Feminist speak-outs became personal and emotive, with prominent feminists like Gloria Steinem recounting tales of their own illegal abortions. With the election of Ronald Reagan in 1980, the abortion issue began to be used as a tool to elect, or alternately defeat, political candidates. In a series of cases that tightened restrictions on access to abortion during both the Reagan and Bush administrations, the Supreme Court turned away from upholding pro-abortion laws. However, neither the Supreme Court nor the George W. Bush administration, which began in 2000, ultimately overturned *Roe*.

Another aspect of the personal becoming political arose from dealing with societal views about the impact on families when women worked outside the home. The media periodically investigated this impact, sometimes warning that children of working mothers suffered more from alcoholism and drugs and performed less effectively in school than children whose mothers remained at home. In the 1970s and 1980s, some studies cautioned that children with absent mothers needed more psychiatric help than other children, sometimes exhibiting eating disorders and higher rates of suicide. Some nutritionists were concerned that

Demonstrators protest anti-abortion candidate Ellen McCormack at the Democratic National Convention in New York City on July 14, 1976.

working mothers cooked far less than nonworking mothers and relied more heavily upon store-bought foods, takeout dinners, and frozen meals. Societal concerns grew over the rising number of children in daycare centers and increases in elderly parents being placed in nursing homes because working women could no longer care for them at home.

In 1989, sociologist Arlie Hochchild identified women's balancing act between work and home as a "stalled revolution," asserting that the major responsibility for childcare and domestic labor remained with women who were often unable to successfully manage their roles as workers, homemakers, and nurturers. In response to pressure by feminist legislators and political groups, Congress passed the Family and Medical Leave Act in 1993, requiring all companies employing 50 or more people to give both female and male employees 12 weeks of unpaid leave for personal reasons, including the birth and care of a newborn or adopted child, the care of an immediate family member with serious health problems, or for major health conditions experienced by employees themselves.

BIRTH OF THIRD WAVE FEMINISM

From the mid to late 1980s onward, the women's movement was becoming fragmented and divided. It was no longer a radical mass movement of feminists agitating for political and social change. Despite this decline, feminist ideas had to some extent entered the mainstream. Feminist scholars had carved themselves a place in the traditionally male-dominated academy, and feminists were influencing policy in government institutions and private companies throughout American society. Women's committees existed in unions and many other public bodies. Despite revolutionary changes in the roles of women since the birth of the second wave of the women's movement, there were strong economic and sociological forces at play that created what feminist writers Susan Faludi and Naomi Wolf labeled a "feminist backlash" against women for demanding too many changes too quickly. In her book *The Beauty Myth*, Naomi Wolf critiqued the role of the "backlash" in manipulating women to buy certain products designed to promote self-esteem. These commercial images have generally been more subtle in their messages than those of previous decades, creating the illusion that women can be all they want to be, balancing both careers and family life, as long as they are beautiful, young (or at least youthful) and most of all, thin. Women's magazines are still replete with beautiful, young, and painfully thin women who supposedly have it all precisely because they have learned how to control their appearances.

By the 1990s, a new generation of feminists who had been raised in a vastly different society from that of their mothers and grandmothers was beginning to redefine the roles of women. One of the key events that triggered a new wave of activism and the birth of the third wave of feminism was the Clarence Thomas–Anita Hill hearings in the Senate in 1991. After Clarence

Rebecca Walker, having negotiated a childhood made turbulent by divorce and race, reflects on her multiracial identity in her memoir, Black, White and Jewish: Autobiography of a Shifting Self.

Thomas, a conservative African American, was nominated to replace civil rights leader Thurgood Marshall on the Supreme Court, reports surfaced that University of Oklahoma law professor Anita Hill, a former employee of Thomas's and also an African American, claimed to have been sexually harassed by him years before.

Conducted amid great controversy, the Senate hearings were broadcast to a national audience, and public debate swirled over the "race card" as well as liberal political motivations for vilifying Thomas, who won the nomination by a narrow margin of 52 to 48. Feminist outrage over the controversy, the failure to question experts on sexual harassment, and the striking image of the all-male, all-white Senate Judiciary Committee during the hearings precipitated a reevaluation of contemporary feminism.

In 1991 feminist writer Rebecca Walker popularized the term the *third wave* to identify the reenergized women's movement. She and other writers such as Christina Hoff Sommers made a distinction between so-called equity or power feminists who sought equity with men because they felt women were entitled to it, and victim feminists, particularly those of the second wave, who identified women as victims forced to fight against injustices. Third wavers claimed that young women (typically those in their late teens to early 30s) rejected the label of feminist because it implied a sense of powerlessness and inadequacy related to their mothers' brand of feminism. Some young women turned away from feminism altogether, convinced that they were already equal to men.

Third wave feminists were determined to be more inclusive, unlike feminists of the second wave, who have been accused of focusing exclusively on the needs of upper-middle-class white women and ignoring the needs and demands of women of color. New feminists rebelled against an "essentialist" definition of femininity, insisting that there was no single road to feminist empowerment, but rather many avenues by which women could develop self-determined identity. This more inclusive interpretation of feminism allowed not only for queer theory, women of color consciousness, and transgender politics, it also embraced post-colonialism and trans-nationalism as well. Terms have been created to distinguish these new sensibilities, such as the label *womanist*, a nomenclature coined in 1983 by writer Alice Walker to denote a black feminist or feminist of color.

CONCLUSION

Women's lives have undergone monumental changes since 1961, profoundly altering the lives of American women and serving as an impetus for women around the world to seek greater freedoms. With education, internet access, and satellite connectivity, the prospects for continued opportunities for women are limitless. Whether future changes will be based upon individual actualization or political group pressure, or a combination of both, only time will tell. The women's movement has grown to encompass women from all walks of life and all political persuasions despite the divisiveness that developed among opposing factions within the movement.

Feminist groups of the 1960s such as the National Organization for Women (NOW) were joined by a plethora of new feminist groups that ranged from EMILY'S LIST (Early Money Is Like Yeast), which funded pro-choice Democratic candidates for office, to the Congressional Caucus for Women's Issues to the Third Wave Foundation—all fighting to improve the lives of women and enhance their social and political rights. Despite a backlash against feminism, feminist women's rights advocates have made their voices heard and have precipitated landmark legislation and court decisions that have redefined women's roles in both the private and public spheres.

Nevertheless, women continue to be bombarded with the notion that they are less than capable if they cannot successfully juggle all aspects of life, leaving many women with a permanent sense of inadequacy.

Myrna A. Hant
UCLA Center for the Study of Women
Rachel Cohen
University of Sussex

Further Reading

Baxandall, Rosalyn, and Linda Gordon. *Dear Sisters: Dispatches from the Women's Liberation Movement.* New York: Basic Books, 2000.

Baxandall, Rosalyn, and Linda Gordon. "Second Wave Feminism." In *Companion to American Women's History,* edited by Nancy A. Hewitt. Oxford: Blackwell, 2002.

Beauvoir, Simone De. *The Second Sex.* New York: Alfred A. Knopf, Inc., 1953.

Cott, Nancy F. *The Grounding of Modern Feminism.* New Haven, CT: Yale University Press, 1987.

Davis, Flora. *Moving the Mountain: The Women's Movement in America since 1960.* New York: Simon & Schuster, 1991.

DPE. "Fact Sheet: Professional Women: Vital Statistics." Available online, URL: http://www.pay-equity.org/PDFs/ProfWomen.pdf. Accessed December 2009.

Dworkin, Andrea. *Heartbreak: The Political Memoir of a Feminist Militant.* New York: Basic Books, 2002.

Evans, Sara M. *A History of Women in America.* New York: The Free Press, 1997.

Faludi, Susan. *Backlash: The Undeclared War Against American Women.* New York: Doubleday, 1991.

Farrell, Amy Erdman. *Yours in Sisterhood: Ms. Magazine and the Promise of Popular Feminism.* Chapel Hill, NC: University of North Carolina Press, 1998.

Fox-Genovese, Elizabeth. *"Feminism Is Not the Story of My Life:" How Today's Feminist Elite Has Lost Touch with the Real Concerns of Women.* New York: A. Talese, 1996.

Friedan, Betty. *The Feminine Mystique.* New York: W.W. Norton and Co., 1963.

Goffman, Erving. *Gender Advertisements.* New York: Harper and Row, 1979.

Hacker, Andrew. *Mismatch: The Growing Gulf Between Women and Men.* New York: Scribner, 2003.

Heywood, Leslie and Jennifer Drake, eds. *Third Wave Agenda.* Minneapolis, MN: University of Minnesota Press, 1997.

Hochschild, Arlie Russell. *The Time Bind: When Work Becomes Home and Home Becomes Work.* New York: Henry Holt and Company, 1997.

Kessler Harris, Alice. *Out to Work: A History of Wage-Earning Women in the United States.* New York: Oxford University Press, 1982.

Kilbourne, Jean. *Can't Buy My Love.* New York: Simon & Schuster, 1999.

Mansbridge, Jane. *Why We Lost the ERA.* Chicago, IL: University of Chicago Press, 1986.

Millett, Kate. *Sexual Politics.* New York: Avon Books, 1969.

Molloy, John T. *The Woman's Dress for Success Book.* New York: Warner Books, 1977.

Morgan, Robin. *Demon Lover: On the Sexuality of Terrorism*. London: Madarin, 1989.
Rogers, Mary F. *Barbie Culture: Core Cultural Icons*. Thousand Oaks: CA: Sage, 1999.
Rosen, Ruth. *The World Split Open: How the Modern Women's Movement Changed America*. New York: Penguin, 2000.
Roth, Benita. *Separate Roads to Feminism: Black, Chicana, and White Feminist Movements in America's Second Wave*. New York: Cambridge University Press, 2004.
Rowbotham, Sheila. *A Century of Women: The History of Women in Britain and the United States*. New York: Viking, 1997.
Sapiro, Virginia. *The Political Integration of Women: Roles, Socialization, and Politics*. Urbana, IL: University of Illinois Press, 1983.
Sommers, Christina Hoff. *The War Against Boys*. New York: Simon & Schuster, 2000.
Wolf, Naomi. *The Beauty Myth*. New York: Doubleday, 1991.
Woo, Liu Ling. "Botox for Barbie." *Time* (January 29, 2009). Available online, URL: http://www.time.com/time/magazine/article/0,9171,1874769,00html#ixzz0hu0x45Rz. Accessed February 2010.

CHAPTER 3

Women's Health

PRIOR TO THE second wave of the women's movement, many women felt helpless when they went to the doctor. When they complained of odd symptoms, many doctors dismissed them as hysterical or ignorant, with a patronizing air of "doctor knows best." As a result, women often felt ignored, humiliated, and powerless. The women's health movement grew, in part, out of the frustration that women experienced in the health care realm—their dearth of information about female biology, the insufficient numbers of female doctors, the lack of decision-making power over their health, the low amount of research dollars earmarked for women's issues, and a lack of female subjects in various health studies. In under a generation's time, feminists were a driving force in transforming the medical community, empowering women and scientists to view women's health in a whole new way.

THE PILL AND THE WOMEN'S HEALTH MOVEMENT

By 1950, Americans were spending approximately $200 million a year on contraceptives. Improvements over the previous decade in condom quality had made them the most popular form of birth control available. Although Planned Parenthood ran 200 birth control clinics across the country, and most doctors approved birth control for married couples, anti-birth control laws in 30 states still prohibited or restricted the sale and promotion of

Gregory Pincus in 1961. In the 1950s, he and John Rock conducted initial birth control pill trials in Puerto Rico, which had no contraception laws.

contraception. In the predominantly Catholic states of Massachusetts and Connecticut, all forms of birth control were illegal; it was a felony in Massachusetts to "exhibit, sell, prescribe, provide, or give out information" about them. Instead of being allowed to provide women with birth control options, doctors in Connecticut performed hysterectomies on women who did not want to have more children. Dr. Richard Hausknecht, a Connecticut physician, described the practice as "prehistoric," explaining that, "From a training point of view we were delighted by this, because we got a chance to operate. But our poor patients suffered enormously. I mean the risks of what we were doing were simply not rational and unacceptable." For decades, women like Margaret Sanger had been advocating for safe and effective birth control for women as a means to economic and personal liberation.

Sanger and heiress Katherine McCormick combined forces to locate Gregory Pincus, a scientist who was conducting hormone research. McCormick, a suffragist and biology graduate from MIT, funded the lab, equipment, and materials for Pincus to continue his research. By 1954, the birth control pill was ready for human trials, so the group recruited Dr. John Rock to help conduct the studies. After nine months of trials in Puerto Rico, Rock and Pincus were ready to apply for FDA approval even though some disconcerting side effects were being reported by women in the studies. The pill was released in 1957 as a prescription to relieve menstrual disorders, with the brand name Enovid.

In May 1960, the FDA approved the pill for birth control purposes. By 1963, 2.3 million women were on the pill; and by 1967, 12.5 million women worldwide were taking the birth control pill on a daily basis. In 1965, a Connecticut couple's fight for access to birth control made it all the way to the Supreme Court. In the historic 7-2 ruling, *Griswold v. Connecticut*, the court ruled that states could not ban access to birth control because it violated rights to privacy. Women on the pill expressed liberation. One woman said, "I really felt

The Rio Piedras Trials

In order to gain FDA approval of the pill, developers needed a large-scale human trial. In the United States in the 1950s, there were still many legal, religious, and cultural roadblocks to birth control research impeding the type of trial that John Rock and Gregory Pincus needed in order to bring the pill to market. They turned their attention to Puerto Rico, which seemed an ideal place because of economic, social, and political circumstances. A U.S. territory, Puerto Rico experienced intense poverty, which led officials to support birth control efforts. Unlike mainland states, Puerto Rico had no anticontraception laws in place. Even though the island was predominately Catholic, Puerto Ricans were much more concerned about alleviating the strains of poverty than in following Vatican mandates on birth control. In 1955 there were over 67 clinics on the island distributing birth control, providing an ideal environment for facilitating trials of the pill. The official trial began in April 1956, and women signed up so quickly that Rock and Pincus decided to expand the trials to other parts of the island to accommodate the requests.

During the trials, a social worker commented that agency phones were always ringing in the office with women asking for the pill. Pincus believed that if they could show the world that uneducated, poor Puerto Rican women could adhere to the daily pill regimen, it would be no problem for most American women.

After one year of the Puerto Rican trials, Dr. Edris Rice-Wray, the doctor overseeing the study, reported to Pincus that the pill was 100 percent effective when taken as directed. However, Dr. Rice-Wray expressed serious concerns that the 10 milligram dose caused "too many side reactions to be generally acceptable," and she was alarmed that 17 percent of women taking the pill complained of nausea, dizziness, headaches, and vomiting. Some women even left the study early because the side effects were so uncomfortable. Rock and Pincus believed that the women's complaints were minor when compared to the benefits of the drug, and even asserted that their ailments were psychosomatic. They also accused social workers of asking leading questions that generated complaints. Three women died during the study, but no investigation or autopsies were performed to find out if the pill had anything to do with their deaths. Excited about the efficacy of the pill, Pincus and Rock rushed it to market without seriously examining the dosage or side effects.

While research involving human subjects was much less regulated in the 1950s than it is today, and trials required minimal tests to safeguard patients, Pincus and Rock were accused of exploiting third world women by not properly informing them of the risks and failing to fully disclose the nature of the trial. Accusations of colonialism, male chauvinism, and deceit during the trials became part of the history of women's health and the experience served to encourage women to question the medical industry.

as if I could have it all." Historian Linda Gordon explained that it created a whole new "contraceptive mentality" that women could actually plan their reproductive lives. By 1965 the pill had become the most common form of contraception among married women, but single women did not begin to use it in large numbers until the 1970s, according to Alan Petigny, a University of Florida history professor and researcher.

The pill was met with suspicion in the African-American community, where many saw it as a form of racial genocide. African-American women had experienced forced sterilization at such common rates that southern blacks called them "Mississippi appendectomies." One African-American newspaper questioned, "Why couldn't blacks get basic health care like a free aspirin, but can get a truckload of birth control pills for free?" Eventually, black women began using the pill at rates similar to those of white women. However, worries over the pill continued to highlight many of the concerns that African-American feminists had about their lack of inclusion in the second wave of the women's movement.

The pill was extremely effective, but no one was listening to women's complaints about its side effects. Barbara Seaman's book, *The Doctor's Case Against the Pill*, called attention to the dangerous side effects, leading Congress to hold hearings in 1970. When Seaman and several other female activists attended the hearings, they were dumbfounded that not a single woman was allowed to testify. When a frustrated Alice Wolfson yelled out during the hearings and asked why no women were testifying, news cameras turned in her direction; the camera lights dramatized the start of the women's health movement. Wolfson accused the medical community of using women as guinea pigs. When Senate Chair Gaylord Nelson accused the women of disrupting the hearings and asked them to sit down, Wolfson replied, "I don't think the hearings are more important than our lives." Wolfson and Seaman organized activists for the remainder of the proceedings, placing some women inside the chambers and others outside to carry on protests. As a result of the hearings and the national attention generated by these women, the FDA required birth control pill manufacturers to include information outlining the potential risks with every prescription. Seaman and the other women then founded the National Women's Health Network, and the women's health movement emerged in full force.

THE BOSTON WOMEN'S HEALTH COLLECTIVE

The same year that Seaman's book was published exposing the risks of the pill, a group of women in Boston held a workshop on women and their bodies. At the conference, woman after woman told personal stories of condescending treatment by their doctors. One woman shared how she was labeled "difficult" for asking questions. Her doctor considered her neurotic because she complained of strange symptoms. A black woman shared how medical students conducted several dozen repetitive pelvic exams on her because she was a charity case. Barbara Ehrenreich wrote of a women's meeting in Cleveland, where the women "discovered that every one of us had been told, at one time or another, that her uterus was undersized, misshapen, or misplaced. How could every woman's body be somehow abnormal and pathological?" Through such conversations, women realized they needed more information about the female anatomy.

In the summer of 1969, the group of Boston women gathered information about anatomy, birth control, physiology, pregnancy and childbirth, venereal disease, and sexuality. Armed with that knowledge, they began to offer classes on women's bodies. One of the founders of the group explained, "We learned that we were capable of collecting, understanding, and evaluating medical information." They also realized that they could "find strength and comfort through sharing some of our most private experiences." In 1971, organized as the Boston Women's Health Collective, they published their findings in *Women and Our Bodies*. That spring, they organized the first Women's Health Conference. By 1973, they had expanded their research and created *Our Bodies,*

Three prominent physicians took an active role in advocating for women's health in the 1960s–80s. Dr. Dorothy Ferebee (left) fought tirelessly for racial equality and women's health care. Dr. Mary Catherine Howell (center), through her involvement with the Boston Women's Health Book Collective, contributed to several projects, including Our Bodies, Ourselves. Dr. Lena Edwards (right), one of the first African-American women to be board certified as an ob-gyn, served and lobbied for health care for the poor, which earned her the Presidential Medal of Freedom in 1964. Well into her 60s, she spoke out against abortion and social welfare, which she felt demeaned and debilitated the poor.

Barbara Seaman

Many historians and feminists consider Barbara Seaman a founding mother of the women's health movement. The *New York Times* asserted that "Barbara Seaman triggered a revolution, fostering a willingness among women to take issues of health into their own hands." Seaman's personal experiences drove her to examine how the medical community—doctors and pharmaceutical companies—treated women. In the 1950s, doctors routinely encouraged women to use formula instead of breastfeeding. When Seaman had a baby in 1957, she told her doctor that she would breastfeed. He disregarded her wishes and prescribed a laxative that was potentially very dangerous for breastfeeding women. It nearly killed her son. Reflecting on that incident, Seaman wrote, "I would never again trust a doctor blindly." In 1959, Seaman watched her Aunt Sally die of endometrial cancer, which the oncologist blamed on the Premarin Sally's gynecologist had prescribed for menopausal symptoms. These incidents inspired Seaman to become a journalist and focus on women's health. Seaman wrote for a variety of women's magazines, encouraging women to ask more questions of their doctors. She argued that medical professionals did not give women enough information to make informed decisions about their health.

In 1969, Seaman's book, *The Doctor's Case Against the Pill,* was released. The book challenged the safety of the contraceptive pill and argued that poor Puerto Rican women were misused during the clinical trials and were not fully informed about the side effects. She also outlined the increased risks of cancer, diabetes, stroke, blood clots, depression, weight gain, and heart disease. Her book, which caused a great stir in the medical world, led to congressional hearings in 1970. After the hearings, Seaman went on to cofound the National Women's Health Network.

In the mid-1970s, only 3 percent of doctors in obstetrics and gynecology were women. Seaman demanded that more women be accepted to medical school, especially in obstetrics and gynecology. She also questioned how research money was allocated for women's reproductive health. She advocated that women should be able to make informed medical decisions, and she worked tirelessly for patient rights. She explained, "Some women want to let their doctors do the worrying for them. But for those of us who don't, it has been extremely difficult to get honest health information."

Her activism and criticism of the established medical community resulted in her being blacklisted or fired from several prominent magazines when pharmaceutical companies refused to place their ads in magazines that published Seaman's articles. She continued to advocate for women by publishing three biographies. For the remainder of her life, Seaman continued to write about women's health issues and the rights of patients. Much of the progress of the women's health movement in the last 30 years owes a great deal to the journalism and political activism of Barbara Seaman.

Ourselves, which became an instant bestseller. This book encouraged women to question the authority male doctors assumed over their health.

Our Bodies, Ourselves also made motherhood an "important feminist life event" and demanded that the process be demedicalized. The Boston Women's Health Collective advocated for a more natural experience, in which women were alert and active while delivering their babies, rather than being drugged throughout the experience. They also rejected the science that advised women to use baby formula, choosing instead to celebrate the experience and benefits of breastfeeding. Over the next several decades, a variety of natural childbirth methods were popularized and standardized, and midwifery made a resurgence both in hospital and home-birth settings. However, it took several lawsuits between 1974 and 1976 before midwives were officially sanctioned to practice. Courts eventually ruled that since pregnancy was not a disease, midwives could not be charged with practicing medicine without a license. The California Supreme Court issued a ruling stating that midwives were covered by the state's Medical Practice Act.

THE SELF-HELP MOVEMENT

To help women gain some control over their bodies, activists began practicing "self-help gynecology." Carol Downer, a feminist activist, realized that most women had never seen a cervix. In April 1971, at Every Woman's Bookstore in Los Angeles, Downer inserted a speculum into her own vagina and showed women how they could use mirrors and flashlights to see each other's cervixes as well as their own. Another such demonstration occurred at the annual meeting for the National Organization for Women. It soon spread across the country, with over 2,000 women attending self-help clinics and leaving with their own speculums. Women began to understand the importance of self-examinations and talking with other women about health issues.

Downer began to question why women always had to turn to doctors for routine problems like yeast infections or birth control. She believed these self-help clinics could give women the opportunity to gain control over certain health issues. Along with another self-help member, Lorraine Rothman, Downer developed a tech-

By 1971, feminist activist Carol Downer was promoting women's self-help care, such as yogurt for yeast infections. In the mid-1970s, the first home pregnancy tests began to appear. Ova II was followed by the more popular e.p.t, which was a complicated, two-hour regimen, but allowed for privacy at home.

nique called "menstrual extraction" in which women used a modified syringe to extract menstrual blood and potential fertilized eggs. They advocated this procedure be performed around the time menses was expected, insisting that this was a much safer method of birth control and would prevent pregnancies.

In September 1972, Downer was arrested for practicing medicine without a license. Authorities considered menstrual extraction a form of abortion, which was still illegal. But when they raided Downer's clinic, their only evidence was a container of yogurt that Downer had recommended to remedy a woman's yeast infection. Feminists were outraged. One newspaper editor wrote, "What man would be put under police surveillance for six months for looking at his penis?" They called the investigation "The great yogurt conspiracy." Historian Linda Gordon identified this incident as the one that set the "precedent that women's genitals were no longer territory reserved for men."

Many in the medical community did not know how to deal with the new "active" female patient. Women started bringing friends to their doctor's appointments to serve as note-takers. Through this process, women gained more confidence to ask questions about their health, be more assertive, get second opinions, do their own research, and approve which tests they would undergo. Historian and journalist Ruth Rosen believes that such health advocacy "sometimes turned women into feminists." The ideas of the women's health movement permeated throughout society. Women began to see themselves as active consumers of their medical care, instead of hopelessly dependent on doctors. The self-help activists began opening women-controlled clinics that offered routine well care. By 1975, there were over 2,000 such clinics throughout the United States.

CONSCIOUSNESS-RAISING GROUPS

The self-help movement encouraged consciousness-raising groups that helped women get in touch with their bodies and their health. Women began to share their sexual experiences, admitting that they often failed to achieve orgasm during sex. One group member described her experience, "I made this absolutely stunning confession and I was convinced that I was the only woman on the planet who had ever been sick enough to [fake orgasm], but I finally confessed ... at which point every woman in the room leaned forward grinning, and said, 'Oh, you too?'" The fake orgasm became a topic of women's groups everywhere. In 1969, *New York Radical Women* magazine published Shulamith Firestone's *Women Rap about Sex* and Ann Koedt's *The Myth of the Vaginal Orgasm*. Women began to explore their feelings about sex and the physiology of the female body. Another activist wrote, "Everyone admitted to faking orgasms ... What I did was stop faking it after that." Through the women's health movement, all sorts of topics about women's bodies were freed from the taboos of previous generations, allowing women to explore their bodies and their sexuality.

DES ACTION

In the 1940s, doctors regularly prescribed diethylstilbestrol (DES) to pregnant women to prevent miscarriages and after delivery to prevent breast engorgement. During the early years of the women's health movement, Berkeley activist Pat Cody began researching the effects of DES on women and formed the grassroots organization DES Information Group to investigate the health problems of children whose mothers had taken DES. They also lobbied Congress for research money. In 1975, Cody published the pamphlet, *Women Under Thirty, Read This!* Cody expanded internationally with DEA Action, demanding that all children of DES mothers be monitored for increased health risks.

The health risks for DES were numerous. For mothers, there was an increased risk for breast cancer. For their daughters, studies showed an increased risk for a wide range of diseases, including clear-cell, vaginal, and cervical cancers; autoimmune diseases; infertility; pregnancy complications; and reproductive disorders. Studies are still being conducted on third-generation effects of DES on the granddaughters of women who were prescribed DES in the 1940s.

Publicity about the long-range effects of DES led to widespread lawsuits against manufacturers. In a 1980 landmark case, *Sindell v. Abbott Laboratories*, the Supreme Court created the standard for market-share liability, which meant that all the companies manufacturing the drug were held liable for paying damages to successful plaintiffs. By 1997, not a single U.S. company was manufacturing DES.

ABORTION

Many self-help activists believed that women needed complete information about their reproductive choices and access to safe abortions. Abortion had been illegal in the United States since the mid-19th century; however, women constantly sought abortions, often resorting to dangerous, dirty, "back-alley" procedures that left them scarred, infertile, or dead. Studies estimated that about 5,000 women died each year from botched abortions. Those involved in the women's health movement sought ways to help women find solutions to unplanned pregnancies. In Chicago, a group of women formed an organization called Jane. Made up of activists, college students, mothers, and housewives, Jane began seeking cheaper and safer solutions for women. One woman who used Jane's services when she was 19 said, "Getting pregnant in those days was a tragedy; it was the end of your life. I knew people who had botched abortions .... You really felt safe once you made contact with the Janes." The group provided birth control and abortion counseling, helped explain the procedure, and even held their clients' hands during abortions. Women were referred to Jane by friends, acquaintances, and doctors. They were listed in small-town newspapers, and even appeared in the phone book under Jane Howe. Other underground abortion networks composed of women, doctors,

Breast Cancer Awareness

Feminist activist and women's historian Ruth Rosen wrote, "The impact of the women's health movement is hard to exaggerate." For her, it became even more personal in 1988, when she had a biopsy for a lump in her breast. Afterward, a nurse advised her to join a women's support group. Rosen wrote in her journal, "What I helped create now returns to comfort me in my moment of greatest need. The circle remains unbroken. Amazingly, a surge of pleasure softens my anguish." In an earlier generation, a woman diagnosed with breast cancer would be faced with a dearth of resource and a code of silence: it was simply not talked about. In little over a decade, the women's health movement transformed breast cancer awareness, treatment, and research.

The protocol for breast cancer used to be a "one-step" process that called for immediate mastectomy, and women had to sign consent to the procedure before cancer was even verified. A series of books prompted women to demand changes. In 1975, medical journalist Rose Kushner questioned this protocol in *Breast Cancer: A Personal History and Investigative Report*. In 1980, when Audre Lorde wrote *The Cancer Journals*, she described her feelings of isolation and terror dealing with her own cancer, opening up dialogue for female cancer patients and the medical community. Women realized that the code of silence not only prevented women from getting vital facts and emotional support, it allowed the medical establishment to continue their unquestioned control over approaches to the disease. Writer Sharon Batt explained that women would no longer be "patient patients."

Women active in the health movement sought ways to get the latest medical research on breast cancer so that women could actively engage in their treatment. They fought to have mammograms covered by health insurance, called for research that questioned the standard procedure of mastectomy, and examined less invasive methods. They also began to question allocation of research dollars and demanded increased funding for breast cancer research.

Not only was breast cancer research underfunded in comparison to other cancers, scientists had been reluctant to examine environmental and social factors as causes of breast cancer. Neither could physicians explain why African-American women had lower overall rates of breast cancer, but had higher rates of mortality from the disease. Self-help and breast cancer support groups have become standard throughout the country. Advocacy groups such as Susan G. Komen For the Cure have gone global with their outreach to women, funding both new and continuing research. The National Breast Cancer Foundation, Avon Walk for the Cure, and other fundraising and awareness organizations now exist throughout the United States. Pink ribbons symbolizing breast cancer awareness have become part of mainstream culture, mass media, and corporate advertising. Feminist advocacy dramatically shifted the public and medical focus on breast cancer, becoming one of the highest-impacting successes of the women's health movement.

Abortion activists demonstrate in Tallahassee, Florida, in 1989. Abortion by this time was an increasingly hot-button topic, and by 1991, federal funds for abortion clinics were curtailed.

and ministers sprung up around the country. In San Francisco, a group began sending women to Mexico for abortions. In New Jersey, a local Methodist church had a message machine where women could call to get the name of a doctor who performed safe abortions.

In 1959, the American Law Institute recommended that abortions be permissible when either the mother or child might suffer from a continuation of the pregnancy. By the 1970s, 11 states had altered their laws to allow abortions under specified conditions. However, that did not give women any more control over the decision than they had before. In California, a woman had to undergo two separate psychiatric evaluations about her mental incapacity in order to be granted an abortion. Women within the movement began to call for a repeal of all laws that restricted a woman's access to abortion. Women started holding public "speak-outs" where they talked about their experiences with illegal abortions. For the first time, women began talking publically about their most private ordeals, helping to galvanize the pro-choice movement.

On January 22, 1973, the Supreme Court issued its historic ruling in *Roe v. Wade*, stating, "We recognize the right of the individual, married or single, to be free from unwanted governmental intrusion into matters so fundamentally affecting a person as the right of a woman to decide whether or not to terminate her pregnancy." The court affirmed a woman's right to abortion during the first six months of her pregnancy. Self-help clinics immediately established abortion services and Feminist Women's Health Centers.

Immediately after the decision, pro-life advocates began to mobilize against *Roe*. In 1977, Congress passed the Hyde Amendment, which prevented the use of federal money to fund abortions, which meant that poor women were ineligible to access abortions through Medicaid. Beginning with the 1980 presidential election, abortion took center stage in national politics. Anti-abortion, or pro-life groups, successfully eroded *Roe v. Wade* at the state level by introducing consent laws and waiting periods. In 1991, in *Rust v. Sullivan*, the Supreme Court upheld the so-called gag rule that allowed the government to cut government funds to clinics that even counseled women about abortion as an option. One of the first actions of Democrat Bill Clinton, who became U.S. president in 1993, was to repeal the gag rule through an executive order. In 2003, under President George W. Bush, Congress passed the Partial Birth Abortion Ban, which prevented doctors from performing a particular type of extraction abortion usually performed between the 18th and 26th weeks of pregnancy. The Supreme Court upheld the law in 2007.

As the national debate over abortion became more heated, clinic violence escalated. Between 1977 and 1989, hundreds of clinics were bombed or became targets of arson, and hundreds more received bomb threats or were vandalized. Between 1993 and 2009, nine people were killed in clinic violence, including a clinic escort, a security guard, two clinic workers, and five doctors. In 1992 the anti-abortion group Operation Rescue created "Wanted" posters of abortion provider Dr. David Gunn. In 1993, as the physician stepped out of his car in front of an abortion clinic during a protest, he was gunned down by Michael Griffin, who acted on his own impulse. Rescue America, the Houston-based anti-abortion group that organized the protest, emphatically stated it did not condone the killing of Dr. Gunn. In May 2009, Dr. George Tiller, the last remaining abor-

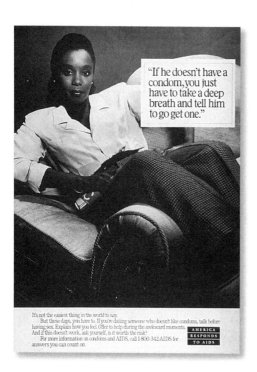

In an effort to overcome skepticism from minority communities about contraception and protection, in 1989 the Centers for Disease Control and the Department of Health and Human Services began a campaign to target specific racial groups of women about making responsible decisions and advocating for their best interests.

tion provider in Wichita, Kansas, was killed in church while he served as an usher. Operation Rescue denounced the killing, again by a gunman acting alone. As of 2010, approximately 85 percent of counties in the United States have no abortion services, and many medical schools do not provide training for the procedure.

NATIONAL HEALTH POLICY

The women's health movement dramatically shaped public policy. Drug manufacturers now have to include information with each prescription about side effects and contraindications. Hospitals are now required to get informed consent signatures from their patients, which have protected women from forced sterilization, unnecessary hysterectomies, and other evasive procedures.

"What you eat has never been so important," was the original caption of this 1983 Healthy Mothers, Healthy Babies poster distributed by United States Public Health Service and sponsored by Gerber Products.

Women's groups pressured the FDA and the National Institute of Health (NIH) for gender equity in medical research funding. Through the work of groups such as the National Women's Health Network and the National Black Women's Health Project, NIH created a Women's Health Advisory Committee. In 1991, the committee introduced the Women's Health Initiative, which dedicated $625 million for studies on women's heart disease, breast cancer, and osteoporosis.

Feminists have also staved off efforts to overturn *Roe v. Wade*, although pro-life groups have been successful in influencing policy that has limited federal funding and minors' access to abortion. Ironically, one voice of opposition is Norma McCorvey, who was the "Jane Roe" in *Roe v. Wade*. In 1995, she reversed her stance and continues to advocate against the procedure.

GLOBAL WOMEN'S HEALTH MOVEMENT

Our Bodies, Ourselves has sold over four million copies worldwide, providing an impetus for the global women's health movement. In 1995, at the NGO Women's Forum in Beijing, many activists for women's health converged to discuss common problems and strategies. The internet has galvanized the movement, making access to health information easier and virtually instantaneous. Transnational groups work on issues of environmental hazards, maternal mortality, breastfeeding, family planning, forced sterilization, AIDS, and infant health and diet. Groups such as the Women's Global Network for Reproductive Rights and the International Reproductive Rights and Research Action Group hold workshops and conferences throughout the world. The United Nations has formed the U.N. Interagency Network on Women and Gender Equality. Its mission statement asserts that "Women have the right to the enjoyment of the highest attainable standard of physical and mental health. The enjoyment of this right is vital to their life and well-being [and to] their ability to participate in all areas of public and private life." The network is drawing attention and resources to health concerns in developing countries and to issues such as reproductive health, drug abuse, female genital mutilation, sterilization, environmental factors, the dangers to female child brides, food and nutrition, and access to medical care. Such efforts are having a dramatic impact on the daily lives and well being of girls and women throughout the world. Shortly after taking office in 2009, President Barack Obama overturned the "global gag rule," a policy instituted in the 1980s by President Ronald Reagan that denied American aid to international health organizations that performed or advocated abortions. President Bill Clinton had overturned it in 1993, but President George W. Bush reinstituted it in 2001.

CONCLUSION

The women's health movement was one of the biggest impacts of second wave feminism. It galvanized support for women to learn about their own bodies and provided them with the tools to speak freely and publicly about the female body. It helped empower women to act as their own advocates to the medical community, challenging existing practices and attitudes. In a single generation, the health movement succeeded in increasing numbers of women entering medical school; increasing funding for breast cancer research; radically changing protocol for a variety of medical procedures concerning cancer, birth control, and child labor; and creating public policies to advance women's health issues. Through increased awareness about health issues affecting women, an entirely new group of women who did not necessarily self-identify as feminists were exposed to issues of gender equality and sexism, which allowed them to see the women's movement in a broader context.

Many argue that the women's health movement still has much work to do. One scholar explains, "Women are at a significant risk of overtreatment if we have medical insurance ... and are under greater risk of undertreatment when we have no form of medical coverage." Poor women lack the funds for health care and health insurance, and often cannot afford regular prenatal care, which leads to increased infant mortality among low-income women. Women of color have higher mortality and morbidity rates than white women.

The health care debates that began during the Clinton administration have yet to be resolved. In 2009, as the Obama administration sought to address health care reform and advocate for a government-managed insurance pro-

These Latina teens, in Brooklyn in 1974, were growing up during a transformation of the way women's health was approached and treated. From the birth control pill to the self-help movement, young women of the era grew up with far more resources to become active in their own health care than their mothers and grandmothers.

gram, Congress and the nation engaged in a contentious debate that resulted in voting almost entirely along party lines. Many activists lamented that until Congress passed meaningful health care reform, the health care gap between rich and poor would continue to increase dramatically, with many poor women remaining unable to benefit from advancements made by the women's health movement. Skeptics cried "socialism" and called the Obama plan an "unsustainable disaster" that could cripple the economy.

Girls today typically learn very early on about their bodies and are encouraged to talk openly and ask questions. They have easy access to information on health issues, reproduction, and sexuality through books, the internet, and local clinics. If faced with illness, women have a multitude of resources to draw from, including support and awareness groups, community-based organizations, women's health clinics, and friends. Women's bodies have gone from being taboo topics in public to entering mainstream discourse and generating powerful public support. While the movement continues to fight for women's access to health care and reproductive options, it has expanded throughout the globe. At the same time, it has transformed American society and millions of individual lives.

Monica Fitzgerald
Saint Mary's College of California

Further Reading

Apple, Rina. *Women, Health and Medicine in America: A Historical Handbook*. New York: Garland Press, 1990.

Bair, Barbara and Susan E. Cayleff, eds. *Wings of Gauze: Women of Color and the Experience of Health and Illness*. Detroit, MI: Wayne State University Press, 1990.

Batt, Sharon. *Patient No More: The Politics of Breast Cancer*. London: Scarlet Press, 1994.

Bawden, D., ed. *The Social Contract Revisited: Aims and Outcomes of President Reagan's Social Welfare Policy*. Washington, D.C.: Urban Institute Press, 1984.

Boston Women's Health Book Collective. *Our Bodies, Ourselves: A Book By and For Women*. Boston, MA: New England Free Press, 1971.

Brownmiller, Susan. *In Our Time: Memoir of a Revolution*. New York: Random House, 2008.

Campbell, Mary. *Why Would a Girl Go into Medicine? Medical Education in the U.S.: A Guide for Women*. New York: Feminist Press, 1973.

Chesler, Phyllis. *Women and Madness*. New York: Doubleday, 1972.

Collins, Patricia Hill. *Black Feminist Thought: Knowledge, Consciousness, and the Politics of Empowerment*. New York: Routledge, 1990.

Davis, Flora. *Moving Mountains: The Women's Movement in America since 1960*. New York: Simon & Schuster, 1991.

Dreifus, Claudia, ed. *Seizing Our Bodies: The Politics of Women's Health*. New York: Vintage Books, 1977.

Ehrenreich, Barbara and Deirdre English. *Witches, Midwives, and Nurses: A History of Women Healers*. New York: Feminist Press, 1993.

Fried, Marlene Gerber, ed. *From Abortion to Reproductive Freedom: Transforming a Movement*. New York: South End Press, 1990.

Gordon, Linda. *Women's Body, Woman's Right: A Social History of Birth Control in America*. New York, Grossman Publishers, 1976.

Kushner, Rose. *Breast Cancer: A Personal History and Investigative Report*. New York: Harcourt Brace Jovanovich, 1975.

Leavitt, Judith Walzer and Ronald L. Numbers, eds. *Sickness and Health in America: Readings in the History of Medicine and Public Health*. Madison, WI: University of Wisconsin Press, 1978.

Lorde, Audre. *The Cancer Journals*. New York: Spinsters Ink, 1980

Morgen, Sandra. *Into Our Own Hands: The Women's Health Movement in the United States, 1969–1990*. New Brunswick, NJ: Rutgers University Press, 2002.

Keen, Cathy. "Coital Conservatism Ended Before Birth Control Pill Arrived, Says Researcher." *University of Florida News* (February 22, 2010). Available online, URL: http://news.ufl.edu/2010/02/22/birth-control. Accessed February 2010.

Ponnuru, Ramesh. "The Fatal Flaw of Obamacare." *Time* (August 17, 2009). Available online, URL: http://www.time.com/time/magazine/article/0,9171,1914973,00.html. Accessed February 2010.

Proctor, Robert. *Cancer Wars: How Politics Shapes What We Know and Don't Know About Cancer*. New York: Basic Books, 1996.

PBS: American Experience. "The Pill." (2002). Available online, URL: http://www.pbs.org/wgbh/amex/pill/timeline/index.html. Accessed February 2010.

Rosen, Ruth. *The World Split Open: How the Modern Women's Movement Changed America*. New York: Viking Press, 2000.

Ruzek, Sheryl Burt. *The Women's Health Movement*. New York: Praeger, 1978.

Seaman, Barbara. *The Doctor's Case Against the Pill*. New York: Wyden Books, 1969.

Shapiro, Thomas. *Population Control and Politics: Women, Sterilization and Reproductive Choice*. Philadelphia, PA: Temple University Press, 1985.

Smith, Susan L. *Sick and Tired of Being Sick and Tired: Black Women's Health Activism in America, 1890-1950*. Philadelphia: University of Pennsylvania Press, 1995.

Solinger, Rickie. *Wake Up Little Suzie: Single Pregnancy and Race Before Roe Versus Wade*. New York: Routledge, 1992.

Starr, Paul. *The Social Transformation of American Medicine*. New York: Basic Books, 1982.

Weisman, Carol. *Women's Health Care: Activist Traditions and Institutional Change*. Baltimore, MD: Johns Hopkins University Press, 1998.

CHAPTER 4

Women's Education

DURING NO OTHER time in history have the gains for women in education in the United States been more dramatic than in the years after 1961. While women of earlier time periods achieved increasing access to education, it was not until the birth of the women's movement of the 1960s that education for women began to flourish. Feminist activists sponsored consciousness-raising groups, demonstrations, and marches, demanding that barriers to equal educational opportunities for women be removed. In response, Congress passed a number of laws, including Title IX of the Education Amendments of 1972, which profoundly altered women's educational possibilities. By the 1970s, universities had begun to understand the need for specialized programs such as women's studies that were designed to inform women about their past and broaden opportunities for the future.

LAYING GROUNDWORK AND CREATING DOUBTS

By the 1960s, demands for educational equality for women had become far more strident and widespread than before. *The Feminine Mystique* by Betty Friedan, published in 1963, delineated many of the problems that educated, middle-class women were experiencing as they tried to fit into lives that were largely limited to the private sphere. During this time, an article in *The New York Times* supported Friedan's contentions, referring to women who felt "stifled in their homes," finding their "routine lives out of joint with their training." According to Kate Millett in her landmark book, *Sexual Politics*, women of the 1960s were educated in the humanities with an emphasis on home economics, nursing, elementary school teaching, and librarianship. They were not being prepared for the technological and scientific jobs of the future. There were clearly dichotomized fields for women and for men. Social science and literature were considered "feminine" subjects, whereas science, technology, business, and engineering were labeled "masculine" areas of expertise. A very few women were iconoclasts, crossing the gender line by becoming federal judges (1 percent female), lawyers (less than 4 percent female), or doctors (7 percent female. Women could be found in all professions; however, they earned an average of only 60 cents for every dollar that men earned.

In the 1960s and 1970s, female students at Miami-Dade Junior College were trained as airline stewardesses, one of the acceptable occupations for women at the time.

Girls began wearing miniskirts in the 1960s. At the same time, boys let their hair grow long in response to what was called the British invasion in rock music. High school principals became involved in measuring skirts and hair with rulers to enforce dress codes, but by the 1970s gradual changes were occurring. Over the course of the decade, schools had less control over how students dressed and wore their hair. A few girls began venturing into shop classes, learning woodworking and carpentry. However, those classes remained predominantly male, just as classes in typing and shorthand continued to be predominantly female. Girls continued to choose to take music, art, and home economics as electives.

At the university level, only 10 percent of faculties were women. In 1971 the University of Michigan became the first university to consciously increase female faculty by adopting an affirmative action plan. Of course, it was the passage of Title IX the following year that forced many educational institutions to revise long-standing beliefs and practices concerning women's roles in education.

Critics of expanding educational opportunities for women, as well as some scholars, questioned women on the advisability of pursuing higher education. A marriage study published conjointly in 1986 by Harvard and Yale received widespread publicity and heavy media coverage. "The popular media have invented a national marital crisis on the basis of a single academic experiment ... of dubious statistical merit," wrote Susan Faludi, then a reporter at the *San Jose Mercury News*. *Boston Globe* columnist Ellen Goodman wrote: "How gleefully they warn that an uppity woman may be overqualified for the marriage market. Reach too high, young lady, and you'll end up in the stratosphere of slim pickings."

According to the study, college-educated unwed women at 30 had only a 20 percent chance of marriage. At 35, their odds dropped to 5 percent; and by the time they were 40 years old, they had a scant 1.3 percent chance of getting married. French researchers had already spread the gloomy news in 1982 that professional women between the ages of 31 and 35 who postponed having children had a 39 percent chance of not being able to conceive at all. Despite the growing number of women who chose not to marry and/or have children, the underlying assumption of such studies was that marriage and children were women's primary goals. These studies contributed to the widespread anxiety of many single career women and served as a minor brake to the continuing progress for women. But these "backlash" tactics were not enough

Vivian Malone, one of the first African Americans to attend the University of Alabama, walks past photographers, the National Guard, and Deputy U.S. Attorney General Nicholas Katzenbach on her way to Foster Auditorium to register for classes in 1963. Governor George Wallace proclaimed his intent to protect segregation, calling federal efforts at integration "tyrannical."

Rep. Martha Griffiths (D-MI) in 1970. In a last-minute hostile move, Howard D. Smith (D-VA) included the criteria of sex to the Civil Rights Act wording in 1964, which he claimed was at the urging of Rep. Griffiths.

to stop women from earning bachelor's and master's degrees. By 1997 female undergraduates made up 55.7 percent of the college population. *Professional Women: Vital Statistics* reported that women have earned more bachelor's degrees than men since 1982 and more master's degrees since 1981. According to Faludi, who authored *Backlash: the War against American Women* (1991), as more women flooded colleges and universities and began preparing to enter previously male-dominated professions, the media continued to engage in a concerted campaign to stem the advancement of women.

ADVANCEMENT AND THE WAGE GAP

Despite these attitudes, progress in education for women in the last 50 years is undeniable. According to *Professional Women: Vital Statistics*, a report published by the AFL-CIO union coalition Department for Professional Employees, in 1961 women received slightly more than 10 percent of all doctoral degrees. By 2008 women were obtaining 48.7 percent of doctorates awarded. *Ladies Home Journal* announced in January 2000 in their millennium predictions that, as a general rule, women were expected to make more than men in the 21st century. They based that assumption on the fact that new technologies would no longer give men an advantage, since they would require brainpower rather than physical effort. In almost every discipline, the number of women students has substantially increased since 1961. In 1960, women made up 5.8 percent of students in medical schools. According to class enrollment for the 2007–08 academic year, women made up 49 percent of medical school students. But the greatest leaps have been in law and dentistry. In 1963, the proportion of women to men in law schools was 3.7 percent. By the 2007–08 academic year, that number had grown to 46.8 percent. Female dental students in 1960 were almost nonexistent, making up only 0.8 percent of dental students. However, during the 2004–05 academic year, 44.5 percent of dental students were female. These numbers indicate an incredible turnaround for women in the last 50 years.

The gap between female and male wages has been persistent, dating from the early 20th century when large numbers of women entered the work world as industrialization expanded in the United States. The pivotal "family wage,"

Gender Bias in American Classrooms

In 1991, the American Association of University Women's Educational Foundation sponsored a study of how girls were treated within American classrooms. Carried out by the Wellesley College Center for Research on Women, the findings of the study, *How Schools Shortchange Girls,* reinforced the findings of studies that had been conducted in the United States since the mid-19th century, concluding that girls repeatedly received less attention from teachers and other school authorities than boys, that the gender gap in science was expanding, that sexual harassment of girls by boys was on the rise, and that standardized testing was gender-biased.

The report also stated that throughout their academic life, girls were discouraged from pursuing fields that were considered the domain of males and found that ongoing experiences of gender bias had resulted in measurably lower self esteem for girls than for boys. The outlook was even grimmer for minority girls and those from low-income families. Other studies had revealed that teachers paid more attention to boys, responding to their questions more often and gearing class activities to their interests. Despite the fact that medical studies suggested that girls were as likely as boys to experience learning disabilities, teachers were more likely to identify such problems in male students.

How Schools Shortchange Girls offered 40 recommendations for improving gender equity in American schools, which ranged from reinforcing compliance with Title IX of the 1972 Education Amendments to providing child care so that teenage mothers could complete high school. The following suggestions were included in those recommendations:

School curricula should deal directly with issues of power, gender politics, and violence against women. Better-informed girls are better equipped to make decisions about their futures. Girls and young women who have a strong sense of themselves are better able to confront violence and abuse in their lives.

Educational organizations must support, via conferences, meetings, budget deliberations, and policy decisions, the development of gender-fair multicultural curricula in all areas of instruction.

Curricula for young children must not perpetuate gender stereotypes and should reflect sensitivity to different learning styles.

---

established for male workers by automaker Henry Ford, was based on the assumption that women were dependent upon males. For generations, scholars have examined the wage gap and attempted to explain why it has continued in the face of women's expanded roles in the American labor force. One such study was conducted by the National Coalition for Women and Girls in Education. By focusing on what they call the STEM subjects (science, technology, engineering, and mathematics), the National Coalition found that considerable progress has been made. At lower educational levels, both girls and boys now study these subjects. In colleges and universities, the number of bachelor's degrees awarded has doubled in the last 20–30 years. The number of females earning doctorates has quadrupled since the 1960s. But despite these gains, women are still earning only 20–25 percent of degrees in physics, computer science, and engineering.

Some scholars believe that the wage gap persists because of female socialization into particular fields that are associated with the traditional role of nurturer, which is generally devalued in American society. In comparison to other fields, most female-dominated professions pay less than those dominated by males. The National Center for Educational Statistics reports that in 1999, doctoral degrees in banking and finance were earned by men 86 percent of the time and by women only 14 percent of the time. Engineering and physics Ph.D.s were awarded to men at a rate of 87 percent as compared to 13 percent for women. Conversely Ph.D.s in nursing were predominantly female (95 percent female versus 5 percent male). Even though Congress allocated $100 million between 1984 and 1998 to hire coordinators to promote equality in education, girls still made up 90 percent of classes that prepared them to enter traditional female-dominated occupations. Conversely, in classes that led to traditionally male-dominated occupations, only 15 percent were female.

Studies are still being conducted on ascertaining gender differences in education that lead to divergent career paths for males and females. Despite years of awareness of how to treat boys and girls equitably in the classroom, male students are still called upon more frequently than females, and professors continue to use sex-stereotyped examples.

SEXUAL HARASSMENT

Since the courts classified sexual harassment as a violation of the Civil Rights Act of 1964, educators have been forced to pay greater attention to the issue of sexual harassment. Most educational institutions have established sexual harassment policies that prohibit particular kinds of behavior. Although instances have been greatly reduced, comments still abound at all school levels concerning the appearances or physical attributes of women as opposed to descriptions of male students. When male professors are accused of sexual harassment, female students may be required to show that they did not wear clothing that was designed to invite sexual advances. As a result of sexual harassment policies, some male college professors, afraid of being accused of improper conduct, may be reluctant to mentor female students. This puts women at a disadvantage since mentoring has proven so beneficial for male students.

Despite considerable obstacles to female educational advancement, girls and women have learned to overcome these barriers, as is evidenced by data from the 2000 census, which reported that women were earning 55.6 percent of bachelor's degrees, 56.8 percent of master's degrees, and 41.3 percent of doctorates. Although these numbers represent impressive gains, they do not delineate the college preparation for traditionally female and traditionally male fields. It is in the STEM subjects that females need to excel in the technological fields of the 21st century.

LAWS, ACTS, AND SUPREME COURT DECISIONS

Without the legal support for equity in education that has occurred since the beginning of the second wave of the women's movement in the 1960s, women would not have made the enormous progress in education that has occurred over the last 50 years. In the 1960s, Lyndon Johnson became a particularly strong proponent of the rights of minorities and women in the workplace, and his advocacy for fairness spilled over into education. After the assassination of President John F. Kennedy in 1963, Johnson was able to parlay the nation's grief and his long congressional career into support for civil rights legislation. The Civil Rights Act of 1964 prohibited discrimination in employment based on race, color, sex, national origin, or religion. The inclusion of females as a protected class was unexpected. Howard W. Smith, a Virginia Democrat, introduced the word "sex" at the last minute on the House floor just before the vote was taken. Many believe he did this to thwart the passage of the Civil Rights Act, which he vehemently opposed. He insisted he did so at the urging of Congresswoman Martha Griffiths (D-MI).

African Americans march through Washington, D.C., in August 1963. Their signs demand equal rights, integrated schools, and decent housing. The following year, the Civil Rights Act was passed.

The impact of the Civil Rights Act of 1964 was substantial in the field of education. In conjunction with a series of court decisions, the act provided the basis for ending segregation in the American public school system. Women used the Civil Rights Act as a rationale for the discussion of all types of discrimination in the school system, for reversing discriminatory practices, and for providing legal support to women and minorities who challenged the status quo. Another significant legal action that occurred during the 1960s was Lyndon Johnson's Executive Order #11246 (1965), which merged the concepts of equal opportunity and affirmative action. To accomplish this, Johnson created the Equal Opportunity Employment Commission. Because of the need to establish goals and timetables for specific action plans designed to employ more minorities and women, contractors began encouraging women and minorities to return to school in order to qualify for jobs that had previously been restricted to white males. Educational institutions established programs for this "non-traditional" workforce, and women even begin entering blue-collar jobs, becoming building contractors, carpenters, electricians, and plumbers.

TITLE IX: IMPLICATIONS AND CONTROVERSY

Perhaps the most significant act passed for the purpose of advancing equity in education was Title IX of the Education Amendments of 1972. The act was renamed the Patsy T. Mink Equal Opportunity in Education Act after Mink, a Democratic congresswoman from Hawaii and the author of the bill, died in 2002. Title IX simply states that "No person in the United States shall on the basis of sex, be denied the benefits of, or be subjected to discrimination under any education program or activity receiving Federal financial assistance." The ramifications were enormous because Title IX included all facets of education. While the public focus was on extracurricular activities such as sports, bands, cheerleading, and clubs, it was also intended to promote the inclusion of females in science, math, and technically oriented classes.

The act also defined sexual harassment as sexual discrimination, which is prohibited under the act. If any educational division or department within an academic institution receives federal funds, the entire institution is covered by Title IX. Most public attention concerning the act has been focused on its application to sports. Ever since the passage of Title IX, there has been a great deal of controversy centered on the amount of money spent for men's and women's athletic activities. Equal opportunities and monies must be made available to both sexes for purchasing equipment, hiring coaches and academic tutors, and providing facilities and services of all kinds. In order to be sure that educational institutions are in compliance, in 1979 the Carter administration established a three-prong test to evaluate athletic spending. The first part requires that athletic opportunities must be offered that mirror the gender proportionality of the school. If one gender is underrepresented,

Title IX at 30

In 2002, the Commission on Opportunity in Athletics, under the auspices of the U.S. Department of Education, conducted an eight-month investigation into the applications of Title IX in American schools. Deborah A. Price served as Executive Director, and Ted Leland and Cynthia Cooper-Dyke acted as co-chairs. The commission was asked to pay particular attention to seven key areas:

Whether or not Title IX was actually promoting equality for male and female athletes.

Whether or not the government was providing adequate support in interpreting and implementing Title IX.

Whether or not additional guidance was needed at the junior and senior high levels to address issues that affected opportunities for athletes to participate in college athletics.

Whether or not activities not defined as spectator sports (i.e., cheerleading and bowling) should be taken into account when determining "equitable opportunities."

How to address inequities inherent in "revenue-producing and large-roster teams" in comparison with other athletic groups.

How to determine the implications of Title IX in providing future opportunities for athletes to participate in the Olympics, professional sports, and community-based sports teams.

Identifying other efforts being employed to promote female participation in athletics, such as those in which the private sector might be involved.

The commission's final report was issued on February 28, 2003. Of 23 recommendations, which were based on the commission's guiding principles of commitment, clarity, fairness, and enforcement, 15 received unanimous approval from commission members. The concept of commitment referred to the desire to remain true to the original intent of Title IX. Clarity, on the other hand, reiterated the need for clear and consistent rules for implementing Title IX. The principle of fairness stated that government should in no way institute policies that undermined enforcement of the original intentions of Title IX. Enforcement dealt with continued aggressive commitment to Title IX but suggested that it would be more productive to promote compliance rather than issuing sanctions against institutions that failed to comply with Title IX.

Patsy T. Mink (D-HI) in 1992. The author of Title IX of the Education Amendments of 1972, Mink died in 2002, and the bill was renamed the Patsy T. Mink Equal Opportunity in Education Act.

the institution must make a concerted effort to expand its athletic programs. The second prong is intended to allow more freedom of action at institutions that have a "history and continuing practice of program expansion" for correcting past inequities. The third part requires academic institutions to "fully and effectively" address the needs of those members of the underrepresented sex who are interested in certain sports programs.

In response to repeated requests to be more explicit on what schools were required to do, the Office of Civil Rights declared in 1996 that proof of nondiscriminatory behavior was based on compliance with any one part of the three-prong test. Under pressure for further clarification, in June 2002, Secretary of Education Rod Paige created the Secretary's Commission on Opportunities in Athletics to investigate the application of Title IX and offer recommendations on how to improve the application of the current standards for measuring equal opportunity to participate in athletics. On February 26, 2003, the commission presented Secretary Paige with its final report, "Open to All: Title IX at Thirty," accompanied by statements from individual members of the commission.

Critics of Title IX have contended that many women are not even interested in participating in sports and, therefore, the use of funds for women's athletics is tantamount to discriminating against men who are more interested in sports and whose sports are more expensive to run. They argue that the effect of funding so many women's programs inevitably leads to the cancellation of sports programs for men. In cases where this has happened, it has resulted in bitter and contentious battles on campuses. These heated disagreements have led to numerous lawsuits over the legitimacy of claims of discrimination. One of the best-known cases filed under Title IX is *Franklin v. Gwinnett County Public Schools,* in which Christine Franklin claimed that under the auspices of Title IX she should receive damages for continual sexual harassment by one of her teachers. In 1992, the Supreme Court agreed, determining that students who experience sexual harassment may be awarded damages. Making school systems responsible for the behavior of their employees created an environment in which all parties were made aware of consequences associated with sexual harassment.

The Family Protection Act, introduced in 1981, called for eliminating all federal laws supporting equal education and prohibited the "intermingling of the sexes in any sport or other school-related activities." Proponents argued that education for girls should be centered on the "career" of marriage and motherhood. And finally, any school that used textbooks portraying women in nontraditional roles should be denied access to federal funding. The act was narrowly defeated.

Several acts and rulings followed that made it clear that the fight for equality in education was an ongoing issue. In 1994 the Gender Equity in Education Act passed, requiring any co-educational institution that received federal money to report the numbers of men and women participating in intercollegiate athletic programs. Grant money was also made available to study discriminatory practices against women. In 1996 the Supreme Court ruled in *United States v. Virginia* that it is unconstitutional for any school receiving public funds to exclude women. This forced the Virginia Military Institute, the last all-male U.S. military college, to begin accepting their first women applicants in 1997.

However, revisions to Title IX in 2006 allowed schools to provide single-sex programs that were not subject to monitoring in regards to their potential for sex stereotyping and discrimination. Early in the 21st century, efforts to expand interpretations of Title IX under the Bush administration and the No Child Left Behind program resulted in a growing number of single-sex schools in the United States, and some experts insist that boys benefit from them as much as girls. Advocates of single-sex education insist that it levels the playing field because in the past such opportunities were restricted to students from wealthy families who could afford to attend exclusive private or parochial schools. Many advocates also argue that taking the opposite sex out of the

Female Douglas High School students in Columbia, Missouri, study science through a program with the University of Missouri and the U.S. Fish and Wildlife Service. By 2002 women were earning nearly 60 percent of all B.A.s and at least half of the Ph.D.s in the humanities, social and life sciences, and education.

Sexual Harassment on College Campuses

Although sexual harassment is not a new phenomenon, women developed much more power to fight against it after the second wave of the feminist movement. Throughout the last three decades of the 20th century, the issue received a good deal of attention on college campuses, where the so-called lecherous professor had had free reign for decades because of the power he held over female students. Even though most female faculty and students knew of the problems that women had with particular professors, victims of sexual harassment were often afraid to come forward because they did not think they would be believed or because they felt others would think they had invited sexual attention. By 1980, the Equal Employment Opportunity Commission had established sexual harassment guidelines based on Title VII of the Civil Rights Act of 1964, which banned discrimination in the workplace on the basis of sex.

In *Alexander v. Yale University* (1977), one of the first cases to deal with sexual harassment in the academic sphere, a lower court determined that students had failed to prove that the university was at fault when a male professor lowered a student's grade after she refused to have sex with him. Additional cases followed, including those at San Jose State University and the University of California–Berkeley, resulting in the firings and suspensions of various college professors. Again and again, the pattern was repeated, with professors receiving minimal censure before returning to the classroom to repeat the same patterns of "lecherous" behavior.

In 1984 Billie Wright Dziech and Linda Weiner described the most likely victims of these professors as nonassertive women, those who were under stress, blondes, nontraditional students, minorities, those pursuing degrees in male-dominated fields, or those who were either uncertain of their academic progress or who were outsiders. Some studies found that professors who fit the profile of "lecherous" had been unpopular or were considered outsiders as adolescents. Therefore, they spent their professional careers trying to reshape their images of themselves as "cool" and "desirable." Others who fit the profile were undergoing professional or midlife crises. They also used their power over female students to improve their self-images. In 1986, in *Meritor Savings Bank v. Vinson* (444 U.S. 57), the Supreme Court clarified the issue of sexual harassment by determining that employers were required to foster a nonhostile working environment, which made them responsible for employees who harassed others. In 1991 the issue of sexual harassment exploded on the national consciousness with the Clarence Thomas Supreme Court hearings. The following year, in *Franklin v. Gwinnett Public Schools* (503 U.S. 60), the Supreme Court held that students who have been sexually harassed may sue educational institutions for damages under Title IX of the 1972 Education Amendments, which bans sex discrimination in education.

daily picture reduces adolescent stress and allows students to concentrate on academics.

WOMEN'S STUDIES

As a result of concentrated efforts by feminists, particularly those in academia, by the 1970s many colleges and universities had begun offering courses in women's studies. In 1970 San Diego University became the first university to establish a women's studies class. According to Beverly Guy-Sheftall in the 2009 spring issue of *Ms.* magazine, which offered a guide to women's studies programs and degrees, there were many reasons for creating courses that focused on women's contributions to a particular field. Before 1970, college courses had focused almost exclusively on men. In humanities classes, students studied the canons of predominantly white Western men such as Chaucer, Shakespeare, and Donne. History was taught from the viewpoint of white males, with barely a mention of women. Standard textbooks ignored even landmark events in women's history such as the woman suffrage movement, which officially started at the Seneca Falls Convention in 1848. Even the passage of the Nineteenth Amendment in 1920 granting female suffrage earned only a brief mention in most history books. The teaching of women's studies encouraged courses that crossed the boundaries among disciplines, promoting a better understanding of what was happening in all disciplines during a particular historical period. By the 1980s, women's studies had introduced the intersections of gender, class, race, and ethnicity. *Ms.* magazine cited examples that supported the value of studying more than just gender. For example, they questioned what happened to low-income girls, often minorities, who could not study math and science due to poorly equipped or nonexistent labs. A number of studies have examined the conduct of white teachers when reacting to African-American girls and compared that conduct to white teachers' interactions with white girls. Results indicate that white teachers had higher expectations for white girls than for African-American girls. When taken in conjunction with studies that reveal that student performance is highly related to teacher expectations, this suggests that African-American girls may not perform up to their individual abilities.

One of the first pioneers of intersectionality was bell hooks, who in her 1984 landmark book, *Feminist Theory from Margin to Center*, examined why women of color could not bond with white women until all systems of domination, encompassing those of gender, race, and class were understood. When Betty Friedan published *The Feminine Mystique* in 1963, she was primarily referring to white, middle-class women who were experiencing "the problem that has no name." According to hooks, Friedan seemed to ignore women of color who were not trying to get out of the house and find a position in the work world, but were dealing with oppressions that existed in response to a capitalist system that served to reinforce materialism and exploitation

Christina Hoff Sommer, author of The War Against Boys, argues that the research cited to support claims of male privilege is "riddled with errors," and that almost none of it has been published in peer-reviewed professional journals.

of the weakest. For these women, she claimed, working outside the home was hardly liberating. For hooks, in order for all women to come together as "sisters," it was necessary to recognize that it was the distribution of wealth that caused so much agony for the poor in American society. Thus, women of color often felt more aligned with men of color than they did with their white "sisters" who had no comprehension of their problems.

Friedan and hooks were addressing the women's movement from different perspectives. Friedan, a liberal feminist, was not attempting to destroy American society. She was concerned with why women like her were not happy when they had done everything that was required of them to fulfill the American dream, and she was trying to change the existing system to accommodate women's rights. As a radical feminist, hooks was reacting to a women's movement that she believed had taken on some of the trappings of the diseased patriarchal system, which she blamed for discriminating against both women and minorities. In response to valid complaints by hooks and others like her, the women's movement became more inclusive as it expanded. Women's studies also served to lay some of the groundwork for gay and lesbian studies. In some cases, such studies have since been absorbed by women's studies programs, while in other cases, they stand alone. More recently, gender studies and men's studies have become outgrowths of women's studies programs. The growth of cultural studies in which gender, race, class, and ethnicity are analyzed is increasingly being developed in universities throughout the country.

Guy-Sheftall reports in *Ms.* magazine that there have been very specific effects of women advocating for social awareness and change due to the courses they have taken in women's studies. For instance, some feminists argue that the Violence against Women Act, which required states to get much tougher concerning violence against women, was a direct result of the practical implications of women's studies courses. In the 1994 act, Congress appropriated $1.6 billion to pay for more extensive investigation into violent crimes, prosecuting perpetrators, and imposing mandatory restitution on individuals convicted of violence against women. Because women are usually the victims of sexual harassment and because it is a persistent problem on college campuses, sexual harassment is another issue that receives a good deal of support from those who have taken women's studies courses. Other issues of concern often assumed to be an outgrowth of consciousness-raising of women's studies classes include fighting to end human trafficking, which had become an extensive worldwide problem; addressing inequities in women's health issues; and promoting subsidized childcare for low-income women.

As of 2009, there were 900 women's studies programs in the United States, offering over 10,000 courses. These programs also existed in 40 countries around the world. Not only do specific women's studies courses exist, but many mainstream courses also now include women as an integral part of the course material. There are at least 31 master's degree programs and 16 Ph.D. programs in women's studies in the United States. The largest of these are at Rutgers University, Emory University, the University of California–Los Angeles, the University of Maryland–College Park, and the University of Washington. According to Layli Phillips in *Ms.* magazine, these graduates are getting jobs in "government, policy and research institutions, foundations, and nonprofits."

LOOKING AHEAD

In 2000 Christina Hoff Sommers published *The War against Boys: How Misguided Feminism is Harming Our Young Men*, arguing that in the past 30 years, efforts for gender equity in the schools have actually harmed boys. She cites numerous statistics to support her hypothesis, arguing that girls now make up a large part of advanced placement classes in schools, undergraduate and graduate students are disproportionately female, and women are catching up in professional schools.

In 2008, The American Association of University Women (the AAUW) countered Sommers's claims by publishing *Where the Girls Are: The Facts about Gender Equity in Education*. The book reported on a study of girls' educational achievements in the past 35 years, making three major points. The first was that "girls' successes don't come at boys' expense." In other words, because girls are continuing to improve their academic achievements, it does not mean that boys are falling behind. On the contrary, the percentage of boys obtaining high school diplomas and college degrees was at an all-time high in 2008. Boys were still doing slightly better on SAT scores on math and verbal skills as well. Among traditional-aged students from high-income families, boys are still more likely to go to college than girls. Among nontraditionally aged students, however, more women than men attend college. Second, according to the AAUW, "On average, girls' and boys' educational performance has improved." Scores on college entrance exams for both men and women have actually gotten higher. Their third, and perhaps most significant argument, is that "understanding disparities by race/ethnicity and family income level is critical to understanding girls' and boys' achievement." Young people who come from low-income families and families of color, regardless of gender, score lower on tests than men and women from high-income white families. African-American and Hispanic boys and girls score lower than white and Asian-American boys and girls. Boys and girls from African-American and Hispanic families are more consistent with each other on their test scores, regardless of gender considerations, than they are with gender comparisons between boys and girls of all races and income status.

CONCLUSION

There is much evidence to support the claim that women have made great advances in the field of education and that they have broken down barriers to achievement that had existed for centuries. Nevertheless, there are arguments that there is still much ground to cover before women are treated equally at all levels of education and before they are encouraged to enter those fields that are still considered best suited to males. While there are distinct advantages to single-sex educational environments, some claim that total segregation by sex is no more acceptable than total segregation by race, class, or ethnicity. Women's studies classes continue to be a significant avenue for teaching students about the contributions that women have made, and helping them to understand the issues that are important to women politically, socially, and

First Lady "Lady Bird" Johnson visits a classroom for Project Head Start in 1968. Inspired by her husband's declaration of "unconditional war on poverty" in 1965, she worked with the Office of Economic Development Chief, Sargent Shriver, to support a program providing underprivileged preschool children with early education skills, basic medical care, and nutrition.

personally. A push for promoting women's inclusion in broader school curricula is intended to ensure that teachers and coursework identify women as significant contributors to American history and society. Some have suggested that for the future of education, more effort and money must be committed to helping youngsters from ethnic minorities, particularly girls in certain cultures, to be able to compete with boys and girls from white families. The extraordinary gains for girls and women in the past 30–50 years serve as a working model for future improvement in the educational attainment of all American youngsters.

Myrna A. Hant
UCLA Center for the Study of Women

Further Reading

American Association of University Women. *How Schools Shortchange Girls.* Washington, D.C.: American Association of University Women Educational Foundation, 1992.

Anderson, Margaret L. *Thinking about Women: Sociological Perspectives on Sex and Gender.* Boston, MA: Allyn and Bacon, 1997.

Beauvoir, Simone de. *The Second Sex.* New York: Bantam Books, 1961.

Commission on Opportunity in Athletics. "'Open to All:' Title IX at Thirty." Available Online, URL: http://www.ed.gov/about/bdscomm/list/athletics/title9report.pdf. Accessed December 2009.

Cressey, Sarah R. *Educational Attainment in the United States: 2007.* Washington, D.C.: United States Bureau of the Census, 2009.

Davis, Sara N. et al., eds. *Educational Success in Girls and Women.* San Francisco, CA: Jossey-Bass, 1999.

Dziech, Billie Wright, and Linda Weiner. *The Lecherous Professor: Sexual Harassment on Campus.* Boston, MA: Beacon Press, 1984.

Faludi, Susan. *Backlash: The Undeclared War against American Women.* New York: Anchor Books, 1991.

Friedan, Betty. *The Feminist Mystique.* New York: Norton, 1963.

Hacker, Andrew. *Mismatch: the Growing Gulf between Women and Men.* New York: Scribner, 2003.

hooks, bell. *Feminist Theory from Margin to Center.* Cambridge, MA: South End Press, 2000.

Howe, Florence and Ellen Bass, eds. *No More Masks! An Anthology of Poems by Women.* New York: Anchor Press. 1973.

Koch, Janice and Beverly Irby, eds. *Defining and Redefining Gender Equity in Education.* Greenwich, CT: Information Age Publishing, 2002.

McGinn, Daniel. "Marriage by the Numbers." *Newsweek* (June 5, 2006). Available online, URL: http://www.newsweek.com/id/52295. Accessed January 2010.

Millett, Kate. *Sexual Politics*. New York: Avon Books, 1969.

Morgan, Robin, ed. *Sisterhood is Powerful*. New York: Vintage Books, 1970.

Renzetti, Claire M. and Daniel J. Curran. *Women, Men and Society*. Boston, MA: Allyn and Bacon, 2003.

Rivera, Lorna. *Laboring to Learn: Women's Literacy and Poverty in the Post-Welfare Era.* Urbana: University of Illinois Press, 2008.

Schneir, Miriam, ed. *Feminism in Our Time*. New York: Vintage Books, 1994.

Guy-Sheftall, Beverly. "Forty Years Of Women's Studies." *Ms.* (Spring 2009).

Sommers, Christina Hoff. "A Threat in Title IX." *The Washington Post* (April 14, 2009). Available online, URL: http://www.washingtonpost.com/wp-dyn/content/article/2009/04/13/AR2009041302119.html. Accessed March 2010.

Sommers, Christina Hoff. *The War Against Boys: How Misguided Feminism Is Harming Our Young Men*. New York: Simon & Schuster, 2000.

Weis, Lois and Michelle Fine. *Beyond Silenced Voices: Class, Race, and Gender in United States Schools.* Albany, NY: State University of New York Press, 2005.

CHAPTER 5

Women in Politics

NEARLY INVISIBLE IN 1960, women political activists and public officials succeeded in transforming politics in the United States over the following five decades, offering new insights into existing social problems and addressing the rights of women and children. The years after 1960 encompassed the tumultuous second wave of feminism, hard-fought battles to defend advances made in women's legal rights and equality during the Reagan and two Bush administrations, and progress under the Clinton and Obama administrations. One of the defining issues of this period was the fight for women to control their reproductive lives. The abortion issue frequently took center stage, and a pro-life or pro-choice stance became a litmus test for being appointed to the federal judiciary. Female politicians and women's rights advocates also turned public attention to issues such as the Equal Rights Amendment (ERA), sexual harassment, violence against women, the feminization of poverty, women's and children's health, and the needs of working mothers and their children.

REBIRTH AND CONTROVERSY
Social movements typically develop from widespread recognition of shared grievances. That was true of the second wave of feminism; many activists were from a generation of women who experienced the contradiction between how women's lives were portrayed in the mass media, and working in an economy

A Brooklyn mother marches with her five-month-old baby along with a ban-the-bomb group outside the United Nations in 1962. Women played a prominent role in early antinuclear activism, citing dangers to their children.

where women faced pervasive employment discrimination. The idealized portrayal of women's lives in popular culture in 1960, with its emphasis on the roles of homemaker and mother, bore increasingly little resemblance to the lives that most American women actually lived. Although a larger percentage of women were employed full time outside the home in 1960 than in previous decades, their incomes were on average only three-fifths those of men. Sexual harassment at work was common. Women with full-time paid employment still found themselves described as "housewives" by the mass media. Survey research in the 1970s showed that although paid employment generally improved a woman's sense of well being, employed women in traditional marriages where housework and childcare responsibilities were not shared with their husbands endured high levels of stress. All of these social forces prepared American women for the revelation that "the personal is political."

Grievances of women long ignored or dismissed by press and politicians became demands for legal reform and political representation because of several events that occurred in the early 1960s. The first was the December 14, 1961, decision of President John F. Kennedy to appoint a President's Commission on the Status of Women, chaired by Eleanor Roosevelt. That decision was followed by a 1962 presidential order directing federal agencies to make employment decisions without regard to sex. Women's issues were ignored during the 1960 presidential election, but Kennedy's advisors were forced to consider the potential of women as voters in relation to his expected 1964 reelection bid and the long-term prospects of the Democratic Party. Women outnumbered men as voters in the 1964 election and in every subsequent presidential election. Although they would not outnumber men as eligible voters until 1980, the higher levels of voting by women that began in 1964 reflected a combination of civic duty, political mobilization, and dissatisfaction with the status quo.

Two books that had an enormous impact on the emerging women's movement were published in 1963: *American Women, Report of the President's Commission on the Status of Women,* and Betty Friedan's *The Feminine Mystique.* The pragmatic public policy goals outlined in *American Women* and the powerful indictment of sexism expressed in *The Feminine Mystique* reawakened interest in social reform and resulted in demands for legislative action. Freidan's book resonated with many women by articulating the dissatisfaction and frustration many felt about how the constraints of domesticity prevented them from achieving their full human potential.

Betty Friedan was also instrumental in bringing together a group of leaders, including attorneys Marguerite Rawalt and Caruthers Berger, and labor activists Dorothy Haener and Caroline Davis, to plan the 1966 conference that launched the National Organization for Women (NOW) in 1965. NOW's initial focus was on expanding career opportunities for women and on lobbying the Equal Employment Opportunity Commission for more vigorous action against employment discrimination. Passage of the Equal Pay Act of 1963 and the inclusion of sex in the list of prohibited categories of employment discrimination in Title VII of the Civil Rights Act of 1964 made it logical to prioritize lobbying for stronger laws and regulatory enforcement for fairness in employment. In October 1967, sex was included as a category

A large crowd gathers at the Capitol March for Equal Rights Amendment (ERA) rally in front of the Florida Supreme Court in 1982. The ERA was introduced into every session of Congress between 1923 and 1972, when it was passed and sent to the states for ratification. However, by the extended deadline, the ERA had only been ratified by 35 states, three states short of the 38 required for ratification. It has been reintroduced into every Congress since that time and has not passed.

in the affirmative action programs mandated for federal agencies and private companies doing business with them.

By the end of the 1960s, NOW had attracted women activists from what became known as the New Left, a political movement that rejected hierarchy and bureaucracy and advocated radical changes in government, politics, and society. The New Left helped NOW to develop from a small interest group focused on employment and education to a mass-membership organization linking the different strands of the women's movement. NOW's agenda expanded to include demands for federal funding for child care, maternity leave rights, Social Security benefits for mothers without paid employment, abortion rights, and ratification of the Equal Rights Amendment (ERA). NOW also helped to focus attention on the problems of sexual violence, domestic abuse, and sexual harassment.

Another important organization in the fight for women's rights was the National Association for Repeal of Abortion Laws (NARAL), which was organized as a national pro-choice lobby in 1969. Following the 1973 U.S. Supreme Court decision in *Roe v. Wade*, which recognized constitutionally protected access to abortion as a privacy right, the group changed its name to the National Abortion Rights Action League, and kept its familiar acronym. In 2009 NARAL had chapters in 22 states and was an ongoing presence in the fight to retain reproductive rights and protect access to abortion.

The attained goals of the feminist women's movement clashed with the objectives of conservative activists, who desired to either overturn or re-

Pro-life marchers demonstrate on Monroe Street in front of the capitol in Tallahassee, Florida, in 1990. Since the Supreme Court decision in Roe v. Wade *in 1973, pro-life groups have argued that the decision was made on faulty and incomplete testimony, and have advocated for the rights of unborn children.*

The Growth of the National Organization for Women

In 1967, the National Organization for Women (NOW) had approximately 1,000 members. By 1972, its membership had grown to a modest 15,000. In 2009 it had 600,000 members, with at least one local chapter in each of the 435 congressional districts. Some of the chapters in more rural southern or western congressional districts are small, often consisting of no more than 100 members and operating from a chapter president's home.

Many college campuses also have NOW chapters. NOW's presence in every district and the large size of the national membership four decades after it was established make the organization a force that cannot be ignored in American politics.

National Organization for Women President Eleanor Smeal during a visit to Florida State University in 1979.

NOW's political clout in the United States is matched only by a handful of dominant mass membership interest groups, such as the environmentally oriented Sierra Club and the American Association of Retired Persons (AARP). Through political action committees (PACs), NOW actively supports women who endorse women's issues for political office. In addition to advocating foundational issues such as reproductive rights and bans against sexual discrimination, NOW actively supports economic justice, lesbian rights, and cultural and racial diversity.

One of the indications that a mass membership organization is viable is the strong, periodical competition for leadership positions. That was certainly true of NOW in June 2009 when its members were faced with what some observers described as an intergenerational contest for the presidency between Terry O'Neill and Latifa Lyles.

Terry O'Neill is a white 56-year-old former law professor who worked as a community activist in New Orleans and campaigned to defeat white supremacist David Duke in his 1991 bid to become governor of the state of Louisiana. She had already served as the vice president for membership for NOW from 2001 to 2005. She promised to tap the grassroots feminist outrage about the ground lost by the women's movement during the two terms of President George W. Bush. Latifa Lyles is a 33-year-old African American who advocated exploiting the internet to recruit younger members. O'Neill won the election by only eight votes.

Women protest the ERA outside the White House in 1977. Women's groups on opposing political spectrums frequently clashed over the issue. Conservative political activist and attorney Phyllis Schlafly (left, in 1967) voiced her opposition to the ERA, prompting liberal activist attorney Florynce Kennedy, on CBS radio in Miami in 1974, to say, "I just don't see why some people don't hit Phyllis Schlafly in the mouth."

duce the scope of *Roe v. Wade*, and opposed ratification of the ERA on many grounds. These voices pointed out that the ERA would harm women and families by reversing women's exemption from military combat duty, dilute the powers of individual states and transfer them to federal courts, and make abortion funding a new constitutional right. Although social conservatives were successful in defeating the ERA, they achieved only a stalemate on the issue of abortion. The struggle over abortion actually began in 1965 with the U.S. Supreme Court decision in *Griswold v. Connecticut*, which struck down the last state law banning contraception. That decision identified the right of married couples to use contraception as a fundamental privacy right and established the right to privacy as the grounds for reproductive freedom that undergirded the Supreme Court's decision in *Roe v. Wade* (1973). A sexual revolution was taking place during this period, and Americans had become more open to the concept of reproductive freedom, despite opposition from the groups such as the Roman Catholic Church, the Mormon Church, and the Evangelical Protestant Church, which were homogenized by the media as the so-called Religious Right. While battles raged over parental and spousal consent, waiting periods for women seeking abortions,

Women of the New Left

Many of the women who energized the second wave of feminism were politically socialized by New Left protests of the 1960s. The New Left, a radical youth counterculture movement, sought to revolutionize American systems and politics and build a new utopia. Similar to the women of the first wave of feminism who rebelled at sexism within the abolitionist movement, many of the leaders in the second wave experienced a feminist political awakening because of the sexism exhibited by their male colleagues in the civil rights and peace movements. Not only were the struggles against racism and imperialism given priority over the struggle against sexism in New Left organizations like the Congress of Racial Equality (CORE), Students for a Democratic Society (SDS), and the Black Panther Party, but men held the majority of leadership positions in those organizations, and the rhetoric they employed was often demeaning to women.

In her memoir *With the Weathermen*, SDS activist Susan Stern diagnoses the weakness of the SDS and the response of women activists during the emblematic protests at Columbia University in 1968:

"Part of the problem with Columbia SDS, and everywhere else, was that it was operating at 50 percent of its potential. Women were almost systematically excluded from anything but secondary role[s] throughout the fall and into the winter ... Toward winter it became clear to all factions of SDS that women intended to be seen and heard. It was gradual and painstaking but relentless. Women began to attend meetings in clusters, to sit in groups, and to raise their hands simultaneously in response to arguments."

By the late 1960s, women had begun to abandon male-dominated, radical New Left groups to establish their own organizations to critique sexism, protest subjugation, and demand equality. Groups such as the Feminists, New York Radical Women, Bread and Roses, the Furies, and Redstockings emerged to do the organizing work that male-dominated New Left groups had deemed secondary to other causes. Although many of the groups were short lived, their activists continued to play important roles in the larger women's movement, and the social problems they identified became part of the feminist public policy agenda. The New York Radical Feminists, for example, held the first Rape Speak Out event in 1970. That and subsequent successful protests in cities and university campuses across the country dramatically increased public awareness about the problem of sexual assault and fostered reforms among police investigators and prosecutors.

The 1970 Black Panther Convention at the Lincoln Memorial.

and whether or not agencies receiving federal funds could mention abortion as a solution to unwanted pregnancies, the Supreme Court steadily turned control over access to abortions to states without ever directly overturning *Roe*. Such was the case with both the 1989 *Webster v. Reproductive Health Services* and the 1992 *Planned Parenthood of Southeastern Pennsylvania v. Casey* decisions. Because of restrictions on access to abortion and the violence that has taken place at some clinics offering abortion services, many physicians have moved to other states or are refusing to provide abortion services. As a result, three states have only one abortion clinic, and many women must travel long distances to obtain abortions. Pro-choice advocates argue that this limited access places an undue burden on poor women who face unwanted or ill-advised pregnancies.

THE ROAD TO POLITICAL POWER

The culture war between American feminists and conservatives exacerbated the gender gap in American elections. The term *gender gap* was coined by Eleanor Smeal of NOW, who used it to call attention to differences in the ways that women and men approached politics. Differences in voting patterns were not new. In the 1952 election, women supported Republican Dwight Eisenhower over Democrat Adlai Stevenson by a margin of 5 percent. At that time, Republicans were seen as slightly more supportive than Democrats of women's issues. Four years later, the gender gap had increased to 6 percent. By 1960, the pattern had shifted, and women became more likely to support Democrats for office. By the late 1960s, public opinion polls were showing that women were more likely to identify themselves as Democrats than Republicans. With the election of Ronald Reagan in 1980 and the political shift to the right, the gender gap widened considerably. Throughout the Reagan administration, feminists argued that women's issues were relegated to the backburner. Outspoken Congresswoman Bella Abzug (D-NY)

Bella Abzug's famous campaign poster from 1970. A leading American feminist and human rights activist, Abzug served in Congress 1970–76. Afterward, she headed the National Advisory Committee on Women; founded Women, USA; and co-founded the Women's Environment and Development Organization.

Progress Without Parity: Elected Women

While women made up approximately 51 percent of the national population and a higher percentage of the electorate, in 2009 only 74, or 23.6 percent, of 314 elected statewide executive positions were held by women. By the first decade of the 21st century, only seven governors, eight lieutenant governors, 13 secretaries of state, and 10 state treasurers were female.

Although the number of women in Congress was higher than it had ever been, women still comprised disproportionately small percentages in both legislative chambers. Only 17 of the 100 seats in the Senate and only 73 or 16.8 percent of the 435 seats in the House were held by women. In 2009, there were no women in 29 of the 50 state delegations to the House. As a point of comparison, in 2009 some 71 countries had higher percentages of women in their national legislatures than the United States. Japan was the only wealthy liberal democracy to rank lower. By contrast, in Canada, usually considered politically and culturally similar to the United States, women held 68 of the 308 seats (22.1 percent) in the Canadian House of Commons, and 32 of 93 seats, or 34.4 percent, in the Canadian Senate.

The picture across the American state legislatures is slightly better than in the U.S. Congress, but is still only approximately halfway to parity. In 2009, women held 1,792 of 7,382 seats in state legislatures, or 24.3 percent. Closest to parity was Colorado, with women comprising 39 percent of its state legislature. Farthest from parity was Oklahoma, with women comprising only 10 percent of its state legislature. Finally, of the 246 major cities with populations of more than 100,000, 36 (14.6 percent) of the mayors are women. Among the 100 largest cities in the United States, only 11 had female mayors. The largest city with a female mayor was Baltimore, Maryland, where Sheila Dixon was the chief political officer.

This limited legislative representation of women means that women's issues often receive little attention, and women who serve in office often have an uphill battle to put the concerns of women and children in a prominent place on the legislative agendas. There is an ongoing debate about whether or not males can adequately represent women's issues, but it is clear that the support of males is essential to successfully addressing women's issues.

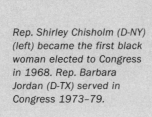

Rep. Shirley Chisholm (D-NY) (left) became the first black woman elected to Congress in 1968. Rep. Barbara Jordan (D-TX) served in Congress 1973–79.

accused Reagan of launching "a massive, across-the-board attack on every government program affecting women and children that had been laboriously won" in previous years.

By the early 1990s, the gender gap in presidential elections had grown to double digits, with analysis showing that the gender gap was largest among those with college educations and those in professional or managerial occupations. In 1996, political candidates began courting so-called soccer moms, a mythical constituency made up of political savvy, educated, middle-class women dedicated to childrearing, because they were considered essential to winning the election. In 2004, in the wake of the terrorist attacks of 9/11, Senator Joe Biden coined the term *security moms* to describe women whose main concerns were security, fighting terrorism, and keeping their families safe. He warned fellow Democrats that the needs of those security moms must be addressed in the upcoming election.

Following the fiasco of the 1991 Clarence Thomas confirmation hearings, women were actively recruited for political office, and news headline writers declared 1992 as the Year of the Woman. The number of women in the House of Representatives rose from 38 to 47, and the female presence in the Senate increased from two to five. Over time, as more women joined the male-dominated world of the U.S. Congress, they began to realize they were stronger when they came together to fight for the rights of women and children. In 1978, female legislators established the Congresswomen's Caucus. Although the group has always been bipartisan, Democratic women generally proved to be more supportive than Republican women of the caucus' agenda. One exception was Olympia Snowe (R-ME) who co-chaired the caucus along with Patricia Schroeder (D-CO). Support for feminist goals dwindled in the conservative years of the Reagan administration, and the caucus broadened its scope in 1981, becoming the Congressional Caucus for Women's Issues

Two notable women who have served in Congress include Jan Schakowsky (left; D-IL), who was elected to the House of Representatives in 1998, and Olympia Snowe (R-ME), who became the first Republican woman with a full-term seat on the Senate Finance Committee in 2001.

and admitting men who supported women's issues as nonvoting members. Although the group underwent major divisions during the what Republicans dubbed the Republican Revolution of the 1990s, the caucus managed to keep the focus on issues such as women's health, violence against women, and human trafficking. Jan Schakowsky (D-IL) and Mary Fallin (R-OK) were elected as co-chairs for the 111th Congress in December 2008.

That more women serve in political office at all levels is due in large part to the efforts of fundraising groups such as EMILY's List, the National Women's Political Caucus, and state groups such as Georgia's WIN and Pennsylvania's Women's Campaign Fund. EMILY's List was founded in 1985 on the premise that "Early Money Is Like Yeast, it helps the dough rise" by 25 women advocating for pro-choice Democratic women to be elected to office. By the 21st century, membership had climbed to more than 100,000. As of 2009 women elected with the help of EMILY's List included 10 U.S. Senators (seven were the first U.S. Senators ever elected from their states), five state governors (three were the first women governors of their states), and 12 new female representatives who joined 38 others in the U.S. House of Representatives. Unlike EMILY's List, the National Women's Political Caucus has always been bipartisan. It was founded in 1971 for the purpose of electing pro-choice women to political office. The National Federation of Republican Women is active in training, recruiting, and funding Republican women for political office.

WOMEN IN POWER

One of the important ways that women have gained political power is by election. No woman has been elected president or vice president of the United States. However, in the 2008 race for the White House, New York Senator and former First Lady Hillary Clinton came close to winning the Democratic Party's presidential nomination. She lost to Illinois Senator Barack Obama and later accepted the post of U.S. secretary of State. That same year, Alaska Governor Sarah Palin was nominated as the Republican Party's vice presidential candidate. This was only the second time that a woman had been nominated by a major party for the second position on its national ticket. The first time had been in 1984, when the Democratic Party nominated Representative Geraldine Ferraro of New York for that position. Women learned a great deal from the 1984 election. Ferraro found that she was treated differently and commented that she often felt like a bridesmaid because she was inundated with flowers at every stop on campaign tours. When her slip inadvertently showed as she raised her hand to wave, the media turned the incident into a major news story. George Bush, Ferraro's Republican opponent, called attention to the fact that as a woman, Ferraro had never served in combat, insisting that she would be reluctant to send males to war or react aggressively to a potential nuclear attack.

Between 1979 and 2009 the percentage of women in the U.S. House of Representatives increased from 3 percent to 16.8 percent. Although that is a major increase, it is still well short of gender parity. The story is the same for the U.S. Senate and for state and local level legislative bodies; women are a long way from making up 50 percent of legislatures at any level. Several factors have prevented American legislatures from achieving gender parity. The first factor is that women, in order to have children, typically wait longer than men to begin their political careers. The responsibilities of being a parent or caregiver for an elderly, ill, or disabled family member is more likely to fall to women than to men. That is why women are sometimes described as working a "double shift," one at the office and another at home. Women are more likely than men to wait until their children are older or have reached adulthood to run for elective office the first time. That not only delays their individual political careers but reduces the total number of women who are available to compete in elections.

The second factor is that because incumbent legislators normally win if they run for reelection, running as a challenger is difficult, for both women and men. As a result, first-time candidates have the best chances of winning in open-seat races or in special elections. Open-seat races occur when an incumbent candidate does not run for reelection, and special elections occur when there is an unexpected vacancy in an elected office due to the death or resignation of the officeholder. Virtually all of the early female members of Congress were "congressional widows" who were selected to fill seats vacated by the deaths of their husbands. For instance, Lindy Boggs (D-LA) was elected to the House in 1973 upon the loss of her husband, Thomas Hale Boggs Sr., in a plane crash. She served until 1990. Likewise, Mary Bono Mack (R-CA) became a member of the House only after the death of her husband Sonny Bono in 1998 in a skiing accident. Bono Mack, who has remarried, continues to represent California's 45th District.

U.S. Secretary of State Hillary Rodham Clinton participates in a ceremonial tree planting at Nairobi University in Nairobi, Kenya, on August 6, 2009. After her unsuccessful presidential primary bid in 2008, Clinton was appointed as secretary of state by President Barack Obama.

Successful first-time candidates often have advantages. Many enjoy name recognition among voters because they have held lower-level elective offices or have had careers as lawyers, business executives, academics, social workers, athletes, or entertainers. U.S. Senator Barbara Mikulski (D-MD) got her start in politics as a social worker who participated in civil rights campaigns. That led to her 1969 decision to run for the Baltimore City Council in an effort to save a neighborhood from a highway project. Growing up in a political family and observing electoral politics firsthand also helps. U.S. Senator Mary Landrieu (D-LA) not only learned how to get elected, but benefited from positive name recognition among voters because her father was Maurice "Moon" Landrieu, who was elected mayor of New Orleans twice in the 1970s and was credited with the passage of laws outlawing segregation based on race and religion.

Alaska Governor Sarah Palin autographs a USO banner during a morale visit to Ramstein Air Base in Germany in 2007. Palin's vice-presidential run, with Senator John McCain in 2008, made her the first female vice-presidential nominee of the Republican Party.

Another important advantage enjoyed by successful first-time candidates is that they can raise enough money to finance their campaigns. Running for a seat in most state legislatures or for most local offices is still relatively inexpensive. However, running for Congress can be very expensive, and good potential congressional candidates are often dissuaded from running by the high cost of campaigns. Multi-million-dollar campaigns are common because of the need to pay television and radio stations to broadcast advertising and to pay the salaries of professional campaign managers, pollsters, and fundraisers. As people would rather back winners, campaigns that begin with more money appear to be more promising to potential donors and to prominent elected officials and newspaper editors who might give their endorsements.

Women have proven more willing than men to risk running for some congressional seats. In most cases, candidates must win the Democratic or Republican primary before they can represent a particular party in the general election. Women have been most likely to contest primary elections in urban districts with larger percentages of African-American and higher-income residents. Many senators served in the House of Representatives before making a run for a Senate seat. In the past, women were more likely to run for Senate

Nancy Pelosi, Madam Speaker

When she was sworn in as Speaker of the U.S. House of Representatives on January 4, 2007, Nancy Pelosi became the single most powerful woman in American politics, the first woman in American history ever to rise to a position of such influence. On taking office, Pelosi stated, "It's an historic moment for the Congress, it's an historic moment for the women of America. It is a moment for which we have waited over 200 years. Never losing faith, we waited through the many years of struggle to achieve our rights. But women weren't just waiting, women were working, never losing faith we worked to redeem the promise of America, that all men and women are created equal."

Elected from the liberal Eighth District of California, which includes most of San Francisco, Pelosi was chosen by the majority of Democrats on the strength of her record of legislative leadership on health care policy, family planning, environmental protection, government ethics, intelligence, and international human rights.

To celebrate Pelosi's success, Representative Rosa DeLauro (D-CT) held an afternoon tea on the eve of Pelosi's swearing-in ceremony to honor both the incoming Speaker and Anne Richards, a former governor of Texas and an outspoken feminist who had died the previous year. DeLauro commented that the sound heard when Pelosi takes the Speaker's gavel, "will be the glass ceiling in this country, and the marble ceiling in this institution, shattering."

Pelosi was able to break through the "marble ceiling" of the congressional leadership less by working her way up from lower-level positions in the party leadership than by effective work on the House Appropriations Committee. Much of the power of Congress is exercised by controlling government funding, and the House Appropriations Committee has immense influence over the amounts of money spent on the programs of federal departments and agencies. Beginning with Ronald Reagan, conservatives regularly blocked funding for family planning and abortion in bills designed to aid developing countries because of the controversy over abortion. Because she sat on Appropriations, Pelosi was able to retain funding for international family planning. Her success as Speaker of the House is attributable to her ability to unite the different factions of the Democratic Party in the U.S. House of Representatives, including liberals, New Democratic Coalition centrists, and conservative Blue Dog Democrats; and to her self-presentation as a mother and grandmother to her five children and seven grandchildren. That approach has been leveraged in deflecting criticism from both conservative Democrats and Republicans who have argued that Pelosi is too liberal.

Nancy Pelosi in 2007.

seats from small-population states, where the numbers of voters in House races were more similar to the numbers of voters in Senate races. In today's Senate races, however, women are just as likely to run and win in large-population states as in small-population states.

Achieving gender parity in legislatures matters because female legislators tend to take on difficult issues that their male colleagues either ignore or treat as low priority. Women in state legislatures are more likely to serve on committees that have responsibility for health care, welfare, and education. California State Senator Carol Liu, for example, serves as chair of the Senate Human Services Committee and is a member of the Education Committee, Budget Subcommittee for Education, and Public Employees and Retirement Committee. Women in state legislatures are also more likely to make families, children, and the elderly their legislative priorities. Georgia State Representative Stephanie Benfield, for example, has authored state legislation providing tax relief for the elderly, reforming child custody laws, requiring equal treatment for girl's athletic programs in public education, increasing patient access to medical records, and punishing perpetrators of domestic violence.

The other route to public office is by appointment. That women are appointed to the cabinet of the president and to positions of equal importance with men is no longer uncommon. The current and two previous secretaries of state are women: Hilary Rodham Clinton, Condoleezza Rice, and Madeline Albright. Women are still underrepresented in the federal judiciary. In 2008, only 24.5 percent of Federal District Court judges and 27 percent of Federal Circuit Court of Appeals judges were women. By 2009 only three women had ever served on the U.S. Supreme Court: Sandra Day O'Connor, Ruth Bader Ginsburg, and Sonia Sotomayor. No more than two women have ever served on the nine-member court at any one time.

The characteristics and political views of those sitting on the federal courts are significant for the rights of women. A recent study of the decisions of judges on U.S. Courts of Appeals, the three-judge panels that hear appeals from cases tried in U.S. District Courts, showed that their decisions reflected the political party and political ideology of the president who appointed them. For example, judges appointed by Republican presidents were more likely to decide against plaintiffs in sexual harassment cases than were judges appointed by Democratic presidents. In most cases, partisanship and ideology were reduced when judges sat on mixed panels with judges who had been appointed by a president of the opposition party. However, that was not true for cases involving abortion. Regardless of the other members of the panels, judges appointed by Republican presidents have tended to take pro-life positions.

CONCLUSION
Since 1960, the American women's movement has established strong lobbying groups, won legislative and judicial victories, survived the defeat of the

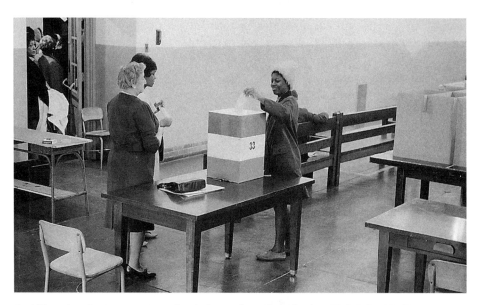

An African-American woman casts her ballot at the polls in Cardozo High School in Washington, D.C., on November 1964. Lyndon B. Johnson won by a landslide in the 1964 presidential elections. Also in 1964, the landmark Civil Rights Act passed in the House and Senate.

ERA, changed public attitudes about the equality of women, and helped overcome some of the gender imbalance in elective and appointive public office. However, women have not achieved parity at any political level, which curtails their ability to make decisions promoting the interests of women and children. Median earnings of women are still only 67 percent those of men, and women are still more likely to be employed in low-status, female-dominated occupations. Violence against women remains a major issue in communities throughout the United States, and in some areas, rape victims are still treated with suspicion rather than compassion. Social conservatives continue to lobby for the appointment of federal judges and Supreme Court justices willing to allow state governments to restrict access to abortion. A woman has been elected speaker of U.S. House of Representatives. However, no woman has ever been elected president or vice president. Nor has a woman ever been named as chief justice of the U.S. Supreme Court. American politics has been dramatically transformed by the women's movement over the last five decades, but there is still a long way for women and society to go.

JOHN HICKMAN
BARRY UNIVERSITY

Further Reading

Abzug, Bella. *Gender Gap: Bella Abzug's Guide to Political Power for American Women.* Boston, MA: Houghton Mifflin, 1984.

Baker, Carrie N., *The Women's Movement Against Sexual Harassment.* New York: Cambridge University Press, 2008.

Barakso, Maryann. *Governing Now: Grassroots Activism in the National Organization of Women.* Ithaca, NY: Cornell University Press, 2003.

Burell, Barbara. "Women Candidates in Open-Seat Primaries for the U.S. House: 1968–1990." *Legislative Studies Quarterly,* v.17/4 (1992).

Burd-Sharps, Sarah et al., eds. *The Measure of America: American Human Development Report 2008–2009.* New York: Columbia University Press, 2008.

Clark, Cal, and Janet Clark. *Women at the Polls: The Gender Gap, Cultural Politics, and Contested Constituencies in the United States.* Newcastle upon Tyne: Cambridge Scholars Publishing, 2008.

Congressional Quarterly, Inc. *Members of Congress Since 1789.* Washington, D.C.: Government Accounting Office, 1985.

Corley, Cheryl. "Two Women Campaign For NOW Presidency." *NPR* (June 19, 2009). Available Online, URL: www.npr.org/templates/story/story.php?storyId=105619536 (accessed June 19, 2009).

Dolan, Kathleen, and Lynne E. Ford. "Are All Women State Legislators Alike?" in *Women and Elective Office: Past, and Future,* edited by Sue Thomas and Clyde Wilcox. New York: Oxford University Press, 1998.

Eagle Forum. "A Short History of E.R.A." Available online, URL: http://www.eagleforum.org/psr/1986/sept86/psrsep86.html. Accessed January 2010.

Embree, Sha. "Meet the Majority." *Campaigns and Elections,* v.28/1 (2007).

Evans, Sara. *Personal Politics: The Roots of Women's Liberation in the Civil Rights Movement and the New Left.* New York: Vintage, 2003.

Falludi, Susan. *Backlash: The Undeclared War against American Women.* New York: Crown, 1991.

Ferraro, Geraldine (with Linda Bird Francke). *Ferraro, My Story.* New York: Bantam Books, 1985.

Freeman, Jo. *We Will Be Heard: Women's Struggles for Political Power in the United States.* Lanham, MD: Rowman and Littlefield, 2008.

Fulton, Sarah A. et al. "The Sense of a Woman: Gender, Ambition, and the Decision to Run for Congress." *Political Research Quarterly,* v.59/2 (June 2006).

Gaddie, Ronald Keith, and Charles S. Bullock, III. "Structural Features of Open Seat and Special U.S. House Elections: Is There a Sexual Bias?" *Political Research Quarterly,* v.50/1 (June 1997).

Hartmann, Susan M., *The Other Feminists: Activists in the Liberal Establishment.* New Haven, CT: Yale University Press, 1998.

Henneberger, Melinda. *If They Only Listened to Us: What Women Voters Want Politicians to Hear.* New York: Simon & Schuster, 2007.

Kolbert, Elizabeth. "Firebrand: Phyllis Schlafly and the Conservative Revolution." *The New Yorker* (November 7, 2005). Available online, URL: http://www.newyorker.com/archive/2005/11/07/051107crbo_books#ixzz0ibbg3rfA. Accessed February 2010.

Mani, Bonnie G. *Woman Power and Political Change.* Lanham, MD: Lexington Books, 2007.

Mansbridge, Jane J. *Why We Lost the ERA.* Chicago, IL: University of Chicago Press, 1986.

Mirowsky, John and Catherine E. Ross. *Social Causes of Psychological Distress,* 2nd ed. Hawthorne, NY: Aldine de Gruyter, 2003.

National Conference of State Legislatures. "Women in State Legislatures: 2009 Legislative Session." Available online, URL: www.ncsl.org/default.aspx?tabid+15398. Accessed July 2009.

Palmer, Barbara and Dennis Simon. "Political Ambition and Women in the U.S. House of Representatives, 1916–2000." *Political Research Quarterly,* v.56/2 (2003).

Pelosi, Nancy. *Know Your Power: A Message to America's Daughters.* New York: Doubleday, 2008.

Peterson, Esther. "Working Women." *Daedalus,* v.93/2 (1964).

Pew Research Center for the People & Press. "Abortion a More Powerful Issue for Women." (April 23, 2004). Available online, URL: http://people-press.org/commentary/?analysisid=88. Accessed July 2009.

Rhode, Deborah. *Speaking of Sex: The Denial of Gender Inequality.* Cambridge, MA: Harvard University Press, 1997.

Rudd, Mark. *Underground: My Life with SDS and the Weathermen.* New York: HarperCollins, 2009.

Saletan, William. *Bearing Right: How Conservatives Won the Abortion War.* Berkeley, CA: University of California Press, 2003.

Seltzer, Richard A., et al. *Sex as a Political Variable: Women as Candidates and Voters in U.S. Elections.* Boulder, CO: Lynne Reinner Publishers, 1997.

Solinger, Rickie. *Pregnancy and Power: A Short History of Reproductive Politics in America.* New York: New York University Press, 2005.

Springer, Kimberly. *Living for the Revolution: Black Feminist Organizations, 1968–1980.* Durham, NC: Duke University Press, 2005.

Stern, Susan. *With the Weathermen: The Personal Journal of a Revolutionary Woman.* Laura Browder, ed. News Brunswick, NJ: Rutgers University Press, 2007.

Sunstein, Cass R., et al. "Ideological Voting on Federal Courts of Appeals: A Preliminary Investigation." *Virginia Law Review,* v.90/1 (2004).

Tolchin, Susan, and Martin Tolchin. *Clout: Womanpower and Politics.* New York: Coward, McCann, and Geohegan, 1974.

Whitaker, Lois Duke, ed. *Voting the Gender Gap.* Urbana and Chicago, IL: University of Illinois Press, 2008.

Witt, Linda, et al. *Running as a Woman: Gender and Power in American Politics.* New York: The Free Press, 1995.

Wolbrecht, Christina, et al., eds. *Political Women and American Democracy.* New York: Cambridge University Press, 2008.

CHAPTER 6

Women in Science and Medicine

AMERICAN WOMEN ARE entering medical and scientific fields in greater numbers than ever before. For instance, between 1971 and 2001, the number of female bachelor's, master's, and doctoral degrees in science, math, and engineering increased by 106, 150, and 267 percent respectively. While 100 years ago women were largely restricted to a limited number of jobs, and many universities had no female faculty members in any of the sciences or medicine, today it would be difficult to think of a field in which women have not made substantial contributions. Women such as anthropologist Margaret Mead, environmentalist Rachel Carson, astronaut Sally Ride, primatologist Jane Goodall, and psychiatrist Elisabeth Kubler-Ross have removed all doubt that women can be successful in science and medicine.

Following in the steps of women who invented the circular saw, the fire escape, the life raft, Liquid Paper, the medical syringe, the windshield wiper, and Scotchguard, between 1961 and the present, female inventors produced a plethora of new inventions that included the canister vacuum cleaner, the Kevlar vest, and the Snugli baby carrier. During that period, women also joined the science and medical faculties of nearly all U.S. universities, including the most prestigious institutions, and many female scientists began heading their own research labs and controlling millions of dollars in research funding.

On the Challenger *spacecraft's middeck, Sally Ride floats alongside the airlock hatch. On June 18, 1983, Sally Ride made history by becoming the first American woman to go into space.*

One way to consider how far women have come is to examine the winners of major awards in the different scientific fields. In recognition that women have historically been discriminated against in the fields of science and medicine, leading scientific societies have distinctive awards reserved for women. For instance, the Garvan Prize (now the Garvan-Olin Medal) of the American Chemical Society is awarded annually to a U.S. female citizen who has made distinguished contributions to chemistry. Over time, however, it became clear that women would only achieve full status within the scientific and medical communities when they were able to compete with men on a level playing field. Once discrimination barriers were removed, women began winning many prestigious awards that were based on outstanding achievement, without regard to sex. Women have made clear gains in such areas as physics, which has traditionally been considered a "male" science. Since 1990, over 60 women have received awards or prizes from the American Physical Society, most of them allotted in competition with men. Women are also well-represented in awards and prizes granted annually by the American Chemical Society.

Six American women won Nobel Prizes for science between 1961 and 2004, and all of those except the first were awarded in the field of Physiology or Medicine. The exception was the win in 1963 for Maria-Göpper-Mayer, the second woman in the history of the Nobel to win the award for Physics. The first was Marie Curie of France, who won in 1903 for her work on radiation. American female award winners in Physiology and Medicine included: Rosalyn Yalow (1977), Barbara McClintock (1983), Rita Levi-Montalcini (1986), Gertrude B. Elion (1988), and Linda B. Buck (2004).

In 2009 Elizabeth H. Blackburn and Carol W. Greider shared the Nobel Prize in Physiology and Medicine with Jack W. Szostak. When Dr. Blackburn was asked how she felt about becoming the ninth woman ever to win in that field, she responded, "Very excited, and hoping that nine will quickly become a larger number."

Linda B. Buck (1947–)

Nobel Prize winner Linda B. Buck was born in Seattle, Washington, and earned her B.S. in psychology and microbiology in 1975 from the University of Washington and her Ph.D. in immunology from the University of Texas Southwestern Medical Center at Dallas in 1980. Buck was a postdoctoral fellow in neurobiology and molecular biology between 1980 and 1984 at Columbia University, where she worked with the neuroscientist Richard Axel. In 2001 Buck achieved full professor status. The following year, she became a Full Member of the Division of Basic Sciences of the Fred Hutchinson Cancer Research Center in Seattle, and in 2003 became an Affiliate Professor of the Department of Physiology and Biophysics of the University of Washington.

Buck's primary research is devoted to understanding how mammals identify and interpret a vast array of chemical stimuli, including those that result in odor or taste, and those that act as pheromones. Her work identified a family of over 1,000 receptors that work in a combinatorial fashion to detect odorants in the nose. She also identified three smaller chemosensory receptor families: one for sweet tastes, one for bitter tastes and one that conceivably detects social cues. These receptor families provide tools to explore the neural mechanisms underlying perception, as well as helping to explain how taste and smell is experienced. She also conducts research into the mechanisms of aging and the possibility that the body has some "central control" system of cells that influence bodily aging as a whole.

Buck and Richard Axel were jointly awarded the Nobel Prize for Physiology or Medicine in 2004 for their work on olfactory receptors. Buck has received many other awards during her career, including the Lewis S. Rosenstiel Award for Distinguished Work in Basic Medical Research in 1997 and the Perl/UNC Neuroscience Prize in 2003. She became a Fellow of the American Association for the Advancement of Science in 2002 and a Member of the National Academy of Sciences in 2003.

EDUCATION AND CAREER DEVELOPMENT

Beginning in the post–World War II era, the government began encouraging young males and females to pursue careers in science and math in the hope that it would make the United States more competitive with the Soviet Union. Efforts to entice women into these fields included legislation passed during the height of the second wave of the women's movement such as the Equal Pay Act of 1963 and Title IX of the Education Amendments of 1972. The National Science Foundation entered the fray in the 1980s and began actively recruiting women and increasing grant money for female scientists. In 1991, the Academies Committee on Women in Science and Engineering began working with Congress and academia to attract more women into these fields.

The upward trend in the number of American women studying science and medicine at the university level has shown dramatic increases in recent years. In 1970 about 9 percent of the students attending medical school in the United States were female; this rose to 44 percent in 1999 and 48 percent in 2008. Similar growth was seen in science and engineering. In 1974, women earned 33 percent of all bachelor's degrees in science and engineering. By 1998, that number had risen to 49 percent. At the master's degree level, women earned 41 percent of all science and engineering degrees in 1998, versus 22 percent in 1977. At the doctoral level, in 1999 women earned 35 percent of the degrees awarded in science and engineering, versus 9 percent in 1970.

With degrees in hand, these women were more successful than women of earlier generations in obtaining positions in both the academic and private sectors. Despite that success, women still made up a small minority of scientific and medical professionals. On the positive side, their progress was steady. In 1973, women constituted 8 percent of the science and engineering workforce. By 1999, they made up 24 percent of the total. However, at the doctoral level, which is the prerequisite for most university faculty positions or independent research careers, proportionately fewer women were employed. A 2001 report from the National Science Foundation (NSF) found that 82.1 percent of men and 75.6 percent of women with science and engineering doctorates were employed full time. When retirees were removed from the calculations (producing a more accurate picture, since a disproportionate percentage of women with doctorates entered the field recently as compared to men) the percentages were more divergent: 91.8 percent of men versus 79.2 percent of women were working full time. A different study found that in 1993, women composed 19 percent of employed doctoral scientists and engineers, and 22 percent of faculties at universities and four-year colleges. However, while 61 percent of male faculty in science and engineering were tenured in 1993, only 35 percent of women faculty members had achieved that status.

Karma Krelle of the University of Alaska Fairbanks holds a reindeer used in a caribou forage evaluation study in 2008. Women have made exceptional contributions to life sciences.

In the NSF study, women working in science fared better in the early stages of their careers relative to men than did those with more years of experience. Among faculty with doctorates who graduated between 1985 and 1992, 57 percent of males versus 50 percent of females were tenured or in tenure-track positions in 1993. For those who graduated before 1985, 85 percent of males versus 69 percent of females were tenured or in tenure-track positions, and 59 percent of males who received a Ph.D. before 1985 were full professors, versus 31 percent of females. Proposed explanations for these phenomena include the fact that women are less likely to receive professional support from males, they are less likely to have mentors, and their networking skills are less developed. Women are overrepresented in low-prestige institutions such as community colleges and underrepresented in research universities, so they spend more time teaching and have less access to the funding and high-level laboratories required for research. Women who have children are more likely to favor a life-work balance. The career paths of women who are married or who do not have children are more similar to those of males. In addition, many women scientists are married to male scientists; and although the anti-nepotism laws are largely a thing of the past, in the competitive world of science, the career of one spouse may take precedence over the other. Social custom dictates that the one taking a back seat is more likely to be female.

MEDICAL CAREERS

In medicine, women's career advancement also lags behind that of men. A 1990 survey of income earned by male and female physicians revealed that women physicians with two to five years of experience earned about 70 percent as much as men with the same years of experience. Even after adjusting for hours worked, women earned only 87 percent as much as their male cohorts. Some of the discrepancy can be explained by choice of specialty. Women are more likely to work in lower-paying fields such as general practice, pediatrics, and general internal medicine while males opt for more lucrative fields. In this survey, 55 percent of women physicians worked in general practice, pediatrics, and general internal medicine as compared to 42 percent of men. Only 14 percent of women worked in the highest-paying fields—radiology, general surgery, anesthesiology, and subspecialty surgery—as opposed to 27 percent of the men.

These statistics raise questions about why women consistently choose relatively low-paying specialties. Although many explanations have been proffered, none have proven definitive. Some argue that this is simply a matter of personal choice, suggesting that women may prefer fields that offer more personal contact with patients; for example, choosing pediatrics or general practice over surgery or radiology. It may also be a case of women choosing caretaking roles, which are associated with female socialization, as is true in many professions. It is also possible that women choose less-demanding specialties that allow them to devote more time to their families. It is also possible that career success and money are less important to women relative to men, or that women prefer to avoid the situations of extreme competitiveness that generally characterize the

Gertrude Belle Elion (1918–99)

Gertrude Belle Elion is an excellent example of a female scientist who used the opportunities given to women in World War II to forge a celebrated career. She was born in New York City and received a B.S. in chemistry from Hunter College in 1937. Four years later, she received an M.S. in chemistry from New York University, but was unable to find a position in a research laboratory. Instead, she worked for several years in commercial laboratories and as a quality control biochemist for a supermarket chain.

In 1944, due to the shortage of male scientists during World War II, she was able to obtain a position at the Burroughs Wellcome Research Laboratories in Tuckahoe, New York. At Burroughs Wellcome, a lab funded by a charitable trust and devoted to research and other activities to advance medical science, she began working with George Hitchings on fundamental research into nucleic acids. Burroughs Wellcome encouraged their staff to publish in scientific journals, and within two years Elion had published first-author papers on her research. She eventually published more than 225 papers.

For several years, Elion pursued her Ph.D. at Brooklyn Polytechnic on nights and weekends, but she dropped out of the program when forced to choose between continuing as a student or keeping her job at Burroughs Wellcome. In 1950 she synthesized two effective cancer treatments: 6-mercaptopurine (6-MP), used to treat childhood leukemia, and thioguanine, used to treat acute myelocytic leukemia. A variant of 6-MP, azathioprine (Imduran), proved to be effective in suppressing the immune system, thus enabling organ transplants. It is still used to treat a variety of autoimmune diseases.

Upon George H. Hitchings's retirement in 1967, Elion became head of the Department of Experimental Therapy at Burroughs Wellcome; and in 1968, she was awarded the Garvan Prize of the American Chemical Society. Also in 1968, she returned to working with diaminopurine, a highly toxic purine compound she had first researched in the 1940s. Discovering that it had active antiviral properties against both the herpes zoster and herpes simplex viruses, she and her colleagues eventually modified it to produce acyclovir, the first effective antiviral drug to be developed. Marketed as Zovirax, it became one of Burroughs Wellcome's best-selling products. Shortly after her retirement in 1983, Elion's former research group at Burroughs Wellcome developed azidothymidine (AZT), at that time the only U.S.-licensed drug to treat AIDS.

After retirement, Elion worked as a consultant and as a research professor at Duke University. In 1988 she was awarded the Nobel Prize for Physiology or Medicine jointly with Hitchings and Sir James W. Black of the University of London, becoming one of the rare winners of a Nobel Prize for science who did not hold a doctoral degree. Burroughs Wellcome gave her a charitable grant matching her prize award to be given to the cause of her choice. She donated it to her alma mater, Hunter College, to support science education for women.

Northern Arizona University postdoctoral research associate Jenna Monroy feeds a cricket to a cane toad during shooting of a Discovery Channel Canada segment in 2008. This study of biomechanics and neural control of movement in toads is part of a National Science Foundation study.

most lucrative specialties. On the other hand, selection of a specialty may not be entirely a matter of choice. Instructors and supervisors may typecast women into those specialties, and the hierarchical structure of American medicine may make such "suggestions" difficult to resist.

The NSF survey found that after adjusting for specialty, practice setting, and other characteristics, including marital status, women earned almost as much (98 percent) as men. However, these results apply to women in the early years of their careers, while evidence shows that the earning gap widens as careers lengthen. In the same survey, women with 10 or more years of experience earned only 86 percent of the salary of men with similar credentials, even after adjustment for the same variables that placed young women at up to 98 percent of men's earnings. This suggests that although men and women start out on a similar economic footing, men's careers develop differently than women's. However, it is also possible that the world of medicine has become less discriminatory, or that women who entered the medical workforce recently are better able to compete (or are more mindful of their careers) than those entering the field 10 years ago.

CHEMISTRY

Women have long excelled in the field of chemistry, and a number of female chemists have made substantial contributions to the profession. For instance, Isabella Lugowski Karle (1921–   ) worked on the Manhattan Project in Chicago until 1946, when she moved to the Naval Research Laboratory in Washington, D.C. In 1959 she became head of the X-ray crystallography lab, and most of her scientific contributions have come in this area. In 1969, she had a breakthrough when she identified the structure of venom that had been extracted from South American tree frogs. In the 1970s, Karle was also able to identify the structures of valinomycin, antamanide, and enkephalin. Throughout her career, Karle published more than 250 scientific papers.

Rather than working with chemical structures, Darleane C. Hoffman (1926–) devoted her career to working with elements. After working at the Oak Ridge National Laboratory and the Los Alamos Scientific Laboratory, Hoffman joined the staff of the University of California-Berkeley. Her primary studies concerned the transuranic elements, and in 1993 she was among the researchers who confirmed the existence of Seaborgium, element 106. She was awarded the National Medal of Science in 1997, and in 2000 became the second woman to win the Priestly Medal of the American Chemical Society. Jacqueline K. Barton (1952–) also honed her skills in the academic world. After teaching at Hunter College and Columbia University, she moved to the California Institute of Technology in 1989. Barton spent most of her career

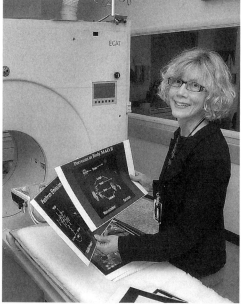

Award-winning chemistry, then and now: in 1978, Barbara Askins (left) patented an award-winning method of enhancing image negatives using radioactive materials for NASA, winning her the National Inventor of the Year award from the Association for Advancement of Inventions and Innovations. Joanna Fowler (right), who developed several unique radiotracer molecules, won the American Chemical Society's Glen T. Seaborg Award for Radiochemistry in 2002, was elected to the National Academies of Science in 2004, and holds a Distinguished Scientist Fellowship from the Office of Biological and Environmental Research in the Department of Energy.

studying DNA, focusing particularly on transverse electron transport along double-stranded DNA, which has many applications in medicine.

Unlike Hoffman and Barton, Joanna S. Fowler chose to work for the Department of Energy. She developed several radiotracers (molecules that can

Rita Levi-Montalcini (1908–)

Like many Jews of the 1930s and 1940s, Rita Levi-Montalcini was a victim of Nazi persecution. She was born in Turin, Italy, and attended medical school at the University of Turin, where she was one of seven female students among 300 males. She received her M.D. in 1936 and remained in Turin for two years, conducting research in neurology and psychiatry in the lab of Professor Giuseppe Levi. Professor Levi was likely an outstanding mentor; three of his students won the Nobel Prize in Physiology or Medicine: Rita Levi-Montalcini, Salvador Luria, and Renato Dulbecco.

In June 1938 Benito Mussolini of Italy issued the *Manifesto per la Difesa Della Razza*, or Manifesto for the Defense of the Race, which forbade Jews from working in professional or academic jobs or for the government. This meant that Levi-Montalcini could no longer practice medicine or continue her research at the university. She built a research lab in the family home and continued her research under makeshift conditions until her family was forced to flee to Florence when the Germans invaded Italy. She rebuilt her lab in the family's country cottage. In 1945 Levi-Montalcini was able to return to Turin, and she began a course of studies in biology at the University. She accepted an offer from Victor Hamburger to be a research associate at Washington University in St. Louis, Missouri, remaining there for the remainder of her career and becoming a full professor in 1958. She maintained her scientific and research ties with Italy and established a research institute in Rome. In 1968 Levi-Montalcini became the tenth woman elected to the National Academy of the Sciences and was awarded the National Medal of Science in 1985. In 1986 she was awarded the Nobel Prize for Physiology of Medicine jointly with Stanley Cohen, with whom she had worked at Washington University.

Levi-Montalcini's research interests were in neurogenesis, the development of the nervous system. While a student at Turin, she developed an improved method of tissue culture that allowed tissues to be grown *in vitro* (in glass, outside a living organism), and her dissertation research demonstrated how specific types of neurological responses were correlated with different stages of development. Her most important work was at Washington University, where she and Cohen discovered nerve growth factor (NGF), a protein that stimulates the growth and differentiation of cells in the nervous system. NGF plays a significant role in understanding both cancers and nervous system diseases such as Alzheimer's and Parkinson's Disease.

be radioactively "tagged" and tracked throughout the body). A tracer form of sugar she developed is used to study brain function and diagnose cancer, and another tracer has been used to study how cocaine is distributed throughout the brain. Fowler won the American Chemical Society's Glen T. Seaborg Award for Radiochemistry in 2002, was elected to the National Academies of Science in 2004, and held a Distinguished Scientist Fellowship from the Office of Biological and Environmental Research from the Department of Energy.

PHYSICS

A diverse group of women have dedicated their lives to employing the science of physics to explain the world in which they live. Mildred Spiewak Dresselhaus, for instance, has been involved in research into carbons. Constantly trying to make physics more female-friendly, she has spent most of her career at MIT and conducting research at Lincoln Laboratory, a research lab funded primarily by the Department of Defense and associated with Massachusetts Institute of Technology (MIT). Within the carbon sciences, she focuses on graphic and carbon fibers, fullerenes, and carbon nanotubes.

Myriam P. Sarachik (1933–) has taken a completely different path within physics. Her field of expertise is low-temperature physics. She collaborated on the discovery of resonant magnetization tunneling in a single-molecule magnet and has also made important contributions to the understanding of superconductivity and the effects of magnetic impurities in metallic alloys. She is also a human rights spokesman, serving on the American Physical Society Committee on the International Freedom of Scientists, the Board of Directors of the Committee of Concerned Scientists, and the Human Rights of Scientists Committee of the New York Academy of Sciences.

Helen Thom Edwards (1936–) has also worked on superconductivity. She played a key role in designing and building the Tevatron at the Fermilab National Accelerator Laboratory in Batavia, Illinois. The Tevatron was the first high-energy particle accelerator based entirely on super-conducting magnets and the highest energy particle collider in the world at the time. The Tevatron accelerates protons and antiprotons around a ring almost four miles in diameter. Completed in 1983 and upgraded in 1993, it was a substantial improvement over any other synchrotron existing at the time. Early in the 21st century, construction of the Large Hadron Collider, which is located in France and Switzerland, relegated the Tevatron to second place.

Renata Kallosh (1943–) who was born in Chernowitz in the Ukraine, has earned an international reputation for her work in theoretical and mathematic physics. After completing doctoral work in 1968 at Moscow State University, where she worked on axiomatic field theory and current algebra, Igor Tamm, a Nobel Prize winner in physics, recruited Kallosh to work at the Lebedev Institute. Kallosh was the first woman scientist to work in the Theoretical Department. In 1990 Kallosh moved to Stanford University, where she continues to pursue research in gravity, sypersymmetry, supergravity, and M-string theory. Another woman, Gail Hanson (1947–   ) has also made an enormous impact on the field of physics. Hanson accepted a position at the Stanford Linear Accelerator Center (SLAC) after finishing doctoral studies at MIT in 1973. While at SLAC, she discovered a phenomenon called "jets" in elementary particle interactions, which led to the discovery of quarks and the development of the Stanford Model, which provides the framework for elementary particle physics today.

MEDICINE

One of the most noted 20th-century women in the field of medicine, Elizabeth Kübler-Ross (1926–2004) was born in Switzerland. She immigrated to the United States in 1958 to continue her training, becoming a U.S. citizen in 1961. She was critical of the manner in which death and dying were approached within the American medical community. The usual practice in hospitals at the time was to avoid discussion of the topic, and physicians did not inform terminal patients of the realities of their conditions. One result was that physicians and nurses were not trained to assist patients and families in the psychological aspects of death and grieving. Kübler-Ross developed a theory that most people needed to work through five stages of grief: denial, anger, bargaining, depression, and acceptance. This theory was popularized through her first book, *On Death and Dying* (1959), which remains her greatest legacy. She wrote over 20 other books and helped to popularize the hospice movement in the United States.

Significant contributions to both science and politics were made by the first two women surgeons general of the United States. In 1990, as the result of an appointment by President George H.W. Bush, Antonia Coello Novello (1944–   ) of Puerto Rico became the first woman to serve as surgeon general. At the University of Michigan Medical Center, Novello had worked with pediatric AIDS, arthritis, and organ transplantation. As surgeon general, she focused

Former U.S. Surgeon General Dr. C. Everett Koop (1981–89) and two of his successors: Antonia Novello (right), the first woman and first Hispanic-American Surgeon General (1990–93), and Joycelyn Elders, the first African-American Surgeon General (1993–94).

Barbara McClintock (1902–92)

Barbara McClintock was a pioneering geneticist whose studies of inheritance in maize (corn) allowed her to discover the principle of genetic transposition long before it could be explained through molecular biology. She was educated in New York and received her Ph.D. in botany from Cornell University in 1928. Her genetics research focused on linkage groups (a set of genes on the same chromosome that are often inherited together). Most work on linkage had been done with the fruit fly, and McClintock applied similar principles to maize.

McClintock encountered many of the difficulties faced by women scientists of her day, including the problem of finding a suitable academic position to support her research. After graduation from Cornell, she was awarded several prestigious fellowships, including grants from the Guggenheim and Rockefeller Foundations, but she had to rely on a personal connection to obtain a faculty position at the University of Missouri (1936–41). When McClintock found herself excluded from faculty meetings and discovered that she was not being informed of career opportunities, she left the university and accepted a position at the Carnegie Institution at Cold Spring Harbor in 1942. This turned out to be the ideal position, as it provided a salary, a laboratory, and the freedom to grow and observe her corn plants. McClintock remained at Cold Spring Harbor for the rest of her career.

She produced the first genetic map for maize in 1931. That same year, she and Harriet Creighton published a paper demonstrating the connection between genetic recombination and chromosomal crossover during meiosis. McClintock was able to demonstrate many fundamental genetic ideas through her maize research, most importantly transposition and the ability of genes to "turn on" or "turn off" physical characteristics. She was recognized early in her career for her research, becoming only the third woman elected to the National Academy of Sciences in 1944. In 1945, she became the first woman president of the Genetics Society of America. However, McClintock's most important work, consisting of her findings on transposition, was not accepted at the time, in part because the field of molecular biology—which today offers an explanation for her observations—was then still in its infancy. In the mid-1950s, after her papers on transposition were met with disbelief and ridicule, McClintock ceased publishing her data for years. During this time, she continued her scientific research at Cold Spring Harbor, performed ethnobotany studies of South American maize, and trained local cytologists in techniques to preserve local strains of maize.

By the late 1970s, molecular biology had advanced to the point where it could explain McClintock's transpositions. She received a number of significant awards in the 1980s, including a MacArthur Foundation genius grant and the Albert Lasker Award for Basic Medical Research in 1981, and the Nobel Prize for physiology or medicine in 1983. She was the first woman to win an unshared Nobel Prize in this field.

on influencing people's health behaviors, seeking to reduce harmful behaviors such as underage drinking and smoking, and increasing positive behaviors such as immunization.

One of the most controversial American female doctors of the 20th century was Minnie Joycelyn Elders, who became the second woman to serve as surgeon general when President Bill Clinton appointed her to that office in 1993. Elders is a specialist in pediatric endocrinology. In 1987, she became director of the Arkansas Department of Health, where she made major improvements in public health practice, including a doubling in the immunization rate for two-year-olds and a tenfold increase in early childhood screenings. Elders advocated for many public health causes that were unpopular among certain segments of the American population, including distribution of contraceptives in schools and encouraging young people to engage in masturbation rather than in riskier sexual behaviors. This latter position was considered too controversial even for the Clinton White House, and Elders left the office in 1994, returning to the University of Arkansas Medical Center and becoming a popular lecturer.

The path that Dr. Linda Laubenstein (1947–92) took was much different than that of Novello and Elders. Laubenstein became a noted AIDS researcher and was the model for the character of Dr. Emma Brookner in Larry Kramer's play *The Normal Heart* (1985). Despite being confined to a wheelchair as the result of a childhood bout with polio, Laubenstein graduated from the New York University School of Medicine and entered private practice in New York City. In 1981 Lubenstein coauthored the first paper on what are now recognized as advanced cases of AIDS: young gay men with Karposi's sarcoma whose immune systems were no longer functioning. Her private practice grew to be largely AIDS patients, and by 1982, she had seen about a quarter of all the known AIDS patients in the country. Laubenstein organized the first national conference on AIDS in 1983 and established the Karposi's Sarcoma Research Fund. With Jeffrey B. Greene she founded a nonprofit organization, Multitasking, to employ AIDS patients, and took the controversial position that the bathhouses in New York City should be closed because they were often the site of unsafe sex and the transmission of AIDS.

LIFE SCIENCES

As with other fields of medicine, the contributions of women to the life sciences were great. Four women serve as examples of the uniqueness of their approach to the field. While attending Cornell University in the 1940s, Ruth Sager (1918–97) studied with Barbara McClintock and Marcus Rhodes. Sager earned her reputation in cellular genetics at Harvard University and served as chief of cancer genetics at Boston's Dana Farber Cancer Institute. Her primary work was with *Chlamydomonas*, a genus of algae, which allowed her to demonstrate that genes appear outside the chromosomes, providing an organism with stability by functioning as a second genetic system. She also conducted important research in identifying factors involved in tumor suppression, and published numerous research articles and books, including *Cell Heredity* (1961) with Francis Ryan and *Cytoplasmic Genes and Organelles* (1972).

Known worldwide for her work with primates, Dian Fossey (1932–85) was one of the premier zoologists of the 20th century and did much to raise interest in preserving gorilla habitats. Her fieldwork was funded by the paleoanthropologist Louis Leakey, the Wilkie Brothers Foundation, and the National Geographic Society. Her primary research area was in the Virunga Mountains of Rwanda. Fossey wrote the popular book *Gorillas in the Mist* (1983) about her work there. The 1988 movie based on the book, which starred Sigourney Weaver as Fossey, earned five Academy Award nominations, including a Best Actress nod for Weaver. Fossey, who continued to lead campaigns against poaching, was murdered in her cabin at the Karisoke Research Center in the Virunga Mountains in 1985. The case has never been solved, but poachers at odds with Fossey have been suspected.

Dr. Gail R. Martin (1944–) spent her career engaged in stem cell research. Along with fellow scientists Mart Evans and Matthew Kaufman, Martin is credited with being the first to develop techniques for extracting stem cells from mouse embryos. She is also credited with coining the term *embryonic stem cell*. Like Martin, immunologist Philippa Marrack is involved in research

Barbara McClintock in the lab at Cold Spring Harbor in April 1963, when her work became increasingly focused on the projects of the Rockefeller-funded races of maize (corn) group.

to improve human life. Although she was born in England, she has spent most of her career at the University of Colorado Health Sciences Center in Denver and the National Jewish Hospital. Her main research areas include HIV, memory T cells, and superantigens—immunological activators that induce toxic shock. Much of her work has been conducted in collaboration with her husband, John W. Kappler.

MATHEMATICS

A number of women have also made their marks within the field of mathematics, including Julia Bowman Robinson, who devoted most of her career to working on a solution to the 10th problem on the famous list of 23 unsolved mathematical problems, which German mathematician David Hilbert posed in 1900 at the International Congress of Mathematicians. That complex problem concerned whether or not mathematicians could find a universal algorithm that would allow them to find a solution to a given Diophantine Equation. In 1970, Robinson's work, in conjunction with that of other mathematicians, led Yuri Matijasevich, a Russian mathematician, to discover that they could not.

Margaret Mead's controversial stance on legalizing marijuana hit the papers in 1969. The then governor of Florida, Claude Kirk, called Mead a "dirty old lady."

Like Robinson, Karen Keskulla Uhlenbeck (1942–) is involved in mathematical research. Through her study of instantons, which examines the behavior of surfaces across dimensions, Uhlenbeck explores the intersections between mathematics and theoretical physics. In 1983, she won the prestigious MacArthur Fellowship to continue her studies in geometry and partial differential equations. She continues to conduct research in the calculus of variations, differential geometry, and topological quantum field theory.

Cathleen Synge Morawetz (1945–), another noted female mathematician, was born in Toronto to Irish parents. Her father was the distinguished mathematician J. L. Synge. Morawetz was educated in New York City, and she remained in the United States after she completed her degrees. Her early research was on viscous flows; but by the 1950s, she had turned her attention to the mathematics of transionic flows, developing a theory for transonic flow with shocks. Afterward, Morawetz focused her research on the propagation of waves. Upon being honored by the National Organization for Women for being able to successfully combine family and professional roles, she quipped that she may have become a career woman because she was so bad at housework.

Women continue to break through barriers in the sciences and medicine. Astronaut Mae Jemison, onboard the Space Shuttle Endeavour in 1992, works with NASA to fulfil their objectives in life sciences, microgravity, and technology research.

CONCLUSION

Before World War II, science and medicine were for the most part dominated by males, but the war opened up new opportunities for women and allowed them to prove themselves. After the war, women began pursuing new subfields of science and medicine, holding their own with male cohorts. Despite these gains and significant contributions, females, particularly those who are mothers, have continued to be discriminated against because of their gender. Women in science and medicine also continue to earn less money, garner fewer grants and fellowships, and win fewer prestigious awards. Notwithstanding these limitations, they have collectively changed not only their individual fields and the overall disciplines of science and medicine, but also the world in which they live. At the same time, they have opened up even greater opportunities for those women who follow them.

Sarah Boslaugh
Washington University School of Medicine

Further Reading

Association for Women in Science, "Women in Science Statistics." Available online, URL: http://www.serve.com/awis/statistics/r_statistics main.html. Accessed September 2008.

Bielby, William T. "Sex Differences in Careers: Is Science a Special Case?" In *The Outer Circle: Women in the Scientific Community*, ed. by Harriet Zuckerman, Jonathan R. Cole, and John T. Bruer. New York: W.W. Norton, 1991.

Byers, Nina and Gary Williams, eds. *Out of the Shadows: Contributions of Twentieth-Century Women to Physics*. Cambridge: Cambridge University Press, 2006.

Committee on Gender Differences in the Careers of Science, Engineering, and Mathematics Faculty, Committee on Women in Science and Engineering, National Research Council. *Assessing Gender Differences in the Careers of Science, Engineering, and Mathematics Faculty.* Washington, D.C.: National Academies Press, 2008.

Committee on Maximizing the Potential of Women in Academic Science and Engineering, National Academy of Sciences, National Academy of Engineering, and Institute of Medicine. *Beyond Bias and Barriers: Fulfilling the Potential of Women in Academic Science and Engineering.* Washington, D.C.: National Academies Press, 2007.

Fossey, Dian. *Gorillas in the Mist*. Boston, MA: Houghton Mifflin, 1983.

Keller, Evelyn Fox. "The Wo/Man Scientist: Issues of Sex and Gender in the Pursuit of Science." In *The Outer Circle: Women in the Scientific Community*, ed. by Harriet Zuckerman, Jonathan R. Cole, and John T. Bruer. New York: W.W. Norton, 1991.

Lambert, Bruce. "Linda Laubenstein, 45, Physician and Leader in Detection of AIDS." *New York Times* (August 16, 1992).

Levin, Beatrice. *Women and Medicine*. 3rd ed. Lanham, MD: Scarecrow Press, 2002.

Lo Chin, Eliza, ed. *This Side of Doctoring: Reflections from Women in Medicine*. Oxford: Oxford University Press, 2003.

Lorius, Cassandra. "An Anatomy of Desire: Gender and Difference in Sex Therapy." In *Women and Modern Medicine*, ed. by Lawrence Conrad and Anne Hardy. Amsterdam: Editions Rodopi, 2001.

McGrayne, Sharon Bertsch. *Nobel Prize Women of Science: Their Lives, Struggles, and Momentous Discoveries*. New York: Birch Lane, 1993.

Montgomery, Sy. *Walking with the Great Apes: Jane Goodall, Dian Fossey, and Birute Galdikas*. New York: Houghton Mifflin, 1991.

Rossiter, Margaret. *Women Scientists in America: Before Affirmative Action, 1940–1972*. Baltimore, MD: Johns Hopkins University Press, 1995.

Sax, Linda J. "Undergraduate Science Majors: Gender Differences in Who Goes to Graduate School." *Review of Higher Education*, v.24/2 (Winter 2001).

Shiebinger, Londa. "Getting More Women into Science: Knowledge Issues." *Harvard Journal of Law and Gender,* v.30 (Summer 2007).

Sonnert, Gerhard "What Makes a Good Scientist? Determinants of Peer Evaluation Among Biologists." *Social Studies of Science,* v.25 (1995).

Valian, Virginia. *Why So Slow? The Advancement of Women.* Cambridge, MA: MIT Press, 1998.

Vare, Ethlie Ann, and Greg Ptacek. *Patently Female: From AZT to TV Dinners: Storiesof Women Inventors and Their Breakthrough Ideas.* New York: Wiley, 2002.

Zuckerman, Harriet. "The Careers of Men and Women Scientists: A Review of Current Research. In *The Outer Circle: Women in the Scientific Community*, ed. by Harriet Zuckerman, Jonathan R. Cole, and John T. Bruer. New York: W.W. Norton, 1991.

CHAPTER 7

Women in the Arts and Literature

TUMULTUOUS CHANGES CHARACTERIZED the 1960s and set the stage for the decades of social revolution that followed. Women in the arts and literature reflected the changes that reshaped the larger culture. More women engaged in cultural production, in forms ranging from journalism to poetry, from music making to mixed media collages. In the first year of his presidency, John F. Kennedy created the Presidential Commission on the Status of Women (PCSW) with Eleanor Roosevelt as its chair. The commission's report in 1963 provided documentation of pervasive discrimination against women. Betty Friedan's *The Feminine Mystique*, published the same year, challenged the entrenched idea that women found fulfillment in their domestic role. Friedan's realization, expressed in the opening line of the preface, struck a nerve with millions of women: "Gradually, without seeing it clearly for quite a while, I came to realize that something is very wrong with the way American women are trying to live their lives today." The book became a bestseller, Friedan became famous, and the second wave of American feminism surged. While it is certainly an oversimplification to suggest that the creative impulses of American women after 1963 were all feminist in nature, the burgeoning movement and varying responses to it served as the dominant force in women's art and literature over the next four decades.

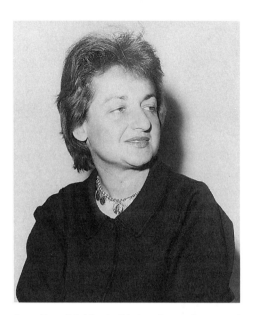

Betty Naomi Goldstein Friedan vigorously pursued political activism and women's rights. Her 1963 book The Feminine Mystique *challenged the idea that women were primarily fulfilled by domestic pursuits such as marriage and children.*

One result of the increasing power of the new feminist movement was a greater emphasis on female experience. Gerda Lerner and Elizabeth Janeway pioneered examinations of women's history and relationships. Women in the visual arts employed female symbols and incorporated such gender-based issues as birth, motherhood, and rape into their work. Women composers created works specifically for women conductors, and novels such as Mary McCarthy's *The Group* (1963) and Sylvia Plath's *The Bell Jar* (1963), which included frank descriptions of sex, contraception, and abortion, became bestsellers. Women also began to question the validity of the canon of the arts and literature and to call for a revision of historical records in painting, sculpture, music, and literature that would include work by women. Despite decades of effort to establish the equality of women in the arts and literature, the number of women identifying themselves as professionals in painting, sculpture, and music remains small. Women writers have fared better in number than those of the past, but the number of those who have achieved canonical status is infinitesimal. In 2006 the *New York Times* asked 200 members of the literary establishment to name the Great American Novel of the past 25 years. Only two women, Toni Morrison and Marilynne Robinson, received more than two votes.

ART AND SECOND WAVE FEMINISM

It is impossible to discuss women who have pursued lives of artistic practice over the past five decades without a concurrent dialogue on the feminist movement. Not only did feminism shape creative form and content for women after 1960, it also prompted recovery and recognition for older artists and set in motion many of the underpinnings for the success of women artists over subsequent decades. Typical of the "clubhouse" atmosphere that shut women artists out were the New York abstract expressionists, a group who inscribed for themselves a romantic and compelling collective biography, built as much around boozing and womanizing as around a common artistic vision. According to the memoirs of women who were affiliated with the painters of the 1950s and 1960s, their secondary status in artistic circles was accepted as part of society's view of women as keepers of the home front. Lee Krasner's subsuming her own career to Jackson Pollock's from the time of their marriage in 1945 until after his death in 1956 was a circumstance replicated in the lives of countless creative women. Even though Krasner produced abstract works at least two years before Pollock developed his signature technique, it was not until her exhibit at the Whitney Museum in 1973 that her contribution to abstract expressionism began to be seriously evaluated.

The feminist art movement did not proceed as the result of a single, centralized effort designed to achieve a well-defined and specific goal. Instead, it began through individual and collective efforts on several fronts, occurred in several locales, and was prompted by specific objectives that were also connected to the larger aims of feminism—liberating women from consignment to domestic servitude (through the institutions of marriage and motherhood) and allowing them to "be all they could be." For women artists, this included expanding professional opportunities and creating representation in art exhibitions that had exercised a double standard by largely excluding women.

The feminist art movement may have been one of the most specific offshoots of the larger feminist movement because of its ties with culture and creativity. Not only did the feminist art movement work on behalf of expanding professional visibility for women, it also bought into the idea that women had a separate culture.

Feminists proposed recognition of a female culture that celebrated the traditional domains of women. Reviewing the work of the earliest prominent women painters, making their mark at the turn of the last century—Mary Cassatt, for example—reveals that they concentrated on domestic scenes, particularly images of mothers and children. While it may be that these were the images a woman could sell or be praised for at that time, they also defined the viewpoint and

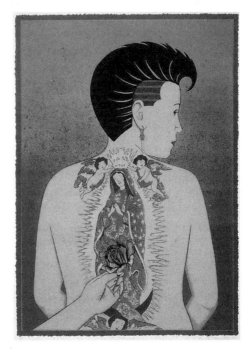

In La Ofrenda II, *a 1988 painting by Ester Hernandez, the Virgin of Guadalupe is represented as a symbol of feminine strength. Hernández is a California painter and graphic artist of mixed Mexican and Yaqui heritage.*

Toni Morrison, Nobel Laureate

Born Chloe Anthony Wofford in 1931, Toni Morrison has become one of the most awarded and respected writers in American literature. Morrison grew up in Lorain, Ohio, where her parents fostered her love of reading and her interest in African-American music, storytelling, and other cultural practices that proved to be central to her fiction. While she was a student at Howard University, Wofford adopted a variation of her middle name and became Toni. After her graduation from Howard, she attended graduate school at Cornell University.

In 1957, she returned to Howard to teach. A year later, she married Jamaican architect Harold Morrison; the couple had two sons. She left Howard in 1964, divorcing Morrison about the same time. After a brief stay in Lorain, she began her long career in publishing, working first at the textbook subsidiary of Random House in Syracuse, New York, and later as senior editor at Random House in New York City. In an act of self-reclamation, she worked on the manuscript that she had begun while at Howard. She recalled that time in a conversation with writer Gloria Naylor: "I was somebody's parent, somebody's this, somebody's that, but there was no me in this world ... I had written this little story earlier just for some friends, so I took it out and I began to work it up. And all of those people were me. I was Pecola, Claudia ... I was everybody." She transformed the "little story" about a young girl's longing for the blue eyes that defined beauty into *The Bluest Eye* (1970), her first novel.

Morrison wove the themes she introduced in *The Bluest Eye*—the nature of identity, the role of the black community, the interplay of past and present, the arbitrariness of cultural norms—into the novels that followed. *Sula* (1973), which examined the lifelong friendship of two African-American women, won the National Book Critics Award, but it was her third novel, *Song of Solomon* (1977), that established her as a major literary voice. In 1980 President Carter appointed Morrison to the National Council on the Arts. In 1981, the year her fourth novel *Tar Baby* was published, she was elected to the American Academy and Institute of Arts and Letters. *Tar Baby* was on the *New York Times* bestseller list for 16 weeks, leading to Morrison's appearance on the cover of *Newsweek*, but it was *Beloved* (1987), a story loosely based on Margaret Garner, an escaped slave who killed one of her children rather than have her returned to slavery, that catapulted Morrison to a new level of fame. *Beloved* won the Pulitzer Prize in 1988. In 1993 Morrison became the first African American and the second American woman to receive the Nobel Prize for Literature. The Nobel Committee praised her prose and her purpose: "She delves into the language itself, a language she wants to liberate from the fetters of race. And she addresses us with the luster of poetry."

Following her Nobel award, Morrison has written three more novels, literary and social criticism, and, in collaboration with her son Slade, children's books. Praised for her universality and for her authentic African-American vision, she is in the 21st century a totemic figure in American letters. Her most recent novel, *A Mercy* (2009), has been called her most powerful work yet.

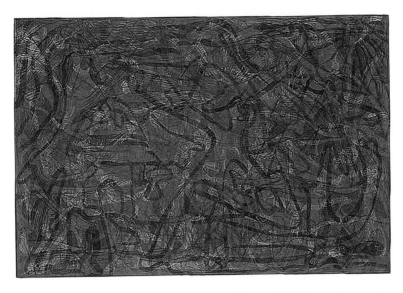

Faith Ringgold's Death of Apartheid (1984). Born in Harlem in 1930, Ringgold created her first quilt in 1980 with her mother, a fashion designer and dressmaker. Since then, she has become renowned for her narrative "story quilts."

experiences of women. In contemporary art, women's culture can be manifested in references of a woman's life and concerns—her relationships with men (or other women), her relationship with her body and appearance, and her constrained role in society among them. Additionally, female culture might be expressed by incorporating the methods of work used domestically by women, such as textiles or needlework. Harmony Hammond, a lesbian feminist artist, used braided rag rugs as an early reference by imitating the form as a surface for paintings or creating sculptures from rags. Miriam Schapiro, who in mid-career became a prominent leader in the feminist art movement, created a series of paint and fabric work that she called "femmages." The materials referenced feminine accessories such as handkerchiefs and lace. She also deconstructed a kimono in a large-scale series. Judy Chicago pioneered the use of china painting in contemporary art practice, and used needlework extensively as a medium.

STORIED ART

In response to abstraction and minimalism, many women began to work in a more narrative way; they fashioned their art around a story. Faith Ringgold's "story quilts" recounted her childhood experiences and those of her ethnic culture in the heyday of the Harlem Renaissance in fabric renditions that evoked similarities with the complex scenes from life painted by the renowned mid-20th century folk painter Grandma Moses. Mixed media artist Betye Saar incorporated her aunt's personal belongings into her early box assemblages and collages. Even a more traditional painter such as Audrey Flack, a practitioner of contemporary photorealism, chose to depict scenes from the realm of feminine identity. Her best-known paintings include *Chanel*, depicting a woman's dressing table. Autobiography, sexuality, one's relationship to nature, childbirth, and menstruation were uncommon themes in traditional (male) art practice, but women's art often turned inward to explore themes of identity, being, and experience. Some argued for an essentialist view of women's ways of seeing and imaging, built around the centralized image, a compositional formulation often found in nature, such as flower centers and the opening to the birth canal.

COLLABORATIONS AND COLLECTIVES

In contrast to the romanticized image of the starving artist working in a garret—or the woman artist working at her kitchen table after the children are in bed—the women of the feminist art movement combined their creative efforts with protests against their status in art and society, and determination to find resolution for these obstacles. Women also worked together to push for more professional recognition of women's work by questioning why art exhibitions and art schools were denying opportunities to women. The women's art movement was generated by grassroots activism as much as by the content of the art. To be a practicing artist in the late 1960s and early 1970s often meant connecting with other women artists to organize exhibitions and engage in community-based projects that raised the profile of artists' work.

What has been regarded as the first public exhibition of feminist art took place at the Lytton Galleries of Contemporary Art in Los Angeles in 1968. Titled *25 California Women of Art*, it was prompted by a concern about women's representation in the visual arts. Similar exhibitions followed in other urban art centers, notably *X to the 12th Power*, organized in New York in 1970 by

Sculptor Anna Hyatt Huntington, in her studio in 1965, is one of the most prolific American artists of the 20th century. The national historic landmark Brookgreen Gardens in South Carolina houses numerous examples of her works, many cast in bronze and some in aluminum.

WAR (Women Artists in Revolution). Other women's art collectives began to form, creating spaces to show women's work and calling for change in the art establishment. Exhibitions such as these may seem unremarkable in the 21st century, but they were radical at a time when few women were included in gallery and museum exhibitions. The Whitney Museum in New York increased its representation of women in its annual exhibition from 5 to 22 percent between 1970 and 1971, at the behest of an ad hoc feminist group.

During the first decade that the feminist movement became widespread, women's art collectives were organized in San Francisco, Sacramento, Minneapolis, Chicago, and Los Angeles. In New York, members of Artists in Residence formed a publishing collective that produced an important feminist journal, *Heresies: A Feminist Publication on Art and Politics*. In 1970 Judy Chicago, a painter, sculptor, and ardent feminist who had been educated at UCLA, established the groundbreaking feminist art program at Fresno State College (now Fresno State University) in California's Central Valley. Although Chicago eventually moved to Los Angeles and relocated her program, a feminist art class continued at Fresno for years under the tutelage of Joyce Aiken.

Although it was not an organization, one of the most important art collaborations of the 1970s was connected with Judy Chicago's titanic installation, *The Dinner Party*. Many women volunteered their time and talents, conducting research and fundraising and helping to execute the ceramics firing and needlework that went into the massive rendition of a dinner table set with abstracted "portraits" of 39 notable women in Western myth and history.

OTHER FORMS OF COMMUNITY

Not all women artists joined feminist art organizations. The demands of organizational work competed with studio time and other responsibilities, and many women had little interest in grassroots activism. But women's art centers benefited their members by providing professional opportunities, critiques of their work, and a sense of group cohesion for an otherwise solitary activity. In addition, the community visibility of cooperative galleries and art centers raised the visibility of art and served educational functions over time. There was a lasting, indirect benefit for women artists, particularly those who worked in contemporary modes, for the feminist art activist groups opened the gate of awareness for women and creativity that had been largely closed before the 1960s.

Not all women artists identified with the feminist art movement, although its influence has been integrated into general art practice since the 1980s. Women such as Agnes Martin, Alice Neel, Louise Bourgeois, Georgia O'Keeffe, and Joan Mitchell, who had been working for decades, may not have been feminist activists, but their careers and visibility benefited from the efforts of the feminist art movement. Audrey Flack was not an active member of a feminist art organization, but her art subjects reflected the concerns of feminine icons and identity that had been championed by feminist artists. Art

Opera singer Leontyne Price with NEA Chairman Dana Gioia at the NEA Opera Honors inaugural awards concert, October 31, 2008, at the Harman Center for the Arts, Washington, D.C. Price received numerous awards and accolades for her performances in the 1960s, when she was welcomed with packed houses and rave reviews all over the world.

by women continues to be highlighted by strong exhibitions, such as *Women Artists 1550–1950* at the Brooklyn Museum in 1994, and the development of the National Museum of Women in the Arts in Washington, D.C., which mounts major, revolving exhibitions of a range of work by women.

MUSIC AND ORCHESTRATING FEMALE SUCCESS

The influence of the feminist movement was less obvious in the world of music, but its impact was no less significant. By the 1960s, women were training as musicians in record numbers. More than half of all music students were female, but only a small fraction made it to the top ranks of professional musicians. Women found it particularly difficult to find employment in the nation's most prestigious orchestras. New members of these orchestras traditionally were chosen by the male music director and the principal player of each section, predominantly male. Positions most often were filled by male students of a select group of teachers. In 1970, only around 10 percent of orchestra members were female. In response to the social changes of the period, orchestras began using blind auditions in the 1970s and 1980s. Open auditions were held in which musicians performed behind a screen that hid them from view with-

Women Conductors

At the end of the first decade of the 21st century, the number of women graduating from conservatories and graduate schools in music equaled the number of men, but only about one-third of membership in the nation's most prestigious orchestras was female. For women as conductors or musical directors, despite the highly publicized achievements of a few, the number remained exceedingly small.

Antonia Brico received accolades upon her 1930 debut with the Berlin Philharmonic, but it was not until after singer Judy Collins made a documentary about her in 1974 that Brico, by then in her 70s, received invitations to conduct widely. Opera conductor Sarah Caldwell's achievements are legendary, but the very fact that *Time* hailed her as Music's Wonder Woman when she appeared on the magazine's cover in 1975 attests to the rarity of her success.

By the late 1980s, women were making inroads into conducting territory. Most prominent among those bridging the gender gap were Marin Alsop, protégée of Leonard Bernstein; and JoAnn Falletta, music director of Buffalo Symphony Orchestra and the Virginia Symphony Orchestra, praised by the *New York Times* as "one of the greatest conductors of her generation." She began conducting at age 18 with a student orchestra. Alsop served as music director of the Colorado Symphony for a dozen years and made history in 2007 when she became artistic director of the Baltimore Symphony Orchestra, the first woman to lead a major orchestra. That same year she was the first conductor to win a lucrative MacArthur Fellowship grant.

Despite the notable achievements of Alsop, Falleta, and a handful of others, fewer than 12 percent of American orchestras are led by women. However, some still doubt women's abilities to conduct men's music and to manage orchestras that are still predominantly male. "Critics used to comment on my hairstyle and what I wore," said Falleta. "They would never refer to me by my last name" [like male conductors]. Nevertheless, Falleta voiced cautious optimism: "The change has been slower than we all thought, but the fact it is slow means it will stick."

In 2009 Laura Jackson was named artistic director of the Reno Philharmonic. The same year, the Berkeley Symphony announced that Lisbon, Portugal, native Joana Carneiro would serve as its third music director, and Elizabeth Schulze was appointed to the same position at the Flagstaff Symphony. Taiwan-born Mei-Ann Chen, the first woman to win the Malko International Conductors Competition and Alsop's assistant in Baltimore, believed her generation would continue to see significant change: "One of the funny things about this profession is that classical music organizations and venues book their schedules three to four years ahead of performances, so shifts don't happen overnight. But I believe very strongly that those of us who have been paying our dues recently will see things start to happen in the next few years."

out altering the sound. Frequently, carpeted floors were laid down in order to muffle the revealing sound of women's high heels. Music educators advised their women female students to avoid wearing perfume and even taught them breathing exercises to disguise their higher pitched voices to be sure the auditions worked as they were intended.

Researchers discovered that blind auditions increased the likelihood of a woman's advancing beyond the preliminary rounds by as much as 50 percent. Blind auditions increased opportunities for women who desired to be professional musicians, but they were not panaceas for inequitable treatment. Women orchestra musicians were more likely to be found in smaller orchestras. By 1995, women players made up 35 percent of the nation's orchestras, but barely 25 percent of those women earned the most lucrative salaries. Prejudice against women in certain fields also persisted. Women brass players remained in substantial minorities even as women string players achieved parity. Composers and conductors also continued to battle for equitable conditions.

Women, working individually and in groups, became their own best advocates in combating inequities. Susan Slaughter joined the St. Louis Symphony Orchestra in 1969 and became the first woman ever named as principal trumpet of a major symphony orchestra four years later. In 1992 she founded the International Women's Brass Conference, an organization providing opportunities and recognition to women brass musicians. From 1981 to 2004, the Women's Philharmonic Orchestra in San Francisco discovered, commissioned, and promoted works by more than 160 female composers. In 1983 Ellen Taaffe Zwilich became the first woman to win the Pulitzer Prize for Music, and by the 21st century Emma Lou Diemer, Ruth Schonthal, Elizabeth Hayden Pizer, and Nancy Van de Vate had won critical acclaim as composers. The Women's Philharmonic also administered a grant to provide training and opportunities for women conductors. Despite the much-publicized achievements of a few women, females still account for less than 10 percent of all orchestra conductors.

BEYOND THE ORCHESTRAS

Women in opera and dance continued to build on the successes of their predecessors. Opera stars such as Beverly Sills, Leontyne Price, and Marilyn Horne gained national prominence larger than opera's limited audience through appearances on television and popular magazine covers. Renee Fleming, a 21st-century diva who achieved celebrity within the larger culture, told *Time Magazine* in 2005 that "a sense of theater and spectacle" was needed to keep a younger audience interested. The 1960s and 1970s marked a period of extraordinary innovation in dance as choreographers, most notably Trisha Brown and Twyla Tharp, brought performances closer to audiences, exploring nonproscenium pieces on city streets, in art galleries, and in public parks.

Today, choreographers such as Noemie Lafrance with her site-specific performances and classically trained Jill Sigman with her audience-participation pieces continue the innovation, redefining dance in the process.

LITERATURE AND LIBERATION

Beginning in the 1960s, the canon of American literature came under attack by women writers and literary scholars who not only challenged the preeminence of dead, white males as authors of the privileged texts of the culture, but also insisted that female experience was as much the matter of American letters as were trips to the territories, sea voyages, and the wounds of war. It is impossible to separate the influence of this period's social revolutions on the literature from the ways in which the literature fueled social changes. Women writers of prose and poetry were laying claim to new terrain in the last four decades of the 20th century, a claim that yielded laudable results in the first decade of the 21st century.

Poet Anne Sexton, educated at a finishing school with a brief stint as a model and years as a suburban wife and mother, might have served as

The Woman's Salon was founded by five women writers in 1975 in New York City as a forum for "an intelligent and receptive audience for writing that generates the personal and communal transformations which are the essence of the feminist world vision." This poster was for the readings and presented talks at the National Women's Conference in Houston in 1977.

> ## The Guerilla Girls
>
> The Guerilla Girls are dedicated to raising public awareness of the marginalization of women and minorities from the institutions of professional art. Founded in New York in 1985, with chapters in other cities that have been active periodically, the group is more a collective than an organization. The women who comprise its membership work together as a coalition of activists who are artists, or who have connections with the art world, to present a voice of radical feminist protest within the art world.
>
> Organized more than a decade after the inception of the feminist art movement, during the so-called culture wars over art that was politicized or that challenged the status quo, the Guerilla Girls responded with art and humor to the threat of an erosion of the gains they had begun to make in being recognized in the art world. As an agitation and propaganda group, they adopted many of the organizing principles of earlier feminist art activities, such as theatrics, adopting a militant pose, producing rhetoric outside of official channels, and celebrating the pantheon of women artists in history.
>
> Known for its theatrical aspects, the Guerilla Girls members make public appearances fully masked in gorilla costuming, combined with miniskirts and high heels, as a visual pun on the idea of guerilla attacks or warfare combined with stereotypes of women's sexuality. The members also act anonymously, adopting as pseudonyms the identities of prominent, deceased women artists in order to create individual public identities, in part because the participants are practicing professional artists who might suffer retaliation if they were "unmasked." Their anonymity also speaks to the broader social perception that, in being excluded from professional recognition and position for so long in history—an exclusion still practiced today by art galleries and museums—women's art was, and is, effectively anonymous. By masking their individual identities, the Guerilla Girls speak collectively on behalf of all women artists.
>
> Although the Guerilla Girls do appear in interviews, they are best known for "taking it to the streets" with posters that appear spontaneously on city sites (one critic likened them to graffiti in professionally produced graphic form) to identify and challenge the representation of women in museum shows, art collections, and gallery endeavors. Using statistics, slogans, and parodies of advertising, they provide information and pose provocative questions about official art institutions and their relationship to women artists. The resulting message they attempt to proffer is that the concerns of women artists are a public concern that requires action.

prototype for the dissatisfied woman Friedan described in *The Feminine Mystique*. Sexton mined her own experience for her poetry, writing about mental illness, abortion, female sexuality, and the ambivalences of motherhood. Established women poets May Swenson, Denise Levertov, and Elizabeth Bishop praised Sexton's work, but male poets and critics generally were made uncomfortable by Sexton's use of taboo subjects. James Dickey was not alone in his valuation of her poems: "One feels tempted to drop [Sexton's poems] furtively in the nearest ashcan, rather than to be caught with them in the presence of so much naked suffering."

The use of formerly taboo subjects was not limited to the work of poets. Two novels, published the same year as *The Feminine Mystique*, shared Sexton's candor about women's lives. Mary McCarthy, who insisted she was no feminist, nevertheless produced in *The Group* a book that revealed in fiction the very issues Friedan identified. The story that followed eight Vassar students from 1933 to 1940 dealt with extramarital affairs, premarital sex, homosexuality, contraception, abortion, and psychoanalysis. McCarthy herself saw it as satire about "the history of the loss of faith in progress, in the idea of progress" for women, an idea supported by Candace Bushnell, creator of *Sex and the City*, in her introduction to the 2009 reissue of McCarthy's most widely read novel. *The Group* topped the *New York Times* bestseller list between 1965 and 1967. *The Bell Jar*, the only published novel of poet Sylvia Plath, reveals the socially imposed restrictions on educated women in the 1950s. Published pseudonymously in England shortly before Plath's suicide, the novel was not published in the United States until eight years later. As surely as the protagonist's psychological struggles mirror Plath's own, the book's rage against the limits imposed on female intelligence and creativity by American culture in the 1950s reflects a common experience for women of the era.

Little more than a decade after Plath's death, Anne Sexton too committed suicide. Speaking at a memorial service for Sexton, Adrienne Rich, one of the most celebrated poets of her generation, called for an end to female self-destruction. "We have had enough," Rich declared. Rich's literary history has been referred to as an emblem of contemporary American feminism. A woman of privilege who followed the socially accepted patterns of her call and time, she was radicalized by the revolutions of the 1960s. Her early formalist poems gave way to experimental, politically charged poems. By the 1970s, she had become a leading voice for women's rights and a self-identified lesbian feminist. By the 1980s, she was examining her status as privileged and white in a movement that excluded those who were neither.

RECLAIMING, RESHAPING, AND REDEFINING
Women writers of the 1970s were reshaping American literature in ways other than their own creations. They reclaimed the women writers of the past whose work had been neglected through decades of a literary field dominated by male works. Feminist Press published such titles as *The Yellow Wallpaper* by Charlotte Perkins Gilman, *A Jury of Her Peers* by Susan Glaspell, and *Life in the Iron Mills* by Rebecca Harding Davis. While teaching in Mississippi, novelist

Amy Tan at Jaszczury, Poland, in 2006, where she met with university students. She discussed her identity as a Chinese-American writer and her childhood in the United States, growing up as the daughter of Chinese immigrants.

and poet Alice Walker read Zora Neal Hurston's *Their Eyes Were Watching God* and found "enough self-love ... to restore a world." In 1979 Walker edited an edition of Hurston's work.

Several women paved the way for female voices of the African-American experience: Nikki Giovanni, already an established poet by the early 1970s; Alice Walker, whose debut novel, *The Third Life of Grange Copeland*, was published in 1970; and Toni Morrison, whose first novel, *The Bluest Eye*, was published the same year. Maya Angelou's first in a series of autobiographies, *I Know Why the Caged Bird Sings*, was published in 1969. Toni Cade Bambara published her first collection of short stories, *Gorilla, My Love*, in 1972, two years after she had edited an important anthology, *The Black Woman*, that included selections by Bambara herself and by other African-American women—Nikki Giovanni, Paule Marshall, and Alice Walker among them. The anthology examined issues like motherhood, politics, racism, and the plight of being black and female. Ntozake Shange (born Paulette Williams) created *For Colored Girls Who Have Considered Suicide/When the Rainbow Is Enuf* (1975), a theater piece on the power of black women to survive, which won the Obie Award and the Outer Circle Critics Award. Both Walker and Lord were nominated for the National Book Award in 1974. Adrienne Rich won for *Diving into the Wreck*, accepting it with Walker and Lord, saying: "We symbolically join here in refusing the terms of patriarchal competition and in declaring that we will share this prize among us, to be used as best we can for women."

African-American women writers were joined by other minority women writers in the 1970s in redefining what was understood as American literature. Asian-American writers also had a widespread impact in translating their cultural experiences to a wider audience. Maxine Hong Kingston became the first woman writer to appear on the front page of *The New York Times Book Review* with *The Woman Warrior*. Amy Tan's story of mothers and daughters, *The Joy Luck Club*, introduced readers to Chinese-American mores while fostering recognition of relationship issues that crossed cultural boundaries. Sandra Cisneros, whose novel *The House on Mango Street* (1984) won the American Book Award in 1985, gave voice to Latina women and to "the shame of being poor, of being female, of being not-quite-good-enough." Louise Erdrich began her multi-voiced, nonchronological stories of Chippewa families caught in the tangles of tradition and extinction with *Love Medicine* (1984) to critical acclaim and commercial success.

Women writers continue to expand the definition of an American writer. Mukherjee Bharati described herself as "an American writer of Indian extraction." Paula Gunn Allen uses both fiction (*The Woman Who Owned the Shadows*, 1983) and non-fiction (*The Sacred Hoop: Recovering the Feminine in American Indian Tradition*, 1986) to explore the centrality of women in Native-American culture. Chinese-American Gish Jen establishes her fiction solidly in American experience and reiterates in interviews that her ethnicity is only one part of her identity.

CONCLUSION

While some women distanced themselves from the women's movement, scarcely any woman engaged in the arts and literature since the 1960s has remained unaffected by the women's movements and other social revolutions of the era, and all women in the arts have benefited from the achievements of the last half-century. Any list of women prominent in the world of music will show the advances women musicians have made, not only in visible fields such as performing and conducting, but also in less visible fields such as composing, publishing, and managing. The National Association of Women Artists was founded in 1889 by five women artists who were barred from full participation in the male-dominated National Academy of Design and the Society of American Artists. The society currently has more than 800 members, and the organization sponsors exhibitions annually that include year-round juried, traveling, and international exhibitions.

Women fiction writers may be excluded from an occasional best-of list, but they routinely achieve recognition that women in earlier eras could only dream of. *Beloved* by Nobel laureate Toni Morrison was selected as the single best work of American fiction published in the last 25 years in a 2006 *New York Times Book Review* survey of 124 prominent authors, critics, and editors; *The Complete Stories of Flannery O'Connor* was selected as the best of 60 years of National Book Award winners in 2009. Marilynne Robinson's first novel, *Housekeeping* (1981), received the PEN/Hemingway award for best first novel and was nominated for the Pulitzer Prize. Her second, *Gilead* (2004), received both the Pulitzer Prize for Fiction and the National Book Critics Circle Award, and she received Britain's Orange Prize for fiction in 2009 for the best writing in the English language by a woman.

Jane Smiley's novel *A Thousand Acres* won the Pulitzer Prize and the National Book Critics Circle Award in 1992, and *Horse Heaven* was short-listed for the Orange Prize in 2002. Annie Proulx, who started writing fiction in her

Women's artistic activism takes many forms. Kaziah Hancock, an artist from Manti, Utah, (here in 2006), devotes all of her work to painting memorial portraits—at no charge—of U.S. military personnel killed in the Middle East.

50s and entered mainstream consciousness when her 1997 story *Brokeback Mountain* became the most surprising movie success of 2005, was the first woman to win the prestigious PEN/Faulkner book award for her debut novel *Postcards* (1992). The following year she won a Pulitzer Prize and the National Book Award for her second novel, *The Shipping News*. In 2007 Natasha Trethewey became the 13th woman poet since 1961 to win a Pulitzer Prize.

Gender continues to be an issue in arts and literature in the 21st century. The continued need for an organization such as the National Association of Women Artists to advance the cause of women artists suggests equal opportunity is still a goal. Marin Alsop's appointment as the first woman to head a major American orchestra (the Baltimore Symphony Orchestra in 2007) received acclaim, but women conductors at Alsop's level are still rare exceptions, as are women instrumentalists in brass sections of top-ranked orchestras.

Female playwrights are so aware of gender discrimination that some have called for blind readings so that their work will be judged on its own merits. Women in all areas of the arts continue the struggle to balance their private and professional lives.

Janis L. Edwards
University of Alabama
Wylene Rholetter
Auburn University (Retired)

Further Reading

Ammer, Christine. *Unsung: A History of Women in American Music.* Portland, OR: Amadeus Press, 2001.

Banes, Sally. *Before, Between, and Beyond: Three Decades of Dance Writing.* Madison: University of Wisconsin Press, 2007.

Broude, Norma, and Mary D. Garrad, eds. *The Power of Feminist Art: The American Movement of the 1970s, History and Impact.* New York: Harry N. Abrams, 1994.

Butler, Cornelia, ed. *WACK! Art and the Feminist Revolution.* Cambridge, MA: MIT Press, 2007.

Cheng, Marietta Nien-hwa. "Women Conductors: Has the Train Left the Station?" *Harmony: Forum of the Symphony Orchestra Institute,* v.6 (1998).

Chicago, Judy, and Donald Woodman. *The Dinner Party: From Creation to Preservation.* London: Merrell, 2007.

Davis, Peter G. *The American Opera Singer: The Lives and Adventures of America's Great Singers in Opera and Concert, from 1825 to the Present.* New York: Doubleday, 1997.

Edwards, Michele. "Women on the Podium." In *The Cambridge Companion to Conducting,* ed. by José Bowen. Cambridge: Cambridge University Press, 2003.

Giles, James R., and Wanda H. Giles, eds. *American Novelists Since World War II. Dictionary of Literary Biography.* Detroit, MI: Gale Research, 1995.

Grubb, Nancy, ed. *Making Their Mark: Women Artists Move into the Mainstream, 1970–85.* New York: Abbeville Press, 1989.

Heinze, Denise and Sandra Adell. "Toni Morrison." In *Nobel Prize Laureates in Literature. Dictionary of Literary Biography.* Detroit, MI: Gale, 2007.

Johnston, Rosie. "Baton of the Sexes." *The Guardian* (April 13, 2007). Available Online, URL: http://www.guardian.co.uk/music/2007/apr/13/classicalmusicandopera.gender. Accessed February 2010.

Jones, Amelia, ed. *Sexual Politics: Judy Chicago's Dinner Party in Feminist Art History.* Berkeley, CA: University of California Press, 1996.

Kester-Shelton, Pamela, ed. *Feminist Writers.* Detroit: St. James Press, 1996.

Lippard, Lucy. *Get the Message? A Decade of Art for Social Change.* NY: E.P. Dutton, 1984.

Miller, Lynn F.and Sally S. Swenson. *Lives and Works: Talks with Women Artists.* Methuen, NJ: The Scarecrow Press, Inc., 1981.

Reckitt, Helena, and Peggy Phelan, eds. *Art and Feminism.* NY: Phaidon Press, Inc., 2001.

Showalter, Elaine. *A Jury of Her Peers: American Women Writers from Anne Bradstreet to Anne Proulx.* New York: Knopf, 2009.

Showalter, Elaine, Lea Baechler, and A. Walton Litz, eds. *Modern American Women Writers*. New York: Charles Scribner's Sons, 1991.

Tsioulcas, Anastasia. "Females Make Inroads Into Conducting." Variety (September 24, 2009). Available Online, URL: http://www.variety.com/article/VR1118009115.html?categoryid=3740&cs=1. Accessed December 2009.

Watanabe, Sylvia, and Carol Bruchac. *Home to Stay: Asian American Women's Fiction*. Greenfield Center, NY: Greenfield Review Press, 1990.

Witzling, Mara R., ed. *Voicing Today's Visions: Writings by Contemporary Women Artists*. London: Women's Press, 1994.

CHAPTER 8

Women in Business

THE ENTRY OF women into the paid workforce has been one of the most dramatic economic developments of the past 50 years. It has led to a remarkable evolution in women's roles and to new challenges and outlooks for women in business. Even before the birth of the women's movement, female participation in the workforce had begun to increase rapidly. In 1960, the labor force participation rate of women, defined as the percentage of women over the age of 16 who are either employed or unemployed and actively seeking employment, was 37.7 percent. By 2008, it was 59.5 percent, driven by a remarkable increase in the labor force participation rate of married women with young children. This increase in the number of working mothers was one of the most significant factors concerning women in business during this period. In 1960, 18.6 percent of married women with children under the age of 6 were in the labor force, as compared to 61.5 percent in 2007. The percentage of women working full time and year round had increased as well. In 1960 only 36.5 percent of working women worked full-time, while in 2000 the percentage was 59.9 percent. This was in contrast to the gradual decline in the labor force participation rate of men from 83.3 to 73 percent during this same period. As women left the domestic realm for the workplace, enormous changes took place within homes and within society as a whole. The dynamics of family life shifted, as fathers were gradually required to take on more responsibilities for childcare and housework, and mothers became more harried as they took on multiple roles. Working mothers were often blamed for everything from juvenile delinquency to childhood obesity.

THE 1960s

The number of employed women, especially wives and mothers, began to climb rapidly in the 1960s, despite significant barriers to paid work. Rising birthrates in the 1940s and 1950s, coupled with social pressure to focus on household responsibilities, made working outside the home particularly difficult. The birthrate per 1,000 population at the beginning of the decade was 23.7, a very slight drop from 24.1 in 1960. Moreover, very few women had the education and training necessary to enter the labor market. In 1960, only 35.3 percent of all bachelor's degrees were awarded to women, and 2.5 percent of law degrees, 5.5 percent of medical doctor degrees, and 3.6 percent of MBAs. Of the 37.8 percent of women in the labor force, the majority were part-time workers without strong attachment to their jobs. Most female workers expected to drop out of the workplace permanently upon marriage, which occurred at an average age of 20.3 years for first marriages.

Women in the workforce continued to face discrimination during this period. Employers segregated women into low-paying jobs that provided little or no chance for advancement. One way to assess the magnitude of differences in the distribution of women and men across occupational categories

A female Census Bureau employee uses a card proof punch to process 1960 census returns. Women in the 1960s tended to hold lower-paying and less prestigious jobs than those held by males.

Title VII of the Civil Rights Act of 1964

Of all laws dealing with discrimination in employment, Title VII of the Civil Rights Act of 1964 and its various amendments have had the greatest impact on American society. The original 1964 law corrected a major deficiency of the 1963 Equal Pay Act by which employers could escape paying male and female employees equally by hiring sexually segregated workforces. Subsequent cases brought under Title VII further defined what constitutes sex discrimination under the law.

When accused of sex discrimination, employers often claimed that the discrimination was not based on sex, but rather on other identifiable factors. In *Phillips v. Martin Marietta Corporation* (1971), for example, Martin Marietta refused to hire Phillips, a woman with preschool age children, although the company had hired similarly situated men. The court ruled against Martin Marietta. Title VII and similar state laws of this type have, however, permitted discrimination based on factors such as intelligence and experience, provided that these neutral factors do not operate to produce discrimination based on any of the prohibited factors of sex, race, national origin, color, religion, age, and disability. Thus, "sex-plus" or "sex-linked" discrimination based on sexually identifiable factors, including pregnancy or the ability to get pregnant, has been prohibited under Title VII.

Dr. Rev. Martin Luther King Jr. during a civil rights march on Washington, D.C., August 28, 1963.

Another defense of sex discrimination is found in the following language of the law, which states that discrimination is permitted only "in those certain instances where ... sex ... is a bona fide occupational qualification (BFOQ) reasonably necessary to the normal operation of that particular business or enterprise." For example, in *Diaz v. Pan American World Airways, Inc.* (1971), Pan Am refused to hire Diaz, a male, for the position of flight attendant, arguing that being female was a BFOQ for the position of flight attendant. The Fifth Circuit Court ruled against the airline, claiming that the nonmechanical aspect of the flight attendant position was not necessary to carry out the normal business operation of transporting passengers. The Equal Employment Opportunity Commission has adopted a restrictive interpretation of the BFOQ exemption in order to further reduce the notion of "men's jobs" and "women's jobs."

is the index of segregation, which gives the percentage of workers who would have had to change jobs in order for the occupational distribution of males and females to be identical. The index would equal zero if the distribution of men and women across occupational categories were identical, or 100 if all occupations were either completely male or female. In 1960, the index was 68.69, indicating a high level of occupational segregation in jobs that were either predominantly female or male. The jobs in which females were clustered were low paying and less prestigious than those held by males. By the end of the decade, the index had fallen to 65.90.

The 1963 President's Commission on the Status of Women documented women's second-class status in all areas of society, including the workplace, resulting in two major pieces of legislation designed to reduce gender discrimination. The Equal Pay Act of 1963 prohibited discrimination by sex for the performance of equal work, and Title VII of the 1964 Civil Rights Act removed barriers to women's opportunities for employment and career advancement. The category of "sex" was not originally included in Title VII. Some legislators saw it as a way to maneuver the defeat of the legislation, but the strategy backfired, and the passage of Title VII outlawed discrimination in all aspects of employment on the basis of sex, as well as race, color, religion, and national origin. The Civil Rights Act also called for the creation of the Equal Employment Opportunity Commission (EEOC) to monitor compliance with the new law. When the EEOC failed to pursue sanctions against sex discrimination in the workplace, women joined together in 1966 to create the National Organization of Women (NOW) to pressure the commission to advance the cause of women in employment as it was doing for minorities.

Women's participation in the labor market during the war proved to many Americans that an employed wife could contribute substantially to her family's material well-being and security, and women learned that it was possible to balance home and work responsibilities to some extent. The expanding definition of

A Yardley Cosmetics advertisement in Seventeen magazine, March 1965. The continuing demand for cosmetics attracted many women to the industry, both in sales and business ownership.

family need, fostered by a consumer economy and by women's impatience with living on one income, received a substantial boost during the war years. Due to the postwar baby boom and the fact that women were marrying at a younger age, there were fewer young, unmarried women available for work, and employers turned to married women as a labor source.

During much of the 1960s, real wages rose, and unemployment was relatively low. The rapid postwar economic growth continued until the mid-1970s, creating a major expansion in jobs for clerks, saleswomen, and service workers. Since women's participation in the labor force was incorrectly seen as temporary, it was not viewed as a threat to male employees.

Another force fueling the movement of women into the workplace was women's questioning of their conventional roles as wives and mothers as discussed in Betty Friedan's *The Feminine Mystique* (1963), which shattered the popular image of the happy housewife. At the time, 74.3 percent of households were led by a married couple, a family pattern that involved substantial division of labor by sex. Men were assigned the role of economic providers, and women managed households and cared for children. Men typically did only specific, male-oriented domestic tasks such as lawnmowing, automobile and household repair, and carrying out garbage.

A few women of the 1960s challenged social norms and proved that women could succeed in the male-dominated business world. In 1963, Mary Kay Ash launched Mary Kay Cosmetics, with a twist on the traditional entrepreneurial model. Its message "At Mary Kay, you're in business for yourself, but never by yourself," emphasized community over competition among her "consultants," the women who sold her cosmetics. Ash's unique business model earned her $198,000 in sales in the first year, which quadrupled to $800,000 after the second year. By 1992, her company was on *Fortune's* list of the 500 largest corporations in the United States.

Like the cosmetics industry, the food industry attracted women entrepreneurs. This field was particularly inviting for minority women who built businesses by bringing ethnic traditions to women's universal role as family cook. Peking-born Joyce Chen expanded her Boston-based Chinese restaurant business by publishing the *Joyce Chen Cook Book* in 1962, and followed it up with a public television show *Joyce Chen Cooks* in 1966, before expanding the business to include Joyce Chen Products and Joyce Chen Specialty Foods.

While the majority of women entrepreneurs were found in traditionally female enterprises, a few gravitated toward nontraditional fields. Katharine Graham took over the *Washington Post* in 1963 after the suicide of her husband, and transformed it from a local newspaper with a modest circulation into one of the country's top-ranked newspapers. By 1993, when she turned the Washington Post Company over to her son, it was included in the Fortune 500 list.

Muriel Siebert, known as "the first woman of finance," became the first woman to have a seat on the New York Stock Exchange (NYSE) and the first

Oprah Winfrey

Best known for *The Oprah Winfrey Show*, Winfrey rose from a childhood of poverty to become one of America's most successful and influential businesswomen. Her love of acting and her desire to bring quality entertainment projects to production prompted her in 1986 to form her own production company, HARPO Productions, Inc. In October, 1988, the company acquired ownership of *The Oprah Winfrey Show* from Capital Cities/ABC, making Oprah Winfrey the first woman in history to own and produce her own talk show. Based in Chicago, the HARPO Entertainment Group includes HARPO Productions, Inc., HARPO Films, and HARPO Video, Inc. Winfrey has also branched out into movie production; cable TV (she is one of the partners in Oxygen Media, Inc., a cable channel and interactive network focused on women); magazines (in 2000, she began *O: The Oprah Magazine*, which topped two million in circulation, making it the most successful startup ever in the industry); radio (*Oprah Radio*); and the Internet (Oprah.com). In 1996 she began Oprah's Book Club to promote reading, recommending a recently published book each month and propelling her choices onto bestseller lists.

In 2003, Winfrey became the first African-American woman to be listed on *Forbes* magazine's list of America's billionaires. She has used her fame and wealth to influence the lives of people in need. Ever since coming to Chicago, Winfrey has given 10 percent of her income to charities, mostly having to do with youths, education, and books. In 2000, Oprah's Angel Network began presenting a $100,000 Use Your Life Award to people who are using their lives to improve the lives of others. In 2007, she opened a school for disadvantaged girls in South Africa, the Leadership Academy for Girls, fulfilling a promise she had made to former President Nelson Mandela.

to own a NYSE brokerage firm, Muriel Siebert & Company. Despite her experience and success as a partner at two leading brokerage houses, Siebert met with ridicule and hostility when she attempted to join the 1,365 male members of the exchange. Among the first 10 men she asked to sponsor her application to the exchange, nine refused. Muriel Siebert was finally elected to membership on December 28, 1967. A decade passed before she was joined by other women. In 1975 Muriel Siebert and Company became the nation's first discount broker when the Securities and Exchange Commission first permitted broker commissions to be negotiable. In 1977 Siebert became the superintendent of banks for the State of New York, with oversight of all of the banks in the state, regulating about $500 billion. Not one bank failed during her tenure, despite significant failures nationwide.

THE 1970s

The postwar baby boom was followed by a baby bust, during which birthrates fell sharply due to factors that included the increasing availability of the birth control pill. The birthrate dipped below the replacement level (the degree to which a population replaces itself when deaths and births are taken into account) in 1972 and hit a low of 1.7 in 1976 before starting to rise again in the late 1970s. Throughout the 1940s and 1950s, birth control advocates had been engaged in numerous legal battles. In 1965 in *Griswold v. Connecticut*, the U.S. Supreme Court struck down the one remaining state law that prohibited the use of contraceptives by married couples. The federal government began to take a more active part in the birth control movement in 1967, allotting 6 percent of funds in the Child Health Act for family planning. In 1970, the Family Planning Services and Population Act established separate funds for birth control, and in 1973, the Supreme Court ruled in *Roe v. Wade* that most U.S. laws against abortion violated the constitutional right to privacy. The ability to control fertility and allow for abortion gave women the flexibility to invest and advance their careers while maintaining intimate relationships. More women began delaying marriage and childbirth to attend college and pursue careers, strengthening their attachment to the labor market.

Estée Lauder applies lipstick on a customer in 1966. Estée Lauder sales have climbed every year since she gained her first counter space in 1948. She attended every launch of a new cosmetics counter or shop; by the time of her death in 2004, Lauder and her two sons were billionaires.

By 1970 the labor force participation rate of women had risen 43.4 percent, largely a response to the dramatic rise in the proportion of married women with children under the age of 6 in the labor force, increasing from 18.6 percent in 1960 to 30.3 percent in 1970. Unfortunately, women's assumption of greater responsibility for breadwinning in American families had not caused a comparable increase in men's homemaking contributions. In response, employed women began to spend more of their income on goods and services to reduce their time spent in cleaning, cooking, and childcare, spending considerably less time on these tasks than their mothers and grandmothers.

The economic boom that began after WWII ground to a halt during the 1970s as unemployment reached 8.5 percent in 1975, a drastic change from the 1969 rate of 3.5 percent. Even during sinking demand for unskilled farm labor and skilled and unskilled manufacturing labor, jobs that were primarily occupied by men, the demand for female-dominated jobs increased. This macroeconomic shift to so-called "female occupations" that required skill without either long-term commitment to work or specialized geographic location allowed women to retain their roles of primary providers of nonmarket output for their families over their lifetimes while following their husbands in their pursuits of higher-paid work.

However, by the mid 1970s, there was a period of revolution for women in the labor force, which was brought on by several developments. First, women had slowly gained access to institutions of higher education. In 1970, women earned 43.1 percent of all bachelor's degrees as compared to 35.3 percent in 1960. In that same year, women earned 5.4 percent of law degrees and 8.4 percent of medical degrees. However, women continued to be limited by institutional policies in which overt or informal quotas limited the number of places available to them, or by those enrollment requirements that held women to higher standards than men. To remedy discrimination in educational institutions, Congress passed Title IX of the Educational Amendment (to the Civil Rights Act of 1964) in 1972. The law prohibited discrimination on the basis of sex in any educational program or activity receiving federal financial assistance, encompassing admissions, financial aid, and access to programs and activities. By the end of the decade, 49 percent of all bachelor's degrees, 30.2 percent of law degrees, 23.4 percent of medical degrees, and 22.4 percent of MBAs were being awarded to women.

The International Ladies' Garment Workers' Union was one of the first U.S. unions to have a primarily female membership when it began in the 1900s. By the 1970s, it struggled under the challenges of cheap imports, restrictive labor laws, and American factories moving overseas.

In 1972 women owned 4 percent of all American businesses, most of which were clustered in service and retail businesses. Frustrated at her employers' failure to provide clothes for working women, in 1976 Liz Claiborne started her own design company, Liz Claiborne, Inc. It was an immediate success, with sales of

$2 million the first year and $23 million in 1978. The company went public in 1981 and made the Fortune 500 list in 1986 with retail sales of $1.2 billion, making Claiborne the first woman to become chairperson and CEO of a Fortune 500 company. Women like Claiborne who had found it difficult to raise startup capital received a boost in 1974 when Congress passed the Equal Credit Opportunity Act, which prohibited creditors, banks, finance companies, credit card companies, and other lenders from discriminating against applicants on the basis of sex, race, color, religion, national origin, marital status, and age (but above minor age).

THE 1980s

The labor force participation rate of women rose to 51.6 percent in 1980 at the same time the fertility rate began rising slightly, reaching the replacement rate shortly after the turn of the 21st century. Other factors affecting the rate of women in the workforce were the rising divorce rate of 5.2 as compared to 3.5 in 1970 and 2.2 in 1960 and the decline in the number of families led by married couples. This rate dropped to 60.8 percent in the 1980s as compared to 70.5 percent in 1970 and 74.3 percent in 1960. The lives of working women were also affected by the stagnating economy, and unemployment reached a postwar high of 9.7 percent in 1982.

Sexual harassment in the workplace, which had long been a significant issue on the feminist agenda, was thrust into the spotlight in 1986 with *Meritor Savings Bank v. Vinson* when the Supreme Court ruled that sexual harassment was illegal under Title VII whenever the behavior in question is unwelcome and is "sufficiently pervasive to alter the conditions of the victim's employment [so as to] create an abusive working environment." This decision was followed in 1993 by *Harris v. Forklift Systems, Inc.*, in which the Supreme Court further defined what constitutes a hostile working condition, determining that victims were not required to prove they had been physically damaged or injured to support claims of sexual harassment. However, the event that hurtled sexual harassment into the national consciousness was the 1991 televised Supreme Court nomination hearing of African-American Supreme Court nominee Clarence Thomas. Reporters had learned that University of Oklahoma law professor Anita Hill, also an African American, had told friends that she had been sexually harassed while working for Thomas, and she agreed to testify. Feminists were outraged with what they considered to be the mishandling of the sexual harassment issue by an all-male, all-white Senate Judiciary Committee. After extensive debate, during which a dozen of his female employees came to his defense, the U.S. Senate confirmed Thomas by a vote of 52–48. However, the highly publicized incident was part of a movement leading employers to create new policies governing behavior in the workplace and a new awareness that more women were needed in both the political and business worlds.

Linda Alvarado

Linda Alvarado is founder and president of Alvarado Construction Inc., a Denver-based firm with an office in San Francisco, which conducts business throughout the western United States. Under her leadership, the company built the Colorado Convention Center; the administration office center at the Denver International Airport; and Mile High Stadium, home of the NFL's Denver Broncos. Further, she is part owner of Denver's Major League Baseball team, the Colorado Rockies, making her the first woman entrepreneur ever to bid for and win ownership of a major league baseball team. She sits on the boards of several major corporations, including 3M, Pepsi Bottling Group, and Qwest Communications. In the early part of the 21st century, Alvarado held more board seats in Fortune 1000 companies than any other Latino, male or female.

Whenever she prepares to vacate a board seat, she suggests a replacement that is either Hispanic or female. Alvarado is a National Women's Hall of Fame inductee and has received numerous awards, including Revlon Business Woman of the Year in 1996, the Horatio Alger Award in 2001, 100 Most Influential Hispanics in America from *Hispanic Business Magazine,* and other honors for her work promoting equal opportunity. She was a founding member and past president of Denver's Hispanic Chamber of Commerce. In addition, she served on President Clinton's Advisory Commission of Educational Excellence for Hispanic Americans.

Another issue facing women that gained increasing attention during this time was the "glass ceiling", a term popularized in a 1986 *Wall Street Journal* article describing the invisible barriers that women confronted as they approached the top of the corporate hierarchy. Statistics provided by the U.S. Department of Labor indicated that only 2 percent of top-level management jobs and 5 percent of corporate board positions were held by women as of 1987. Other significant work during this time was by the Center for Creative Leadership and Catalyst, a New York-based research organization that advised corporations on how to foster the careers of women. The conclusions of these studies pointed to few true differences between men and women in psychological, emotional, or intellectual qualities, but found that contradictions in expectations for women were a major factor in the glass ceiling. Women were expected to be tough without displaying "macho" characteristics, to take responsibility while remaining obedient, and to be ambitious without demanding equal treatment. Secretary of Labor Elizabeth Dole created the Glass Ceiling Initiative in 1989 to identify problems, causes, and solutions to the ceiling.

THE 1990s

Continuing the work begun in the previous decade, Congress passed Title II of the Civil Rights Act of 1991, also known as the Glass Ceiling Act, which mandated the appointment of a commission to identify barriers to female and minority advancement faced in the workplace. The commission's 1995 report revealed that at the highest levels of business, there was indeed a barrier only rarely penetrated by women or persons of color, stating that 97 percent of senior managers of Fortune 1,000 industrial and Fortune 500 companies were white, and 95 to 97 percent were male. Obstacles to women's advancement included the existence of a male-dominated corporate culture, women's exclusion from informal networking, management's belief that women were less career oriented, and the lack of female mentors.

Not surprisingly, childcare became an increasingly important, controversial, and emotional issue as more mothers of preschool age children moved into the workforce. Debate centered on whether childcare was harmful to children, particularly care by non-family members, and the extent of government subsidies and regulation. There was also growing concern over the extent of low-quality childcare in the United States. Programs and credits to assist working parents and their children were developed, such as the Dependent Care Tax Credit, the Child Tax Credit, and the Child Care and Development Block Grant. New women-owned business sprouted up as many saw

Children at Alumni Village Day Care Center in Tallahassee, Florida, in 1987. The availability of childcare continued to open opportunities for women in paid employment, but also sparked controversy as to the economic and personal cost. In the 1990s, women increasingly took advantage of work-at-home ventures made more widely available by the growth of the Internet.

business ownership as the answer to the problem of juggling work and family. By 1991, women-owned businesses comprised 38 percent of all U.S. businesses and were responsible for $4 trillion in sales and employment of 27 million workers. Unlike corporate workplaces, entrepreneurship offered women the autonomy and freedom to set their own schedules and control their own work. Moreover, at-home businesses were particularly appealing to mothers of young children, offering them the ability to incorporate work and family within a single space. By the mid-1990s, women had founded an estimated 3.5 million home-based businesses. Turning their backs on the separation of work and family, the rise of computer technology opened up previously unimagined opportunities to recreate a new version of the old preindustrial model, where work and family were integrated into the household, allowing women to run businesses or work without leaving home.

THE 21ST CENTURY
Changing demographics and social norms, as well as reduced discrimination in education and the labor market, have motivated women to explore new frontiers. Women currently receive about 57 percent of all bachelor degrees, 45.9 percent of law degrees, 42.7 percent of medical degrees, and 39.8 percent of MBAs. Demographic trends of the last 40 years that motivated women to attach themselves more firmly to the labor force continued into the new century. The divorce rate per 1,000 population in 2000 remained high at 4.0, and the total birth rate held steady at 2 children per woman, only increasing to the replacement rate of 2.1 children per woman in 2006. The percentages of all births to unmarried women rose from 5.3 percent in 1960 to 33.2 percent in 2000, and the percent of all family households led by a married couple declined to only 52.8 percent. The median age at first marriage rose to 25.1 years, while the average age of first childbirth for women was 24.9 years of age. The result was that in 2000, the labor force participation rate of all women was 59.9 percent, and 62.8 percent for married women with young children. Almost half of all workers in the United States were women.

Women continued to lead the growth in new businesses: 10.1 million firms were owned by women in 2008 as compared to 6.5 million in 2002, employing more than 13 million people in 2008 compared to 7.1 million people in 2002, and generating $1.9 trillion in sales in 2008 compared to $939.5 billion in 2002. These firms accounted for 40 percent of all privately held firms in 2008. Some 1.9 million firms, or approximately one in five women-owned businesses, are owned by women of color in the United States. These firms employ 1.2 million people and generate $165 billion in revenues annually. Between 2002 and 2008, firms owned by women of color grew faster than all other privately held firms.

One important measure of progress is the changing nature of the types of businesses that women now pursue. As opposed to the previous 30–40 years, women of the 21st century have been successful in almost every industry—from telecommunications to building and manufacturing to information technology. In 2009, 15 women were CEOs of Fortune 500 companies, including Angela Braly of WellPoint; Patricia Woertz of Archer Daniels Midland; Indra Nooyi of PepsiCo; Irene Rosenfeld of Kraft Foods; and Ursula Burns of Xerox, who succeeded another woman as CEO, Anne Mulcahy, the first time that has happened in a Fortune 500 company. In 2008, women held 15.2 percent of directorships at Fortune 500 companies, a slight rise from the previous year's 14.8 percent, and substantially higher than the 9 percent rate of 1993. However, the number of Fortune 500 companies with no women on the board directors increased from 59 in 2007 to 66 in 2008, although the number of companies with three or more women on the board directors increased from 83 in 2007 to 92 in 2008. Women of color held just 3.2 percent of all Fortune 500 directorships and made up slightly more than one-fifth of women directors.

CONTINUING CHALLENGES
Women continue to face challenges in the business world. Due to differences in the socialization process, most women are not taught to be risk takers or to be competitive or aggressive. Such dynamics often prevent women from reaching their full potential as business owners. As caretakers of the home, women are taught to value security and tend to take fewer financial risks such as taking out a second mortgage to finance a business venture. Women are still perceived negatively when they exhibit aggressive or competitive behaviors.

Another challenge is balancing work and family. Bearing most of the responsibility for the family has been a consistent and far greater challenge for women than men because women have different expectations of themselves regarding their role in their families, and children tend to have different expectations of mothers and fathers. Even among women who own their own businesses, the freedom implied by entrepreneurship, working at home, and the latest technology has not always enabled women to transcend the continuing struggle to balance work and family.

For many women business owners, continuing disparities in access to networks, mentors, and capital for starting and expanding their businesses have been the most pressing issues that they face. All-women organizations have developed to support and mentor women, including the National Foundation for Women Business Owners, the National Association of Women Business Owners, the National Women's Business Council, the Small Business Administration's Office of Women Business Ownership, the Commonwealth Institute, and the Committee of 200.

While access to capital has improved, significant disparities remain, and women still are not on equal footing with men when it comes to obtaining business funding because of biases and expectations of lending program officials and representatives, availability of venture capital for woman-owned businesses, and lack of technical knowledge on the part of women business owners in certain male-dominated industries. The Equal Credit Opportunity Act has loosened credit restrictions on women consumers more than entrepreneurs. In a report published by the *Journal of Developmental Entrepreneurship* in 2002, Susan Coleman wrote that characteristics typical of many women-owned firms, including small size, limited prospects for growth and profitability, and lack of collateral lower women's chances of obtaining a business loan. Smaller firms, then, may have their loan opportunities constrained by the characteristics of the firm, rather than by the choices of the owner-manager.

Even as women's businesses grow in number, size, and revenue, women entrepreneurs receive a remarkably small 4 percent of available venture capital funds. Access to capital continues to be even more difficult for minority women. As a result, women have continued a familiar pattern: reliance on personal savings or funds from family and friends. Linda Alvarado, for instance, went to six banks, all of which rejected her business plan, before she turned to her parents, who mortgaged their home to help her get started.

The wage gap was 80 percent in 2000, a significant improvement over 1960 when it was 61 percent. However, that 61 percent represented a gap that had

A pregnant women had little recourse if fired for her condition until 1978, when President Jimmy Carter sponsored the Pregnancy Discrimination Act, which required employers to treat pregnancy like other medical conditions and provide job protection for pregnant women.

widened three percent since 1955. By the 1970s, in response to the women's movement and a heightened awareness of the issue of comparable worth, the wage gap narrowed, and women began earning around 70 cents for every dollar paid to male workers. Nevertheless, the wage gap persists even in occupations dominated by females. According to the Institute for Women's Policy Research, in 2009, the weekly median wage of male nurses was $1,168 as compared to $1,011 for female nurses. Among elementary and middle-school teachers, the comparable figure for males was $994, but only $871 for females. Even among cashiers, a job that required no educational degree, males made $798 as compared to $638 for females.

Some elements of the wage gap can be explained by the fact that women continue to occupy lower-wage jobs as compared to men; therefore, efforts to reduce occupational segregation is likely to reduce the wage gap. However, unequal pay for equal work still exists, as evidenced by the need for the Lilly Ledbetter Fair Pay Act of 2009, which amended the Civil Rights Act of 1964, stating that the 180-day statute of limitations for filing an equal-pay lawsuit regarding pay discrimination resets with each new discriminatory paycheck.

FLEX-TIME AND OTHER DEVELOPMENTS

After the 1960s, many employers became aware that women were a significant part of the modern workforce and began understanding that women who were not stressed about their families were more productive workers. Consequently, they began experimenting with various ways to help women balance the dual roles of mother and worker. One such innovation was flex-time, part-time, and share-time positions for working mothers. Flexible working hours allowed women to arrange nontraditional work schedules to accommodate the needs of their families, while part-time work permitted mothers to work only a few hours a day or a few days a week. With share-time, two workers divided the same job so that it was covered throughout a typical working day. Compressed time allowed workers to work typical hours within a shorter work week. Telecommuting expanded the flexibility of working schedules still further, allowing mothers to work without having to leave their homes for regularly scheduled work days.

Another way in which some companies accommodated working mothers was with the so-called mommy track, which allowed mothers to opt for a slower professional track that allowed them more time with their families. It soon became evident that women on the mommy track were making less money and losing out on promotions to males and women on regular tracks to success. In 2009, among *Working Mother's* top-100 companies, all offered flexible working schedules and telecommuting, 98 percent offered job sharing, 94 percent offered compressed work schedules, 86 percent provided backup childcare, and 62 percent provided childcare for sick children.

Before the women's movement, pregnant women were regularly fired from their jobs. Insurance companies often refused to pay the birth costs for female employees even though they offered this benefit to the wives of male employees. Before the late 1970s, women found no redress for this discrimination in the courts, but in 1978, President Jimmy Carter sponsored the Pregnancy Discrimination Act, which required employers to treat pregnancy the same as any other medical condition and required employers to provide job protection for pregnant women who took maternity leave. In 1993, the Congressional Caucus for Women's Issues worked with President Bill Clinton to pass the Family and Medical Leave Act, which allowed either parent to take time off from work to care for newborns, adopted children, and family members who were seriously ill. Many companies now allow pregnant women to save up vacation and personal leave time so they receive full pay while on maternity leave.

CONCLUSION

A half-century ago, the response of the labor market to the entry of large numbers of women workers was to segregate them into low-paying, dead-end jobs. The situation has improved greatly, and women have made significant contributions to the labor force. Nevertheless, women continue to earn less than men on average, and they continue to face barriers when entering the job market and when seeking career advancement.

Regrettably, progress in education and the labor force for women masks differences by race and ethnicity. As a result of urbanization, improved educational opportunities for minorities, civil rights activism, and laws such as the Title VII, many African-American and Hispanic women in recent decades have moved into traditionally female service, clerical, and sales jobs from which they had been previously excluded. However, racism still limits the opportunities of women of color. Although some change has occurred in recent years, women still shoulder a dis-

A 2005 study found that the probability of receiving a loan is about five percentage points lower for female-owned/managed firms than for male-owned/managed firms.

proportionate share of unpaid childcare and domestic work, which limits the time and energy they can devote to paid work.

DONNA ANDERSON
UNIVERSITY OF WISCONSIN, LACROSSE

Further Reading

Blackwelder, Julia Kirk. *Now Hiring: The Feminization of Work in the United States, 1900–1995.* College Station, TX: Texas A&M University Press, 1997.

Blau, Francine D. "Trends in the Well-Being of American Women, 1970–1995." *Journal of Economic Literature*, v.36/1 (1998).

Blau, Francine D., et al. *The Economics of Women, Men, and Work.* Upper Saddle River, NJ: Pearson Prentice Hall, 2006.

Baxandall, Rosalyn, and Linda Gordon, eds. *America's Working Women: A Documentary History, 1600–1995.* New York: Norton, 1995.

Bernard, Michelle D. *Women's Progress: How Women Are Wealthier, Healthier, and More Independent Than Ever Before.* Dallas, TX: Spence Publishing Co., 2007.

Catalyst. *2008 Catalyst Census of Women Corporate Officers and Top Earners of the Fortune 500*, and previous issues, New York, various years. Available online at http://www.catalyst.org. Accessed May 2009.

Coleman, Susan. "Constraints Faced by Women Small Business Owners: Evidence from the Data." *Journal of Developmental Entrepreneurship*, v.7/2 (August 2002).

Drachman, Virginia G. *Enterprising Women: 250 Years of American Business.* Boston, MA: Vernon Press, 2002.

National Women's Business Council. *Enterprising Women: The Legacy and the Future.* Washington, D.C.: National Women's Business Council, 2003.

Goldin, Claudia. *Understanding the Gender Gap: An Economic History of American Women.* New York: Oxford University Press, 1990.

Government Accounting Office. "Women's Pay: Converging Characteristics of Men and Women in the Federal Workforce Help Explain the Narrowing Pay Gap." (April 28, 2009). Available online, URL: http://www.gao.gov/new.items/d09621t.pdf. Accessed December 2009.

Hunt, Vilma R. *Work and the Health of Women.* Boca Raton, FL: CRC Press, 1979.

Kay, Herma Hill, and Martha S West. *Sex-Based Discrimination.* St. Paul, MN: West Publishing Co., 2006.

Kesler-Harris, Alice. *Out to Work: A History of Wage-Earning Women in the United States.* New York: Oxford University Press, 1982.

Koziaro, Karen Schallcross, et al. *Working Women: Past, Present, Future.* Washington, D.C.: Bureau of National Affairs, 1987.

Lindgren, J. Ralph, and Nadine Taub. *The Law of Sex Discrimination.* Minneapolis, MN: West, 1993.

Mills, Kay. *From Pocahontas to Power Suits: Everything You Needed to Know about Women's History in America.* New York: Penguin, 1995.

Lindgren, J. Ralph and Nadine Taub. *The Law of Sex Discrimination.* Minneapolis: West, 1993.

Sellers, Patricia. "The Business of Being Oprah." *Fortune* (April 1, 2002).

Thistle, Susan. *From Marriage to the Market: The Transformation of Women's Lives and Work.* Berkeley: University of California Press, 2006.

United States Department of Labor. *Good for Business: Making Full Use of the Nation's Human Capital, a Fact-Finding Report on the Federal Glass Ceiling Commission.* Washington, D.C.: U.S. Department of Labor, 1995.

United States Department of Labor Women's Bureau. Available online, URL: http://www.dol.gov/wb/. Accessed May 2009.

Warner, Deborah J. *Perfect in Her Place: Women at Work in Industrial America.* Washington, D.C.: Smithsonian Institution, 1981.

Working Mothers. "Working Mothers 100 Best Companies 2009." Available Online, URL: http://www.workingmother.com/BestCompanies/work-life-balance/2009/08/working-mother-100-best-companies-2009. Accessed December 2009.

Yeager, Mary A., ed. *Women in Business.* Northampton, MA: Edward Elgar Publishing Company, 1999.

CHAPTER 9

Women in Entertainment and Sports

IN RESPONSE TO the women's movement and the changing role of women, the latter decades of the 20th century and the early years of the 21st century were marked by an increased presence of women in entertainment and sports and by new perceptions of how much women could achieve. During this period, women joined the ranks of high-profile newscasters and achieved major successes in acting, directing, and producing, and in less visible fields of entertainment. In television and film and on the stage, women refused to be stereotyped as helpless victims who needed to be rescued or as women who were only fulfilled as mothers and wives. At the same time, female musicians forged new paths for themselves in all genres. On athletic fields, women proved they could draw audiences and attract both sponsors and fans.

WOMEN AND THE NEWS MEDIA

Female journalists made huge strides on the small screen after 1961, moving from coverage of the local weather and human-interest stories to investigative journalism and war correspondence. The first woman to break the barrier of the male-dominated position of news anchor was Barbara Walters, who in 1976 was hired as the first female anchor for an evening network newscast at an unprecedented annual salary of $1 million. Due to tense relationships with male colleagues, Walters's run was not successful. However,

Barbara Walters interviews President Ford and First Lady Betty Ford in December 1976. She broke down the all-male barrier of U.S. network news when she was hired as anchor on NBC, but her seven-figure salary and "infotainment" approach to the news allegedly led to her dismissal. She became a household name as a result of her Barbara Walters Specials, 20/20, *and* The View.

she developed a reputation as a candid, intuitive interviewer and scored major interviews with sitting and former presidents, foreign dignitaries, and Hollywood elite. Walters also paved the way for reporters such as Christine Amanpour, Campbell Brown of CNN, and Rachel Maddow of MSNBC, who landed major political interviews and won awards for their reportage. In 2008 Katie Couric made history by becoming the first female anchor of an evening TV news broadcast. Later that year, Diane Sawyer proved that the glass ceiling of broadcast journalism was definitely cracking when she became the first female evening anchor on the ABC network. While women still face challenges surrounding age and race in seeking careers in broadcast journalism, the female faces appearing on the nation's small screens have become increasingly diverse.

While female war correspondents had been around since Kit Coleman first covered the Spanish-American War in 1898, they broke new ground in the post-1961 era, covering U.S. military actions in the Vietnam War (1961–75), the Persian Gulf War (1990–91), and the 2003 invasion of Iraq. Female war correspondents covered the stories of war with new attention to the consequences of war on civilians. They also examined incidences of sexual assault and post-traumatic stress disorder among women in the military, challenging decades of silence on such topics.

Super-Heroines: Women in the Comics

From Wonder Woman to Catwoman to Buffy the Vampire Slayer, female characters in comic books have both reinforced and challenged social stereotypes about women's roles. The busty, long-legged Wonder Woman and pinup-girl characters of the World War II era, and the cheerleader and housewife characters of the 1950s, reinforced a physical standard of beauty.

It was not until the late 1960s that a significant change in women's comic book roles emerged, partially as a result of the women's movement. One notable series that introduced women characters of a variety of ages, powers, and body types was the *X-Men* series. Throughout the 1970s and 1980s, characters like Storm, Jean Grey/Phoenix, and Kitty Pryde gave teen readers the chance to encounter complex women in engaging story lines. In the 1990s, characters from other media drew new attention to the potential of comic books, such as Buffy the Vampire Slayer, which had originated in a 1992 film about a teenage girl who emerged as a reluctant heroine. Buffy-related comics were published beginning in 1998. After the *Buffy* television show concluded at the end of its seventh season, season eight was published as a comic book. For younger girls, the Powerpuff Girls were introduced on a TV show first broadcast in 1998, and featured in comic books beginning in 2000. These kindergarten-age characters encouraged young girls to dream of "saving the world before bedtime."

At the turn of the millennium, *manga* (Japanese comic books) became popular in the United States. *Shojo manga*, or Japanese comics aimed at a teenage female audience, had been around since the late 1960s. However, Japanese animated films (*anime*) were far more accessible to American audiences than manga until the 1990s, when U.S. publishers began to publish manga in the wake of the popularity of anime such as *Akira* and *Pokémon*. By the early 21st century, Cartoon Network was regularly showing Japanese anime based on successful manga series on its Adult Swim lineup. The result was an explosion of interest in the genre and in Japanese culture. By 2006, 60 percent of all manga readers were female. Ironically, one of the most popular manga types among female readers is *yaoi*, which focuses on the relationships of gay males. At the many annual anime conventions, female attendees regularly dress as their favorite male heroines, but cross-dressing males are still a small minority. The female characters in manga range from innocent schoolgirls on adventures to powerful super-heroines that offer readers a wide variety of role models. As more women became illustrators, a more authentic variety of girls' and women's experiences began to be reflected in the comics. Contemporary "superwomen" in manga include Mikami of *Ghost Sweeper Mikami*, Gally of *Gunnm*, and Natsuki of *Natsuki Crisis*. However, there is considerable concern over the contemporary tendency of heroines to become more traditional over the course of a manga series.

Print journalism went through major transformations during this time, as one new technology after another challenged the supremacy of print news. The women's movement also transformed coverage of women's issues as the 20th century evolved. While the women's pages of the early 1960s largely contained social announcements, fashion tips, recipes, and advice columns, select urban newspapers began incorporating investigative journalism and human-interest stories into women's pages. Katharine Graham, who had taken over the *Washington Post* after her husband's death, was at the helm when the Watergate scandal broke, and she was instrumental in allowing reporters Bob Woodward and Carl Bernstein to pursue the story when other newspapers dropped it.

By the mid-1970s, women's issues had become more integrated within newspapers, but stereotypes continued to exist. It was a headline-seeking male journalist who started the myth of feminist bra-burnings. By the 1980s, the fight for passage of the Equal Rights Amendment had become front-page news, and the "women's pages" became the "lifestyles section" of many newspapers.

The ever-provocative Helen-Gurley Brown was editor-in-chief of Cosmopolitan magazine for 32 years. She was known to say, "Good girls go to heaven, bad girls go everywhere."

The rise of internet culture from the 1990s onward gave birth to web logs. By 2007, estimates indicated that approximately 112 million "bloggers" worldwide were writing on a plethora of topics. Female bloggers maintained personal or group web pages with short diary entries (posts) on topics ranging from personal hobbies to politics to parenting. Most personal blogs had less than 100 regular readers and were largely used to keep in touch with friends and family by posting pictures, videos, and family updates. Exceptional personal blogs were able to support their authors through advertising revenue. One of the first of these was Dooce, a blog written by Heather B. Armstrong, about her mothering and marital adventures. She was the first documented woman to be fired from her job for blogging about work.

Corporations also created blogs for business purposes. Perhaps the most widely known blogs were group-written and political in nature: notable women in this field created the *Huffington Post,* edited by Ariana Huffington; the politically sarcastic *Wonkette,* founded by Ana Marie Cox, and *MichelleMalkin.com,* founded by the award-winning blogger Michelle Malkin. In 2007, a group of well-known women created Women on the Web (www.wowowow.com), which offers daily blogs written by the likes of Candice Bergen, Marlo Thomas, Whoopi Goldberg, Lesley Stahl, Liz Smith, and Cynthia McFadden.

WOMEN IN FILM

In the 1960s, actress Audrey Hepburn, the Belgium-born daughter of an English banker and a Dutch baroness, won America's hearts in movies such as *Breakfast at Tiffany's* (1961) and *My Fair Lady* (1964). Her classic style on and off the silver screen made her an icon for a generation. An icon of a different sort was actress Jane Fonda, who began her career with the western *Cat Ballou* (1963), then became a sex symbol with the 1968 sci-fi parody *Barbarella.* Her career took a serious turn in 1971 when she played a prostitute in *Klute,* for which she won a Best Actress Oscar. She also became an outspoken antiwar activist, which cost her both box-office popularity and opportunities to act. Perhaps her most famous role was as the daughter in *On Golden Pond* (1981), in which she acted with her father Henry Fonda and Katharine Hepburn, another nontraditional actress. Hepburn, whose mother was a feminist and birth control activist, won two Best Actress Oscars in the 1960s for *Guess Who's Coming to Dinner?* (1967) and *The Lion in Winter* (1968). A second two-time Oscar winner in the 1960s was Elizabeth Taylor, a violet-eyed star known for her frequent marriages, tempestuous affairs, and a love of large diamonds. Taylor won Oscars for roles in *Butterfield 8* (1960) and *Who's Afraid of Virginia Woolf?* (1966).

In the 1970s, crossover stars moved back and forth between film and television, creating a new dimension of Hollywood celebrity. For example, Sally Field began her career in television with the sitcoms *Gidget* and *The Flying Nun.* Anxious to avoid being typecast, Field won rave reviews for her title role in *Sybil* (1976), the tale of a tormented woman with multiple personalities. At the urging of screen idol Bert Reynolds, with whom she became romantically involved, Field returned to her comedy roots in the *Smokey and the Bandit* series. However, she returned to drama in 1979, taking on the role of Norma Rae, a woman who fights to unionize her town's textile mill. Field won the Oscar for Best Actress for her work in *Norma Rae,* and followed that up with a second Academy Award for Best Actress for *Places in the Heart* (1984). While such substantial roles for female actresses were often hard to come by in a male-dominated industry, social-topic dramas occasionally offered juicy roles to women who were unafraid to take on challenging investigations of controversial subjects. Meryl Streep rose to stardom in the late 1970s and moved

Older, Bolder Women in Film

The sexism and ageism of Hollywood became a key concern for women in entertainment after the 1970s. Film studies scholars drew attention to the fact that older men were often featured with leading ladies a few decades younger, while women over 40 were relegated to supporting roles, rarely coupled with younger men. Flaunting tradition, at the age of 42, Sally Field played opposite Tom Hanks (32) in 1988's *Punchline*. Six years later, she played Hanks's mother in *Forrest Gump*. A few films challenged the double standard in cinema, including *The Graduate* (1967) and *How Stella Got Her Groove Back* (1998). In *The Graduate,* Anne Bancroft, who was approaching 40, had an affair with Ban Braddock (Dustin Hoffman), an immature, recent college graduate who was still searching for the meaning in life. The entire plotline of *How Stella Got Her Groove Back* focused on an older women (played by 40-year-old Angela Bassett) finding a new passion for life with a younger man (played by 27-year-old Taye Diggs). Feminist scholars have generally found that older women are less likely to be positively portrayed, to have clear goals, and be shown as sexually attractive.

A 1993 study of Academy Award nominees in the Best Actor, Best Actress, and Best Supporting Actor/Actress categories found that women over 39 had comprised only 27 percent of award nominees since 1927, as compared to 67 percent in the male acting categories. A study that analyzed the top films of 1996 found that women over 50 made up less than 4 percent of leading roles onscreen, although they represented over 28 percent of the U.S. population. Seven years later, researchers again turned to consideration of older women by examining the top 100 grossing films of 2002, and found that matters had improved slightly. Female characters over 50 had doubled to 16 percent of leading characters, although this figure still fell far short of representing the 36 percent of women of that age in the U.S. population. In 2002, moviegoers over 50 represented 22 percent of box-office sales, indicating a growing market for positive representations of older women in film.

In the 21st century, as the baby boomer generation began to reach retirement age, more attention was paid to the limited number of roles available for women over 40. This phenomenon raised the possibility that baby boomers might be successful in replacing the stereotypes of women as nurturing grandmothers or controlling mothers-in-law with portrayals of women with strengths, flaws, and goals similar to those of their real-life counterparts. The actress who seems most likely to succeed at this is Meryl Streep, who has been nominated for Best Actress 15 times and is generally considered the greatest living American actress. At the age of 59, in the role of Donna Sheridan in *Mamma Mia!* (2008), Streep's love interest was popular leading man and former James Bond portrayer Pierce Brosnan (55). A year later, in *It's Complicated,* Steep was romantically involved with two men played by Alec Baldwin (51) and Steve Martin (64).

on to build a lasting career in film. Between 1979 and 2009, Streep was nominated for Best Actress 15 times. She won for *Kramer v. Kramer* (1980), which addressed the question of child custody after a divorce, and *Sophie's Choice* (1983), which dealt with the heartbreaking dilemma of a mother arriving at the Auschwitz Concentration Camp and being forced to choose whether to save the life of her daughter or her son.

The rise of a new film genre aimed at teens created a young generation of movie stars in the 1980s that became known as the Brat Pack. These actors and actresses starred in films like *The Breakfast Club* (1985), *St. Elmo's Fire* (1985), and *Less than Zero* (1987). Molly Ringwald, Demi Moore, and Ally Sheedy were the three key women in this celebrity circle, and their taste in fashions influenced teenagers around the world. Their teen and early adult films usually showcased them as suburban teenagers on the brink of adulthood, either in romantic comedies or in dramas involving heavy alcohol and drug use.

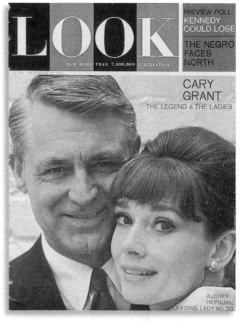

Audrey Hepburn graced the cover of LOOK magazine with Cary Grant in 1963 to promote their romantic thriller Charade.

Many of the attention-getting films of the 1990s featured strong women. An early blockbuster of the decade was *Pretty Woman*, starring Julia Roberts as a prostitute who falls in love and wins the heart of a man who hired her as an escort. This modern-day Cinderella story grossed over $400 million at the box office, and demonstrated Roberts's star power. While she often played romantic heroines, as in *My Best Friend's Wedding* (1997), she also took on dramatic roles that won her critical attention, including the title character in *Erin Brockovich* (2000). Roberts won the Oscar for Best Actress for her portrayal of Brockovich as a feisty, nontraditional environmental activist. Another notable actress of the 1990s was Jodie Foster, who matured from a popular child star to win Oscars for leading roles in *The Accused* (1988), which was based on the true story of a victim of gang rape, and *Silence of the Lambs* (1991), in which she played Clarice Starling, an FBI cadet who is forced to work with the notorious, cannibalistic Hannibal Lector to catch another serial killer who is known for skinning his victims. Foster also worked behind the scenes as

Elizabeth Taylor gently holds a bird between filming on the set of The Sandpiper (1965), about a young, unwed mother who seduces an Episcopalian priest.

a director and was lauded for her work on *Little Man Tate* (1991).

Women's involvement on production aspects in the film industry has yet to equal the numbers of women working in silent film prior to the introduction of sound. Women directors, specifically, comprised only 7 percent of the directors with the top 250 highest-grossing films in 2006. While female producers and directors have been regularly passed over for awards, in 2010 Kathryn Bigelow made history as the first woman to win the Academy Award for Best Director. She won for her 2008 film *The Hurt Locker*, which won five other Oscars, including for Best Picture. Other aspects of film production, notably funding, impacted the hiring of other creative personnel. Women behind the camera increased in number during these decades, as women producers and executive producers began to mentor younger women hoping to build careers in film. While only 16 percent of film's executive producers and 20 percent of film's producers were female, their films employed greater percentages of women in all creative roles. Women were most likely to work on documentary films and were least likely to be employed on films in the science fiction and horror genres.

WOMEN IN TELEVISION

Television, particularly situation-comedy, continued to exert its influence in the post-1960 period. One of the first attempts to bring feminism to television occurred in the mid-1960s, when Marlo Thomas, daughter of popular comedian Danny Thomas, began appearing as *That Girl* (1965–71). When network executives balked at introducing a sitcom about an independent young woman living alone in New York City while pursuing an acting career, Thomas handed them Betty Friedan's *The Feminist Mystique*. Throughout the series, Thomas's character of Ann Marie remained in a romantic relationship with news reporter Don Hollinger (Ted Bessell), but control over her show provided her with the ammunition she needed to steadily refuse audience and network demands to end the show with a wedding. Instead, the last show of the series featured Ann taking Don to a women's liberation meeting.

By the 1980s, feminism was being openly addressed on television sitcoms. In 1998, Diane English cast Candice Bergen, the daughter of ventriloquist Edgar Bergen, as the crusty, recovering alcoholic *Murphy Brown* (1988–98), a reporter for the fictional news show *FYI*. In response to feminist outrage over the Clarence Thomas appointment to the Supreme Court despite charges of sexual harassment, Murphy appeared before a fictional Senate Judiciary Committee. When the character chose to become a single mother on the show, Vice President Dan Quayle accused Murphy Brown of perpetuating the notion that fathers were unnecessary in the lives of children. In response, Bergen's character addressed the changing definition of American families on *FYI*.

In the 1990s, the marriage scene changed in many sitcoms. In *Mad about You* (1992–99), for instance, Paul (Paul Resier) and Jamie (Helen Hunt) Buchman lived in a big city rather than the suburbs, they were both college educated and serious about their careers, and they accepted one another as equal partners in the marriage. The lives of single women had also changed, and sitcoms were reflecting the ambiguousness of many young women about the goals of feminism. In *Ally McBeal* (1997–2002), Calista Flockhart played a Harvard-educated lawyer who was always on the lookout for Mr. Right and was well aware that her biological clock was constantly ticking while she devoted time and energies to her career. The most defining comedic series of the late 1990s and early 2000s for many women was *Sex and the City* (1998–2004), in which four women frankly discussed and pursued sex in ways that would have been unthinkable before the 1970s.

WOMEN IN MUSIC

Unforgettable artists added to the American dominance of popular music in the 1960s. While boy bands dominated pop-music stations for much of the decade, rock, soul, and folk music provided the backdrop for stars that included Janis Joplin, Aretha Franklin, and Joan Baez. Janis Joplin became a hippie poster child and rock legend. She was famous as much for her drug and alcohol abuse and vagabond lifestyle as for her music, which included hits like "Me and Bobby McGee" and "Mercedes Benz." Aretha Franklin, dubbed the Queen of Soul, brought a gospel sensibility to popular music, empowering women with songs like "Respect" and "Think." Joan Baez became famous for her original songwriting, her performances of traditional folk songs, and her Bob Dylan covers.

The genre of country music gave solo artists like Tammy Wynette, Loretta Lynn, and Patsy Cline a chance to shine. Tammy Wynette's 1968 song "Stand By Your Man" became a number one hit, but was reviled by the women's movement. Unlike Wynette, Loretta Lynn, both as songwriter and recording artist, refused to promote traditional stereotypes for women. In 1964 Lynn recorded "Don't Come Home A-Drinkin (With Lovin' on Your Mind)." She also broke ground in 1975 with "The Pill," in which she cautioned husbands that the birth control pill was ending the cycle of continuous pregnancy. Patsy Cline, singer of

Barbra Streisand in 1962, the same year she made her smash debut in the Broadway show I Can Get it For You Wholesale, for which she won the New York Drama Critics Award and a Tony nomination. At the age of 20, she signed with Columbia Records, then released her first album in 1963.

"Walkin' After Midnight" and "Crazy" died in a 1963 plane crash, but her silky vocals and work on Decca Records left a legacy for women in both country and popular music. Cline, more than any other female singer of her day, paved the way for female country artists to receive their due, and she was generous in her mentoring of other female performers.

In the 1970s, women often provided the backup to male leads during the era of disco, but a few exceptions set the tone. Diana Ross left the Supremes to become a star in her own right. Donna Summer's song "I Will Survive" became an anthem for a generation of feminists. In the realm of country and western music, the Grand Ole Opry produced a generation of influential female singers, including Barbara Mandrell and Dolly Parton. Judy Collins sang crossover hits ranging from Broadway tunes like "Send In the Clowns" to traditional folk and church music. Rhythm and blues artist Roberta Flack landed several number-one tunes on the pop charts, including "The First Time Ever I Saw Your Face" and "Killing Me Softly."

The rock tradition was carried on by the women of Heart, sisters Ann and Nancy Wilson, and by Linda Ronstadt, who blended rock with country in songs like "Blue Bayou." In 1972 Australian singer Helen Reddy recorded "I

Am Woman," which American feminist women embraced as the anthem of the women's movement:

I am woman, hear me roar
In numbers too big to ignore
And I know too much to go back an' pretend
'cause I've heard it all before
And I've been down there on the floor
No one's ever gonna keep me down again.

With the birth of MTV in 1981, the combination of music with video created a powerful new means of reaching audiences. It also put new emphasis on female appearance, as artists were seen as well as heard. The 1980s brought Madonna to the world stage, and her breakthrough album *Like a Virgin* and the related movie *Desperately Seeking Susan* altered fashion standards for a generation of teenagers. Other key influential solo pop artists during the 1980s included Cyndi Lauper, Janet Jackson, Pat Benatar, Tina Turner, and Whitney Houston. Girl groups remained popular during the 1980s, including the Go-Go's, the Bangles, and Bananarama. Female front women led bands to international fame, including Joan Jett and the Blackhearts, and Gloria Estefan and the Miami Sound Machine. Punk rock bands had begun their rise in the United Kingdom in the 1970s, and reached U.S. shores with notable women like Chrissie Hynde of the Pretenders, Kim Gordon of Sonic Youth, and Deborah Harry of Blondie.

In the late 1980s, the United States was on the brink of transforming world music with the new genre of rap. Rap combined African and African-American rhythms with spoken-word

Talented in both film and music, country star Dolly Parton performs on stage at the Grand Ole Opry in 2005, when she was honored by Secretary of Defense Donald H. Rumsfeld for her support of American troops.

Women's Soccer: Victory at the Olympics

It has been said that women's athletics came into its own in the United States on August 1, 1996, in Athens, Georgia, when the women's soccer team scored a gold medal victory over China at the Summer Olympics. It was the first time that women's soccer had been included as an Olympic sport. Playing to an audience of 76,481 at the University of Georgia's Sanford Stadium, with some 22 minutes left in the game, Mia Hamm passed the ball to Joy Fawcett, who sent it on to forward Tiffeny Milbrett, who scored the winning goal, bringing the score to 2 to 1. The first goal of the game had been scored by Shannon Macmillan. Milbrett later said, "I was wide open, and I just tapped it in." The roar of the crowed that followed the goal proved that women's sports could be as exciting as men's sports.

After the clock ran out, the team ran around the field waving American flags. The crowd was so exhilarated that most of them stayed to watch the celebration and the medal ceremony that followed. In 1996, no women's sport had ever drawn such a large crowd. Despite the popularity of the sport, the event was not broadcast on television, and the team expressed disappointed that television audiences were denied the opportunity to see their victory live. Other members of the team also included Michelle Akers, Brandi Chastain, Joy Fawcett, Julie Foudy, Carin Bagarra, Mary Harvey, Kristine Lilly, Carla Overbeck, Cindy Parlow, Tiffany Roberts, Briana Scurry, Tisha Venturini, and Staci Wilson.

The breakout star of the women's soccer team turned out to be Mia Hamm, who is considered the best female soccer player in the history of the sport. Hamm, who had been born in Selma, Alabama, was 24 years old in 1996. She had honed her athletic skills playing soccer for the University of North Carolina-Chapel Hill, which won NCAA national championships for the four years she was on the team. Hamm remained on the national team for 17 years and was named FIFA World Player in 2001 and 2002. Hamm, along with teammates Michelle Akers, Brandi Chastain, and Kristine Lilly, was on hand to carry home the gold again in 2004. Hamm's many awards included being chosen as Soccer USA's female athlete of the year each year between 1994 and 1998, winning three ESPY awards, and becoming one of only two female soccer players to be named to the list of 125 greatest living soccer players. The other woman on the list was Hamm's teammate Michelle Akers. The two women were the only Americans named to the list of soccer greats. Hamm retired from the sport after the 2004 Olympics.

rhyming, often at great speed. While this heavily male genre usually bragged of violence, wealth, and sex, a few witty women including MC Lyte, Queen Latifah, and Salt n' Pepa held their own on stage and opened the door for later female rappers. By the 1990s, rap diversified into several subgenres, from battle rap to hip-hop. Hip-hop used samples from older rock and soul songs, remixed them with a strong beat, and often added soulful vocals. Female hip-hop and R&B groups that rose in popularity during this time included TLC, En Vogue, and Destiny's Child. The lead singer of Destiny's Child, Beyonce, went solo in 2003 and became a superstar in the recording industry.

During the same decade, the rise of grunge music led a generation of "alternative" musicians to sing about topics rarely discussed in the popular music of previous generations. The musical style incorporated heavy electric guitar and dissonance, drawing on both punk and heavy metal influences, but otherwise used fairly sparse instrumentation. Grunge's influence also touched solo pop female singers such as Tori Amos, Courtney Love, and Alanis Morrisette, who sang about love, heartbreak, and brutality with a raw and candid angst rarely heard on the radio. Canadian singer Sarah Maclachlan headlined the first Lilith Fair tour in 1997, which quickly became the biggest-selling women's tour in history. Lilith Fair was an all-women's music festival that toured North America for three years, featuring over 100 female solo and duo artists, including the Indigo Girls, Tracy Chapman, and Sheryl Crow.

At the end of the 1990s, a return to bubblegum pop mixed innocence with a come-hither sexuality that many adults found disturbing. Britney Spears and Christina Aguilera began their music careers on Disney's Mickey Mouse Club in their early teens, but went on to major pop solo careers. Spears's breakthrough album, *Baby One More Time* (1999), made her a pop-culture idol and popularized a schoolgirl-gone-wild fashion with midriff-baring shirts and miniskirts. Aguilera's self-titled debut album showcased her wide vocal range, but she did not want to be limited to teenage bubblegum pop. Her next album, *Stripped* (2002), was much more sexual in nature, and it disappointed critics in spite of its popular success. Her third album, *Back to Basics* (2006), featured another image transformation into a 1940s glamour girl who sang in jazz and cabaret styles. A third teen superstar, Miley Cyrus, rose to prominence playing the dual roles of Miley Stewart and Hannah Montana on Disney's *Hannah Montana,* launching an entire industry of Hanna Montana-related paraphernalia and making Cyrus a sometimes questionable idol to young girls throughout the United States.

WOMEN IN SPORTS

Thanks to Title IX legislation, the growing talent pool in the nation's high schools and colleges improved many women's sports. One of these was golf, which continued to be a popular and prestigious women's sport. On professional tours, the women's prize money remained low in comparison with men's, but purses grew with each passing year. By 1972, the Dinah Shore Tournament offered the first six-figure first prize; by the 1990s, total prize monies topped $20 million. Increased prize money aroused public interest, and people watched golfers such as Nancy Lopez and Kathy Whitworth win

Nancy Lopez drives one out of the rough in the Centel Classic in Tallahassee, Florida, in 1991. In 1987, Nancy Lopez was inducted into the World Golf Hall of Fame.

one prize after another in the 1970s. In the 1980s, women became part of the governing board of the U.S. Golf Association with the election of Judy Bell in 1987. She eventually became the USGA's first female president. In the 1990s, the rise of very young female players such as Michelle Wie and Annika Sorenstam drew renewed media and public interest to golf. In 2003, Sorenstam became the first woman since 1945 to qualify for and play in a men's professional tour event. She retired from professional golf in 2008 at the age of 38.

Professional tennis grew exponentially during these decades in the United States, beginning with the founding of the Women's Tennis Association in 1973. One of the WTA's earliest champions was Billie Jean King, who defeated former men's number-one champion Bobby Riggs in a Battle of the Sexes match on September 20, 1973. King beat Riggs 6–4, 6–3, 6–3. The rivalry between male and female champions was carried out in the public eye for decades. A second battle of the sexes between Jimmy Connors and Martina Navratilova was held in 1992. Connors won in two sets. Key American women's champions in these decades included Navratilova, Chris Evert, and Monica Seles. Two African-American sisters, Venus and Serena Williams, dominated women's tennis at the turn of the millennium. Venus led a crusade to get the major tennis tournaments to pay the same prize monies to male and female champions, and this equality was finally achieved in 2007.

Women's basketball first struggled, then scored in attempts to create a league for the best female players. The short-lived Women's Basketball League (WBL) lasted only from 1978 to 1981. The creation of the Women's National Basketball Association (WNBA) in 1996 met with greater success. In part, this may be because the WNBA was created in conjunction with, and supported by, the men's NBA. Also, during the 1980s and 1990s, amateur women's success on U.S. women's basketball teams at the Olympics created a new generation of fans, many of whom were players themselves. Three of the women's 1996 Summer Olympics basketball superstars announced the creation of the WNBA: Rebecca Lobo, Lisa Leslie, and Sheryl Swoopes.

Basketball was not the only sport that Olympic media coverage influenced. Television coverage of women's gymnastics and soccer teams influenced generations of young girls to become competitors and fans of these sports. While women's gymnastics had been an official Olympic event since 1928, television brought Romanian Nadia Comenici's 1976 performances into millions of U.S. homes as she won seven perfect 10 scores. (She later became a dual citizen of the United States after her marriage to U.S. Olympic gymnast Bart Conner). In 1984, Mary Lou Retton won America's hearts and two gold medals with two perfect 10s on floor and vault. Her infectious smile and cheery demeanor brought her opportunities for professional sponsorship far outside her sport, and she became the first woman to appear on a Wheaties cereal box. Twelve years later, in 1996, gymnast Kerri Strug became a heroine to many young girls when she performed her final vault in spite of an injury to guarantee the women's U.S. team the gold medal.

Women's soccer came fairly late to the professional field, with

Vonetta Flowers (left) and Jill Bakken sprint down the track in the sled USA-2 for the women's two-man bobsled event in Park City, Utah, during the 2002 Winter Olympic Games. They won a gold medal in the event.

the creation of the FIFA Women's World Cup in 1991. The U.S. women's team has won this World Cup twice, most memorably in 1999, with key players Mia Hamm, Brandi Chastain, and Michelle Akers. Women's soccer has been part of the Olympics since 1996, and the U.S. women's team has brought home gold medals from three of the four Olympics to date.

Volleyball was yet another sport that received public attention through a combination of expanded opportunity and Olympic coverage. The chance to play on indoor volleyball teams with six players on a side drew thousands of junior high and high school girls into athletic participation. Because six-player volleyball was both a men's and women's sport, where there were advantages with skill regardless of size, co-ed volleyball became a popular social sport for adults well past their college years. Indoor leagues formed in recreation centers and gyms across the country. Outdoor sand, or beach, volleyball featured two-player teams that used considerably different skills in terms of speed and strategy; the first men's beach tournament was held in 1960, and women's tournaments soon followed. Female players like Missy May-Treanor and Kerri Walsh became household names in the United States thanks to their medal wins on the volleyball court in the 2000s.

CONCLUSION

By the 21st century, a large number of pioneering women had broken down numerous barriers that had long prevented women from being seen as equals in the fields of entertainment and sports. Although women continued to constitute minorities in both fields, they made great strides in advancing their own careers and in opening doors for women and girls who followed. Actresses such as Meryl Streep proved that women could still be viewed as attractive after the age of 40. Television stars such as Marlo Thomas and Candice Bergen proved that women could carry their own shows without resorting to stereotypes. Newswomen such as Barbara Walters, Diane Sawyer, and Katie Couric demonstrated that women could bring both professionalism and female insight to the task of interpreting the news. In the world of music, women from Janis Joplin to Brittany Spears made their mark on popular culture. However, the most successful artist of the period and the most critically acclaimed tended to be male. When *Rolling Stone* composed its list of the 100 Best Guitarists of All Time in 2003, only Joni Mitchell (72) and Joan Jett (87) made the cut. Bonnie Rait was notably absent. In the sports world, athletes such as Mia Hamm, Mary Lou Retton, and Serena and Venus Williams redefined women's sports by refusing to accept outdated limitations on women's athletic abilities.

Heather A. Beasley
University of Colorado, Boulder

Further Reading

Bazzini, Doris, et al. "The Aging Woman in Popular Film: Underrepresented, Unattractive, Unfriendly, and Unintelligent." *Sex Roles,* v.36/7–8 (April 1997).

Carson, David A. *Grit, Noise, and Revolution: The Birth of Detroit in Rock 'n' Roll.* Ann Arbor: University of Michigan Press, 2005.

Case, Sue Ellen. *Feminism and Theatre.* New York: Routledge, 1988.

Cheslock, John. *Who's Playing College Sports? Money, Race, and Gender.* East Meadow, NY: Women's Sports Foundation, 2008.

Chinoy, Helen Krich, and Linda Walsh Jenkins, eds. *Women in American Theatre.* 3rd Ed. New York, NY: Theatre Communications Group, 2006.

Cramer, Judith. "Radio: A Woman's Place is On the Air." In *Women in Mass Communication,* ed. by Pamela J. Creedon. Thousand Oaks, CA: Sage, 1993.

Eschholz, Sarah, et al. "Symbolic Reality Bites: Women and Racial/Ethnic Minorities in Modern Film." *Sociological Spectrum,* 22 (2002).

Goren, Lily J., ed. *You've Come a Long Way, Baby.* Lexington, KY: University Press of Kentucky, 2009.

Halper, Donna L. *Invisible Stars: A Social History of Women in American Broadcasting.* Armonk, New York: M.E. Sharpe, 2001.

Hart, Linda. *Making a Spectacle: Feminist Essays on Contemporary Women's Theatre.* Ann Arbor: University of Michigan Press, 1989.

U.S. Golf Association. "History." Available online, URL: http://www.usga.org/aboutus/usga_history/usga_history.html. Accessed February 2009.

Hogshead-Makar, Nancy and Andrew Zimbalist, eds. *Equal Play: Title IX and Social Change.* Philadelphia, PA: Temple University Press, 2007.

Izawa, Eri. "Gender and Gender Roles in Manga and Anime." Available online, URL: http://web.mit.edu/rei/www/manga-gender.html. Accessed January 2010.

Klein, Allison. *What Would Murphy Brown Do? How the Women of Prime Time Changed Our Lives.* Emeryville, CA: Seal Press, 2006.

Lavin, Michael R. "Women in Comic Books." *Serials Review,* v.24/2 (1998).

Lauzen, Martha M., and David M. Dozier. "Maintaining the Double Standard: Portrayals of Age and Gender in Popular Films." *Sex Roles,* v.52/7–8 (2005).

Lotz, Amanda D. *Redesigning Women: Television after the Network Era.* Chicago, IL: University of Illinois Press, 2006.

Marcic, Dorothy. *Respect: Women and Popular Music.* Mason, OH: Texere, 2002.

Markson, E.W. and Taylor, C.A. "Real World Versus Reel World: Older Women and the Academy Awards." *Women and Therapy,* 14 (1993).

Marzolf, Marion. *Up From the Footnote: A History of Women Journalists.* New York: Hastings House, 1977.

Master, Coco. "America Is Drawn to Manga." Available online, URL: http ://www.time.com/time/magazine/article/0,9171,1223355-1,00 .html. Accessed January 2010.

Moraga, Cherrie, and Gloria Anzaldua, eds. *This Bridge Called My Back: Writings by Radical Women of Color*. Watertown, MA: Persephone Press, 1981.

O'Reilly, Jean and Susan K. Cahn, eds. *Women and Sports in the United States*. Boston: Northeastern University Press, 2007.

Press, Andrea L. *Women Watching Television: Gender, Class, and Generation in the American Television Experience*. Philadelphia, PA: University of Pennsylvania Press, 1991.

Robbins, Trina. *From Girls to Grrlz: A History of Women's Comics from Teens to Zines*. San Francisco, CA: Chronicle Books, 1999.

Rowbotham, Sheila. *A Century of Women: The History of Women in Britain and the United States*. New York: Viking, 1997.

Sochen, June. *From Mae to Madonna: Women Entertainers in Twentieth-Century America*. Lexington, KY: University Press of Kentucky, 1999.

Spangler, Lynn C. *Television Women from Lucy to Friends: Fifty Years of Sitcoms and Feminism*. Westport, CT: Praeger, 2003.

Trecker, Jim and Charles Miers, eds. *Women's Soccer: The Game and the World Cup*. New York: Universe Publishing, 1999.

Wolf, Naomi. *The Beauty Myth: How Images of Beauty Are Used Against Women*. New York: Anchor Books, 1992.

CHAPTER 10

Women and Family

DEFINITIONS OF MOTHERHOOD and family have undergone massive transformations since the social revolutions set off by the 1960s. As that decade began, 45 percent of American families were defined as nuclear, made up of a mother, a father, and one or more children. By 2001, U.S. census data had revealed that less than a fourth of American families fit that definition. Today, families are more likely to be headed by one parent, or to be blended together with stepparents or life partners of either the opposite or same sex, and half, step, or adopted siblings. In 2006, 10.4 million American families were headed by a single mother, while only 2.5 million families were headed by single fathers.

Because women's salaries continue to lag behind those of men, families headed by mothers continue to be more likely to be poor than those headed by fathers. The lives of mothers have also undergone watershed changes in response to the rise in the number of women in the workforce and the success of the women's movement in fighting discrimination of working mothers. Although changing social patterns and unprecedented leaps in technology have transformed family life far beyond the traditions of earlier generations, American mothers have continued to bear the lion's share of responsibility for childrearing and homemaking, creating new demands, expectations, and stresses.

While this mother of 11 children in 1961 was single, it was due to widowhood, not divorce, which began to climb by the mid-1960s. Her children were also in the minority with their single-parent status; only 9 percent of children under age 18 lived with one parent in 1960.

DEMOGRAPHICS

The average age of first marriage increased in the last four decades of the 20th century as more young people delayed marriage for economic and educational reasons. By 2005, the median age of 25 at the time of a first marriage for women was the highest since it was first measured in 1890. For men, the median age was just over 27 years of age. By the age of 30, 71 percent of Americans had married; and by the age of 65, that number climbed to 95 percent. In 2007, 4.2 million U.S. women gave birth. One-third of those women gave birth outside marriage. This shift in societal norms is notable when compared with 1960, when less than 10 percent of births occurred among unmarried women. While those critical of such changes focus on the moral issues surrounding the gradual rise of childbearing outside marriage, significant research efforts have focused on public policy issues related to this shift. Since poverty rates, infant mortality, and marital status are linked, an ongoing political discussion centers on ways to improve the likelihood that children will be born to married mothers. The average age of mothers at the birth of their first child has increased significantly. In 1960, the average age was 21.6 years old. By 2006, it had risen to 25.2. This change was due to increased educational and work opportunities that caused many women to delay marriage and motherhood.

The average number of children per married couple declined over this time period. Advances in birth control methods allowed couples to limit family size, and economic concerns about the cost of raising a child to adulthood made small families more sustainable for many couples. Couples also faced societal pressure to limit family size because of global concerns about overburdening the planet. In 1960, U.S. married couples had an average of 2.3 children; by 2008, that number had fallen to 1.9 children per family. Thus, the population of the United States, like those in many other industrialized nations, fell below the population replacement rate.

The most notable demographic change was the number of marriages that ended in divorce. Beginning in the second half of the 1960s, the first marriage rate began to decline, and the divorce rate began to increase. While the divorce rate increased sharply from 1970 to 1975 as no-fault divorce laws spread across the United States, it gradually leveled off. By 2005, the divorce rate had fallen to 3.6 per 1,000 people, the lowest rate since 1970. At the same time, the number of single-parent families increased significantly. In 1960, roughly 9 percent of all children under 18 lived with only one parent. By 2008, that number had almost tripled.

MARRIAGE AND DIVORCE

After 1960, trends in wedding and anniversary celebrations moved toward diversity. While low legal barriers in cities like Las Vegas, Nevada, made it possible for couples to marry quickly and inexpensively, an opposite trend toward consumerism made the average cost of a wedding rise significantly during this time period. While high-society weddings have always been occasions to display wealth in addition to celebrating a couple's union, the middle class also increasingly embraced the idea of a wedding ceremony as the event of a lifetime. In 1960, the average wedding ceremony cost $3,300. With a median annual income of $4,970, wedding events were taking center stage in American family's lives. As weddings became increasingly secular and receptions more elaborate, an entire wedding industry emerged over the decades, with

The trend toward more expensive and lavish weddings began to increase by 1960, when the average mean cost of a wedding was $3,300—about two-thirds of that year's median annual income. According to the Consumer Price Index, that equates to $24,000, the average mean cost of a wedding in 2008, but at just one-half of the 2008 U.S. median income of $50,303.

The Commune Movement

In the 1960s, the "hippie" movement took root in California and spread to youth subcultures around the world, promoting peace activism, folk music, recreational drug use, and freedom from sexual moral codes. Experiments with religion-based communal living had begun in the United States and elsewhere in the 1800s, but the communes of the 1960s were notable for being organized around the hippie values of peace, community, and free love.

Adult commune members often shared a framework of politics and philosophy. Men and women who sought to escape what they considered the oppressive structures of traditional marriage and societal living hoped that, by living communally, they could create a more equitable distribution of work. Some also participated in nonmonogamous sexual arrangements.

Without the nuclear family as a basic structure, however, the number of people involved in making even the simplest decisions sometimes made communal life quite difficult. Almost as soon as they joined, commune members found themselves negotiating to distribute the work of cooking, cleaning, and earning enough to cover living expenses. Many communes organized and dissolved within a few years, as arguments broke communities apart. In secular communes, those who joined as couples often found intense pressure put on their primary relationships. Jealousies and rivalries often caused relational breakups and strife among the entire communal group. Within some communes, members reverted to traditional gender roles with men making most of the decisions and women providing most of the unpaid labor. This failure to live up to the ideals of social equality also divided communes and led to the eventual formation of women-only communes such as Alapine in Alabama and the Pagoda in Florida.

The issue of mothers and children created challenges for a structure based on social equality, as questions about childcare could create tension throughout a commune as members were forced to distribute responsibilities for children. In most communes, the biological parents retained primary responsibility and decision-making power regarding their children. Women-only communes faced special difficulties surrounding male children, and members sometimes left upon the birth of a son as a result of the difficulties of combining radical feminist ideals with the realities of living with boys and men.

By the late 1970s, communal experiments came to an end for a variety of reasons, including the tragedy of the communal People's Temple mass suicide at Jonestown, Guyana, in November 1978. The public horror of these cult deaths led to renewed calls to strengthen traditional family models. Another primary factor was the increasing challenges members faced as they moved from the mobile lifestyle of young adulthood into the roles of wage earners and parents. Working adults who wanted to control their own earnings without paying the expenses of others often left communal lifestyles behind.

hired professionals taking on responsibility for planning weddings in exotic locales or depicting certain themes. Wedding expenses not only included bridal gowns, tuxedoes, flowers, and photographers, but also the salaries of wedding planners, stipends for videographers, and costs of elaborate receptions that sometimes lasted for days and/or included paying expenses for family and friends to be flown to other parts of the world. Later on, anniversaries also provided occasions for families, friends, and communities to celebrate. While couples continue to celebrate silver and golden wedding anniversaries, they have also added a new tradition in which couples periodically renew wedding vows. In some cases, these celebrations have been as elaborate as first-time weddings.

While the vast majority of Americans consider it immoral for a married person to have sex with someone besides their marriage partner, infidelity continues to occur and is a major factor in the rising divorce rate. Statistics on incidences of infidelity are based on self-reported admissions, so it is highly probable that conclusions drawn from existing data are flawed. There is considerable evidence, however, that suggests that men are more likely than women to have sex outside of marriage. Studies also show that infidelity is more likely in marriages where at least one partner is unhappy and in those where one partner became sexually active at an early age. In 2007 roughly a third of divorces in the United States cited adultery as the reason for the breakup of the marriage.

Divorce has become a more common event than at any previous time in U.S. history. The frequently reported and misleading statistic that 50 percent of all marriages end in divorce has not been true since 1985. In 2005 the divorce rate was closer to 40 percent, and rates varied considerably according to the age of the couple being married and the number of previous marriages. In 2001 the U.S. Census Bureau estimated that the average length

An anti-war hippie protester refreshes herself between demonstrations at the 1972 GOP National Convention in Miami. Hippies of the 1960s and 1970s shunned traditional norms and chose to live in alternative social arrangements.

Blondie Bumstead of Chic Young's comic strip Blondie *was still the quintessentially trim and domesticated housewife in this 1964 panel. The prior year,* The Feminine Mystique *by Betty Friedan debunked the concept that women felt primarily fulfilled as mothers and housewives.*

of a marriage that ended in divorce was eight years, and 15 percent of all recorded marriages were remarriages. Rising divorce rates have led to a greater reluctance to remarry. As a result, the number of couples living together without marrying has steadily increased since 1960. According to the 1960 census, 439,000 couples were reported as cohabitating. By 2008, the number of opposite-sex cohabitating couples had climbed to 6.8 million. The increase in divorce, remarriage, and cohabitating heterosexual and homosexual couples has entailed numerous social changes in relation to family structure. Recognizing changes in social patterns, schools have had to develop more complex systems of gathering information on students' families. A variety of studies have documented the negative impacts of divorce on children, suggesting that they are more likely to experiment with drugs and with premarital sex and to struggle academically and be disruptive in school. A key consideration in these factors is the age of the children at the time of divorce; older adolescents tend to experience more negative outcomes than very young children. In recent years, the impact of divorce on children has been reexamined, and one 2002 study revealed that 75 percent of children from divorced families exhibited none of these previously-identified negative behaviors.

CHANGING PATTERNS OF MOTHERHOOD

Several trends in pregnancy and birthing practices gave mothers-to-be a new range of childbirth options. Natural childbirth advocates recommended breathing, visualization, and movement practices to help women through the pain of labor without drugs or surgery. Within the medical realm, Caesarian (C) sections became more common, and by the turn of the century were used in almost a third of live births. A variety of factors contributed to the sharp rise in C-sections. Hospitals that wanted to avoid possible lawsuits encouraged doctors to recommend surgery in cases of fetal or maternal distress. Efficiency and financial concerns also led doctors to suggest C-sections rather than drawing out labor. A reduction in the number of birth assis-

Myth of the Supermom

In the wake of Betty Friedan's *The Feminine Mystique,* many American women began to believe they could "have it all." They were told that they could find fulfillment as mothers and as career women at the same time and in equal measure. As Kathy Buckworth wrote in *The Secret Life of Supermom: The Tricks and Truths about Having It All,* no one warned supermoms that they would have "to give up all personal time, self-identity, leisure activities, and patience." Even though women of the second wave of feminism and their daughters had become convinced that they had a right to develop an identity other than that of wife and mother, many husbands, and most of society, still expected supermoms to accomplish all that stay-at-home moms had done—and more. As a result, women were coming home frazzled after a full day at work to deal with the needs of their children, cooking, cleaning, doing laundry, chauffeuring, serving on committees, and a host of other activities.

Ultimately, women began to understand that even though they might be able to have it all, they could not give equal amounts of time and energy to family and careers and have anything left for themselves. They began to make choices. Female academics, for instance, began delaying motherhood until after they achieved tenure. Female celebrities put off having children until their careers were established. Many career women bypassed the supermom phenomenon by choosing not to have children at all.

In the fictional world of the sitcom, women dealt with the dual roles of motherhood and career women according to their own lifestyles and social classes. On *The Cosby Show* (1984–92), attorney Clare Huxtable (Phylicia Rashad), was portrayed as having a relatively easy time because her pediatrician husband (Bill Cosby) worked at home. In *Who's the Boss* (1984–92), wealthy advertising executive and single mother Angela Bower (Judith Light) hired live-in housekeeper Tony Micelli (Tony Danza) to clean house and share parenting responsibilities. At the other end of the social spectrum, on *One Day at a Time* (1975–84), divorced mother Ann Romano (Bonnie Franklin) frequently had a difficult time fulfilling her dual role as the custodial parent of two teenage daughters. On *Roseanne* (1988–97), working-class mother Roseanne Connor (Roseanne Barr) never quite succeeded as the supermom, even though her husband Dan (John Goodman) was very much involved in his family. Instead, she hammered home the message that the supermom was always a myth rather than a reality.

tants who focused on the mother's needs during delivery, such as doulas or midwives, also meant that the likelihood of labor induction and C-sections increased. Despite the popular belief that many C-sections are scheduled for convenience, a 2006 survey revealed that only one in 1,600 women who had a C-section in 2005 had done so at her own request without an underlying medical reason.

Changing social patterns have transformed the lives of American mothers in other ways. In the decades following 1960, mothers entered the workforce at unprecedented levels. In 1960, roughly 20 percent of mothers of preschoolers worked outside the home. While most of these women worked out of economic need, a significant number worked in part-time or temporary jobs to make additional money for specific purchases. By 2005, the number of mothers with preschoolers in the workforce had risen to 60 percent. For married couples with children, the median family income was $60,374. For single mothers, the median family income was $29,829. Balancing family and work proved a difficult task for most women. Studies have revealed that working mothers were not spending less time with their children than they did in the past, but they did spend less time alone with their spouses, less time on housework, and less time sleeping than in previous decades. Increased numbers of women in the workforce led to demands for more government responsibility in recognizing the needs of working mothers and for recognition of a father's role in parenting and caring for ailing family members.

A mother and two children enjoy an outing in their boat in 1966. Mothers working outside the home brought in more income to the household, often earmarked for specific family purchases.

In 2006, less than 5 percent of U.S. employees had access to paid parental leave upon the birth of a child. The 1993 Family and Medical Leave Act (FMLA) mandated up to 12 weeks of unpaid parental leave for both men and women after the birth or adoption of a child. However, it applied to only 45 percent of U.S. workplaces, and only to those employees who had been at their jobs for at least a year. As a result, the majority of American mothers returned to work while their children were still infants, creating a greater demand for quality infant and childcare. Only a small portion of these expenses were offset by tax credits. As part of the public and political backlash against what were perceived as "welfare mothers," major welfare reforms were instituted in the 1990s. These "workfare" policies set mandatory hours-of-employment targets for low-income working mothers who accepted government support. While women receiving welfare had to work or face sharply reduced payments, corresponding support for daycare for their children was limited or lacking. Many mothers were forced to choose between putting their children in substandard childcare and earning enough money to meet basic needs such as food and rent. Such approaches led to inconsistent social and economic policies toward mothering.

FERTILITY AND CONTRACEPTION

As the average age of childbearing increased, fertility issues became increasingly common among married couples. Improved birth control options led many women to delay pregnancy in order to focus on their careers, which led to the increased need for fertility treatments as women wished to have children in their 30s and 40s. Several new technologies became available to aid couples in bearing children, including in vitro fertilization (IVF), hormonal methods of ovulation induction, and working with egg donors. Artificial insemination, which had been widely practiced agriculturally to improve animal breeding rates for decades, was used to impregnate infertile women with increasing success after the 1980s. Several of these technologies, particularly IVF, had a tendency to lead to multiple births, which also increased the likelihood of pregnancy complications. Miscarriage, once thought to be the result of divine will or of a woman's weak physiology, was increasingly viewed as a medical issue and a personal tragedy. New medical technologies were employed that vastly decreased the number of miscarriages, stillbirths, and deaths resulting from premature birth.

A variety of reproductive technologies increased the chances of preventing unwanted pregnancies as well, especially after the legal battles of *Griswold v Connecticut* (1965) and *Eisenstadt v. Baird* (1972) made birth control widely available. Such technologies included condoms, diaphragms, intrauterine devices, and spermicides. The most popular and effective method of birth control has proven to be the birth control pill, which contains estrogen that mimics pregnancy when introduced into a woman's body, preventing the release of eggs available for fertilization. With a success rate of 99.5 percent, tubal

The Mommy Wars

During the 1990s, numerous books and articles noted a growing social divide between stay-at-home mothers and those with paid employment outside the home, a division called the "mommy wars" by *Child* magazine in the late 1980s. Social tensions over the life choices of women with college degrees led some authors to claim that stay-at-home mothers had deserted the feminist movement. Journalist Lisa Belkin coined the term *the opt-out revolution* to describe the demographic group of highly educated, affluent white women who increasingly dropped out of the work force with the birth of a child to focus on motherhood. These women, who were the direct beneficiaries of the 1970s second wave of feminism, chose family over career advancement in a way that puzzled and angered many women of their mothers' generation.

The battle was fierce, and both sides had roots in the feminist movement as well as in the mores of the upper middle class. Mothers who returned to the workforce argued that stay-at-home mothers abandoned feminist ideals by becoming dependent on their husband's incomes, damaging their future careers, and impacting their ability to care for themselves in areas like retirement funding. Authors such as Linda Hirshman argued that "Bounding home is not good for women and it's not good for the society ... their talent and education are lost from the public world to the private world of laundry and kissing boo-boos." They viewed the return home as nothing more than the perpetuation of an outdated model of domestic life and argued that daycare would not harm children emotionally or academically over the long term.

Women who left their careers to stay at home with young children argued that one of the goals of the feminist movement had been to give women choices. Therefore, women should have the choice to stay home and raise their young. They accused the feminist movement of abandoning motherhood to focus on economic advancement. Authors on this side of the battle also argued that the economic impacts stay-at-home mothers suffered were a result of society's bias against parents, suggesting compromises in tax laws and leave policies to address this bias. Some emphasized the dangers of daycare and wrote books and articles that heightened parental anxiety about threats to healthy development, the possibility of producing overly aggressive children, and damaging the future academic potential of children who grew up in daycare.

Most stay-at-home mothers believed this media-fueled war had little to do with their daily lives. Working-class and middle-class women often had to work in order to provide enough money for their families' basic needs, and thus had to utilize daycare while their children were too young for public education. Race also played a role in the stay-at-home mothering phenomenon, as African-American married mothers were more likely across all economic classes to work outside the home than were white, Asian, or Hispanic women. By creating guilt and anxiety in a new generation of mothers, regardless of career and family decisions, the mommy wars ended in a vicious stalemate.

ligation, or female sterilization, has become the second most popular method of birth control in the United States. After the 1973 Supreme Court case *Roe v. Wade*, abortion became a hotly debated social and political issue.

CHILDREN AND FAMILIES

Life within American families changed in conjunction with changing patterns of motherhood. Despite this, mothers continued to bear the major responsibility for child rearing. As a result, parenting advice was dispensed across every form of media, assaulting mothers with a bewildering array of options on childcare and child-related consumer products. The once-simple nursery exploded with potential gadgets and gizmos ranging from bottle and wipe warmers to swings and bouncy seats. Mothers faced a selection of texts from Dr. Spock's post–World War II parenting guides to hundreds of parenting manuals written by pediatricians, nurses, sociologists, and other experts who often disagreed with one another. Mothers were compelled to choose between environmentally questionable disposable diapers and cloth diapers that were more inconvenient and energy-consuming.

Whether or not to let an infant cry itself to sleep was a hot-button issue with both mothers and experts. Another issue of burning concern was whether or not to breastfeed. Based on a plethora of evidence that breastfed babies were healthier, many mothers scorned infant formulas, choosing to pump breast

These women in Rand, West Virginia, in 1973 are surrounded by poverty; their town is cluttered with unpaved roads, substandard houses, and junked cars. The tendency for women and children to make up the largest segment of those living below the poverty line is called the feminization of poverty.

milk after they returned to work, and workplaces were urged to accommodate the needs of nursing mothers. When the availability of no-fault divorce spread throughout the United States in the 1970s, it became easier for women in unhappy or abusive marriages to leave their spouses. While divorce became easier, raising children did not. The same expenses of child care, education, and basic needs took a much larger share of the household budget when only one parent provided income. Mandatory child support laws were passed in every state, but enforcement was often difficult, leaving single mothers to face what became known around the world as the feminization of poverty.

Between 1970 and 2000, the number of families led by single parents increased from 5 percent to 9 percent of all U.S. households. In 2008 roughly 25 percent of U.S. children lived with only one parent, and six out of seven of those lived with their mothers. The percentage of single mothers as a total of the population varied by race, with Hispanic women having the highest birthrates outside of marriage since 1990, at a rate slightly higher than African-American women and more than twice the rate of white women. Asian-American women had the lowest reported birthrate outside marriage over the same time span. Another contributing factor to these shifting percentages is the decrease in children among married women. As married mothers bear fewer children, unmarried mothers appear as though they increase in number when their number is actually remaining constant or declining slightly as the nation's birthrate falls.

Many single mothers are divorced women who had children within marriage, but an increasing number of unmarried, single women also become mothers. In 2007, 36 percent of births in the United States occurred among unmarried women. Roughly a third of out-of-wedlock births occurred among women 19 and younger, but the number of teen pregnancies has decreased steadily since peaking in 1990. Another growing trend concerned the number of unmarried professional women who chose to become mothers without partners for a variety of reasons. This issue received a good deal of public attention in 1992 during an ongoing debate over family values when Vice President Dan Quayle lambasted fictional television reporter Murphy Brown (Candice Bergen) for having a baby out of wedlock and "calling it just another lifestyle choice."

EDUCATIONAL CHOICES FOR FAMILIES

Even though more mothers were working than ever before after 1961, they continued to be heavily involved in the education of their children, and the number of educational options available to families skyrocketed during these decades, ranging from charter schools and online/home schooling to traditional public and private schools. In addition to participating in parent/teacher organizations and transporting children to and from extracurricular activities, parents managed to stay in touch with their children's schools through emails and the internet.

The Feminization of Poverty

Globally, women and children make up the largest segment of the population living below the poverty line. This phenomenon is known as the *feminization of poverty*, a term coined in 1976 by sociologist Diana Pearce. In the United States, many women and children only become poor after a divorce or the loss of a job. For others, it is a cycle that follows them throughout their lives as a result of insufficient education or inadequate job skills. Working women may also be poor because they consistently earn less than men, and those with small children must often pay childcare expenses out of minimum-wage salaries. Because women are paid less than men and because they live longer, pension funds and social security payments tend to be lower. Thus, elderly women are often plunged into poverty. Internationally, the United Nations has designated female poverty as a violation of women's human rights.

The 1980s was a time of particular vulnerability for women and children in the United States when the Reagan administration made significant cuts to Aid to Families with Dependent Children, the food stamp program, and WIC, a federally funded program that provides nutritional assistance to poor women and children. By 1989, 25 percent of children under the age of six were living in poverty. In the 1990s, Congress and the Clinton administration overhauled the existing welfare apparatus, implementing the Personal Responsibility and Work Reconciliation Act, which transformed AFDC into a temporary emergency-assistance and work program. By 1998, three-fourths of the nation's poor were women and their dependent children, and one in five American children was living in poverty.

In 2008, as the economic situation worsened, the U.S. Census Bureau reported that 13.1 percent of all Americans were living in poverty, up from 12.5 percent the previous year. Poverty rates were expected to continue to rise, along with increases in unemployment and a decrease in the number of employees working full-time jobs. Because women are more likely than men to fit into this latter category, they continue to be more at risk for falling below the poverty line. Between 2007 and 2008, the rate of child poverty rose from 18 to 19 percent for all children and from 10.1 to 10.6 for Hispanic children. The rate of poverty among African-American children remained static at 34.7 percent. Among families headed by females, the poverty rate was 28.7 as compared to 5.5 percent for two-parent families. Overall, more than 14 million American children were living in poverty in 2008.

Three young girls in Brooklyn in 1973. By the end of the 1980s, one quarter of children under six lived in poverty.

Barbara Sadler reads to Nicole, one of her two adopted daughters. In recent decades, the number of American children available for adoption has declined due to changing family patterns and the availability of birth control, but that decrease applies mainly to white infants.

In 1965, roughly one in four American families with children under 18 had two working parents. By 2000, that number had increased to almost one in two families. A new trend developed in which fathers also exercised the option to be stay-at-home parents. In 2006, 159,000 fathers were fulfilling such duties. However, stay-at-home mothers still outnumbered them by far (5.8 million). As women gained economic power outside the home, working fathers were expected to take on greater roles in housework and childcare. According to research involving family-time use data, some household tasks have become more equal across genders, while others tend to remain segregated by traditional gender roles. In dual-earner families, both men and women spend more time performing childcare tasks than in earlier generations. Since 1965, the number of hours fathers spend performing childcare as their primary activity in an average week has doubled. For mothers, it has increased by a third. Some of the change is due to the fact that new social patterns encourage both parents to spend more time with their children.

In the 1960s, children under 18 spent most of their time between school and home, while older teenagers often took on paid employment as well. Over the decades, increased emphasis on schooling beyond high school, and on getting into the "right" college, has significantly increased the time children have spent on education. The school year has grown longer in many parts of the country. In 1960, the average school day was six hours long, and children spent about

180 days per year in school. In 2008, the typical school year was still around 180 days in length, but children spent close to seven hours per day in school, with additional hours spent on homework depending on the child's age.

A 2002 study showed that, as contemporary children grow older, they spend more time in organized activities, rather than in free play as in past decades. Organized sports leagues and city recreation classes begin for children as young as three or four years of age, and arts and music enrichment activities begin around the same age. By elementary school, over half of American children are participating in at least one organized activity outside of school. The typical child spends about three hours a week playing a sport of some sort, and another hour each week on arts or attending sporting or cultural events.

CONCLUSION
The period between 1961 and the present resulted in a plethora of social, political, and legal transformations concerning women and their families. In 1971, for instance, the Supreme Court ruled in *Phillips v. Martin Marietta Corp.* that corporations could not refuse to hire women with preschool children unless they also refused to hire men with preschool children. The Pregnancy Discrimination Act of 1978 made it illegal to discriminate against women in hiring or while on the job due to potential or actual pregnancy. As the health benefits of breastfeeding became widely known, 40 states passed laws protecting mothers' rights to breastfeed in public; several states also required employers to designate locations with sanitary conditions for nursing mothers. Lawyers schooled in family law used their training to deal with the needs of families experiencing divorce, child custody, and adoption. In the 1980s, gay and lesbian activists in the United States began to achieve legal recognition for their relationships and gained protections for their families through health insurance coverage and property inheritance rights. Family patterns have also shifted concerning adoptions as the number of children available for adoption, particularly white infants, has declined in response to the widespread availability of effective birth control and the growing acceptance of single motherhood. As a result of decreases in American children available for adoption, many couples have opted for international adoptions. In 2008, 17,439 such children were adopted, most from Guatemala, China, and Russia. The increase in single parenting, couples bearing children without marrying, and rising divorce and remarriage rates have all served to redefine the American family. In response to those changes, mothers have taken on a plethora of new roles while continuing to be responsible for caring for their families on a day-to-day basis.

Heather A. Beasley
University of Colorado, Boulder

Further Reading

Askeland, Lori, ed. *Children and Youth in Adoption, Orphanages, and Foster Care.* Westport, CT: Greenwood Press, 2006.

Blakely, Kristin. "Busy Brides and the Business of Family Life: The Wedding Planning Industry and the Commodity Frontier." *Journal of Family Issues,* 29/5 (2007).

Booth, Cathryn L. et al. "Child-care Usage and Mother-Infant 'Quality Time.'" *Journal of Marriage and the Family,* 64/1 (2002).

Buckworth, Kathy. *The Secret Life of the Supermom: The Tricks and Truths about Having It All.* Naperville, IL: Sourcebooks, 2005.

Carp, E. Wayne. *Adoption in America: Historical Perspectives.* Ann Arbor, MI: University of Michigan Press, 2002.

Coleman, Marilyn, et al. *Family Life in 20th-Century America.* Westport, CT: Greenwood Publishing, 2007.

Coleman, Marilyn, and Lawrence H. Ganong, eds. *Handbook of Contemporary Families: Considering the Past, Contemplating the Future.* Thousand Oaks, CA: Sage Publications, 2004.

Cubbins, Lisa A. and Daniel H. Klepinger. "Childhood Family, Ethnicity, and Drug Use over the Life Course." *Journal of Family and Marriage,* v.69/3 (2007).

Edin, Kathryn, and Maria Kefalas. *Promises I Can Keep: Why Poor Women Put Motherhood Before Marriage.* University of California Press, 2005.

Eisenstadt v. Baird, 405 U.S. 438 (1972).

Fildes, Valerie. *Wet Nursing: a History from Antiquity to the Present.* New York: Basil Blackwell, 1988.

Golden, Janet Lynne. *A Social History of Wet Nursing in the United States: From Breast to Bottle.* New York: Cambridge University Press, 1996.

Gordon, Linda. *The Moral Property of Women: a History of Birth Control Politics in America.* Chicago: University of Illinois Press, 2002.

Griswold v. Connecticut, 381 U.S. 479 (1965).

Hirshman, Linda. *Get to Work: A Manifesto for Women of the World.* New York: Penguin, 2006.

King, Valarie, and Mindy E. Scott. "A Comparison of Cohabiting Relationships among Older and Younger Adults." *Journal of Marriage and Family,* v.67/2 (2005).

Kukla, Rebecca. *Mass Hysteria: Medicine, Culture, and Women's Bodies.* Lanham, MD: Rowman and Littlefield, 2005.

Leavitt, Judith Walzer. "'Science' Enters the Birthing Room: Obstetrics in America Since the Eighteenth Century." *Journal of American History,* v.70/2 (1983).

Macunovich, Diane J. et al. "Echoes of the Baby Boom and Bust: Prospective Changes in Living Alone Among Elderly Widows in the United States." *Demography,* v.32/1 (1995).

Marsh, Margaret S, and Wanda Ronner. *The Empty Cradle: Infertility in America from Colonial Times to the Present*. Baltimore, MD: Johns Hopkins University Press, 1996.

Miller, Timothy. *The 60s Communes: Hippies and Beyond*. Syracuse, NY: Syracuse University Press, 1999.

Mitchell, Barbara A., and Ellen M. Gee. "'Boomerang Kids' and Midlife Parental Marital Satisfaction." *Family Relations*, v.45/4 (1996).

National Association of Child Care Resource and Referral Agencies. "Child Care in America: 2008 State Fact Sheets." Available online, URL: http://www.naccrra.org/policy/docs/ ChildCareinAmerica.pdf. Accessed February 2009.

Olen, Helaine. "A Truce in the Mommy Wars." *Salon* (March 15, 2007). Available online, URL: http://www.salon.com/life/feature/2006/03/15/mommy_wars. Accessed March 2010.

Onderko, Patti. "Work and Family: Married vs. Single Moms." *Parenting* (September 2007).

Sidel, Ruth. *Keeping Women and Children Last: America's War on the Poor*. New York: Penguin, 1998.

Smith, William L. *Families and Communes: An Examination of Nontraditional Lifestyles*. Thousand Oaks, CA: Sage Publications, 1999.

Smolensky, Eugene, and Jennifer A. Gootman, Eds. *Working Families and Growing Kids: Caring for Children and Adolescents*. Washington, D.C: The National Academies Press, 2003. Available online, URL: http://books.nap.edu/catalog.php?record_id=10669#toc. Accessed January 2010.

Strow, Claudia W. and Brian K. "A History of Divorce and Remarriage in the United States." *Humanomics*, v.22/4 (2006).

Treas, Judith, and Deirdre Giesen. "Sexual Infidelity among Married and Cohabiting Americans." *Journal of Marriage and the Family*, v.62/1 (2000).

U.S. Census Bureau. Available online, URL: http://www.census.gov. Accessed January 2010.

U.S. Department of Labor Bureau of Labor Statistics. Women in the Labor Force: A Databook. (September 2006). Available online, URL: http://www.bls.gov/cps/wlf-databook2006.htm. Accessed February 2009.

Wallerstein, Judith S. and Sandra Blakeslee. *The Good Marriage: How and Why Love Lasts*. Boston, MA: Houghton Mifflin, 1995.

Wallerstein, Judith S. and Sandy Blakeslee. *The Unexpected Legacy of Divorce: A 25-Year Landmark Study*. New York: Hyperion, 2000.

Wolf, Jaqueline H. *Don't Kill Your Baby: Public Health and the Decline of Breastfeeding in the Nineteenth and Twentieth Centuries*. Columbus, OH: Ohio State University Press, 2001.

INDEX

Index note: page references in *italics* indicate figures or graphs; page references in **bold** indicate main dicussion.

A
AARP (American Association of Retired Persons) 81
AAUW (American Association of University Women) 63, 73
Abernathy, Ralph 7
abortion 80, 92. *See also Roe v. Wade*
   activists *51*
   clinic violence 52
   funding 82
   health x, xi, 34, **49–53**
   Jane underground abortion network 49–50
   Partial Birth Abortion Ban 52
   politics 77
Abzug, Bella 84, *84*, 86
Academies Committee on Women in Science and Engineering 99
Academy Awards 110, 155, 156, 157
Accused, The 157
activism vii, x. *See also* feminist activism
   animal rights 1
   anti-nuclear *78*

Index

civil rights 4, 148
   in colleges 7
   lesbian 183
   new forms 6–7
   pro-life 1, 52, 77, *80*, 91
Adams, Abigail viii
adoption 177, *182*, 183
AFDC (Aid to Families with Dependent Children) 181
affirmative action 66, 79–80
African Americans x, 4, 33, 74, 89, 138, 148
   arts/literature 128
   contraceptives campaign *52*
   elected in federal offices x–xi
   feminists 23
   health care and 44, 53
   march on Washington, D.C. (1963) 4, 6, *65*
   needs of 36
   Poor People's Campaign (1968) *7*
   sterilization 44
   voting *92*
   whites compared to 71
Against Our Will (Brownmiller) 24
ageism 152, 156
"age of majority" 31
Agnew, Spiro 9, 10
Aguilera, Christina 163
Aid to Families with Dependent Children (AFDC) 181
AIM (American Indian Movement) 6
airline stewardesses *60*
Akers, Michelle 162, 166
Alabama 22, *61*, 172
Alapine 172
Alaska 16, 87, *89*, *100*
Albert Lasker Award for Basic Medical Research 108
Albright, Madeleine 5, 33, 91
Alexander v. Yale University 70
Allen, Paula Gunn 129
Alliance for Progress 2
Ally McBeal 159
Alsop, Marin 123, 130
alternative energy 10, 16
Alumni Village day Care Center *143*
Alvarado, Linda **142**, 146

Alvarado Construction, Inc. 142
Alvarez, Ada 5
Amanpour, Christine 152
American Association of Retired Persons (AARP) 81
American Association of University Women (AAUW) 63, 73
American Book Award 128–129
American Chemical Society 98, 102, 104, 106
American Law Institute 51
American Physical Society 98, 106
American Women, Report of the President's Commission on the Status of Women 79
America through Women's Eyes (Beard) ix
Amos, Tori 163
Angelou, Maya 128
animal rights 1
anorexia 32
Anthony, Susan B. vii
anti-birth control laws 41–42
anti-nuclear activism *78*
anti-pornography laws 24
Archer Daniels Midland 145
Arkansas 12–14, 109
Armstrong, Anne 5
Armstrong, Heather B. 154
arts/literature **115–130**
    abstraction 119
    African Americans 128
    collaborations/collectives 120–121
    dance 124–125
    liberation and 125–127
    minimalism 119
    minorities 126
    music 122–124
    opera 124–125
    photorealism 120
    reclaiming, reshaping, redefining 127–129
    second wave feminism 116–119
    storied art 119–120
Ash, Mary Kay 137
Asian-Americans 23, 33, 128
Askins, Barbara *104*
Avon Walk for the Cure 50
Axel, Richard 99

B

Baby Boomers 14–17, 137, 156
baby bust 139
backlash 62
    feminist xi, 35, 37
    political 177
    tactics 61
Backlash: The War Against American Women (Faludi) 62
Baez, Joan 159
Bagarra, Carin 162
Bakken, Jill *165*
Baldwin, Alec 156
Bambara, Toni Cade 128
Bananarama 161
Bancroft, Anne 156
Bangles 161
Barbarella 155
Barbie Doll Syndrome **32**
Barr, Roseanne 175
Barton, Jacqueline K. 104–105
basketball 165
Bassett, Angela 156
Bates, Daisy x, 4
Bay of Pigs Invasion 3
Beard, Mary ix
beauty ideal 6
beauty pageants 6
Bell, Judy 164
Bell Jar, The (Plath) 116, 127
Beloved (Morrison, T.) 118, 129
Benatar, Pat 161
Benfield, Stephanie 91
Bergen, Candice 155, 159, 166, 180
Bergen, Edgar 159
Berger, Caruthers 79
Berlin Wall 3, 12
Bernstein, Carl 10, 154
Bernstein, Leonard 123
Bessell, Ted 158
Beyonce 163
BFOQ (bona fide occupational qualification) 135
Bharati, Mukherjee 129
Biden, Joseph 86

birth control viii, x, 17, 41–44, 177. *See also* childbirth; contraceptives; pro-choice; pro-life
birth control pill 42–44, 139
birth defects x
Bishop, Elizabeth 127
Black, James W. 102
Blackburn, Elizabeth H. 98
black feminists 37
Blackhearts 161
Black Panther Party 83, *83*
black power movement 23
Black Unicorn, The (Lorde) 23
blogs 154–155
Blondie 161
Blondie comic strip *174*
"Blue Bayou" 160
Bluest Eye, The (Morrison, T.) 118, 128
Boggs, Lindy 88
Boggs, Thomas Hale 88
Bolton, Roxcy *22*
bona fide occupational qualification (BFOQ) 135
Bono, Sonny 88
Bono Mack, Mary 88
Boston Women's Health Collective 44–47
Bourgeois, Louise 121
bourgeois feminists 29
Bradstreet, Anne viii
brainpower 62
Braly, Angela 145
Brat Pack 157
Bread and Roses 83
Breakfast at Tiffany's 155
Breakfast Club, The 157
breast cancer **50**
    risk 49
    studies 53–54
Breast Cancer: A Personal History and Investigative Report (Kushner) 50
breastfeeding 46, 47, 53, 179, 183
breeding viii
Brico, Antonia 123
British Invasion 60
Brokeback Mountain (Proulx) 130

Brown, Campbell 152
Brown, Helen-Gurley *154*
Brown, Jerry 15
Brown, Trisha 124
Browner, Carol 5
Brownmiller, Susan 24
bubblegum pop 163
Buck, Linda B. 98, **99**
Buckworth, Kathy 175
Buffalo Symphony Orchestra 123
Burns, Ursula 145
Burroughs Wellcome Research Laboratories 102
Bush, George H. W. 1, 5, 12, 69, 87, 107
Bush, George W. 12, 15, 34, 54, 81
   "faith-based presidency" 16
   women appointments 5
Bushnell, Candace 127
business **133–149**. *See also* glass ceiling
   continuing challenges 145–147
   cosmetics industry *136*, 137
   "female occupations" 140
   flex time 147–148
   food industry 137
   mommy-track 147
   1960s 134–139
   1970s 139–141
   1980s 141–143
   1990s 143–144
   21st century 144–145
   women-owned 143–144, 146
Butterfield 8 155

C

cable television 1
Caldwell, Sarah 123
California 47, 51, 70, 73, 90, 91, 104, 120
California Women of Art 120
Camelot 2
Camp David Accords 10–11
Cancer Journals, The (Lorde) 50
career development 2
   advancements 136, 139, 148, 178
   balancing with family 35

divergent paths 64
expanding 79
film 158
focus 177
fostering 142
lacking 143
networking 27
political 88
reshaping 70
science/medicine 99–103
single women 61
supermoms 175
Carneiro, Joana 123
Carson, Rachel x, 97
Carter, Jimmy ix, 13, 118, 148
    Camp David Accords 10
    human rights and 10–11
    women appointments *4*, 5
Carter, Rosalynn 10
Cassatt, Mary 117
Cat Ballou 155
Cell Heredity (Sager/Ryan) 110
cell phones 1
Center for Creative Leadership and Catalyst 142
Chanel 120
Chao, Elaine 5
Chapman, Tracy 163
Chastain, Brandi 162, 166
Chavez, Cesar 6
chemistry 103–106
Chen, Joyce 137
Chen, Mei-Ann 123
Cherry, Gwen 22
Chicago, Judy 119, 121
Chicano Movement 6
Chicanos 1, 6, 23. *See also* Hispanics; Latinas
childbirth 47, 170
    Caesarian 174, 176
    miscarriages 177
    out-of-wedlock 180
    pregnancy and 174
    premature 177

child care x, 21, 35, 73, 80, 134, *143*
   debate 143
   low-quality 143
   unpaid 149
Child Care and Development Block Grant 143
Child Health Act 139
Child magazine 178
children 13, 15, 32, 54, 139, 143, 170. *See also* childbirth; child care; motherhood; mothers
   adoption 177, *182*, 183
   AFDC 181
   divorce and 174
   family and 179–180
   female child brides 54
   No Child Left Behind 69
   rearing 179–180
   working mothers and 34–35
Children's Health Insurance Program 15
Child Tax Credit 143
China 10
Chisholm, Shirley x, 85
Christian feminists 30
Christianity 28, 30
Cisneros, Sandra 128–129
Civil Rights Act (1964) x, 6, 12, 64, 65–66, 70, 79, **135**, 147. *See also* Title IX
   EEOC established 136
   Title VII 135, 136, 141, 148
Civil Rights Act (1991) 12, 143
Civil Rights Movement 23
   activists 4, 148
   grassroots 4
   momentum x
   rejuvenated 1
Claiborne, Liz 140–141
class viii–x, 23
   exploitation 25
   gender and 26, 71–72
   protected 65
   second-class status 136
   segregation 74
   working 175, 178
Cline, Patsy 159–160

Clinton, Bill 5, 8, 12, *14*, 52, 54, 109, 148
    administration 77
    election 14
    impeachment 14–15
Clinton, Hillary x–xi, 5, **13**, *14*, *88*, 91
    children's/women's issues 15
    as presidential contender 16, 33, 87
    as Secretary of State 16–17, 33, 87
clubhouse 116
Cody, Pat 49
Cohen, Stanley 105
cold war 10
    Cuban Missile Crisis and 3
    escalation 12
Coleman, Kit 152
Coleman, Susan 146
colleges 182. *See also specific colleges*
    activism 7
    degrees earned 61–62, 63, 100–101
    sexual harassment in 70, 73
Collins, Judy 123, 160
Colorado Symphony 123
color consciousness 37
Comenici, Nadia 165
Committee of 200 145
Committee to Reelect the President (CREP) 10
Commonwealth Institute 145
commune movement **172**
communism 9, 12
community service x
condoms 41, 177
conductors **123**
Congressional Caucus for Women's Issues xi, 8, 37, 86–87, 148
Congress of Racial Equality (CORE) 83
Connecticut x, 31, 42–43, 139, 177
Conner, Bart 165
Connors, Jimmy 164
consciousness-raising meetings x, 25, 48
contraceptives 41, 177. *See also* birth control; birth control pill
    banning 82
    campaign *52*
    condoms 41, 177
    diaphragms 177

intrauterine devices 177
spermicides 177
Cooper-Dyke, Cynthia 67
CORE (Congress of Racial Equality) 83
Cosby, Bill 175
Cosby Show, The 175
cosmetics industry *136*, 137, *139*
counterculture 7, 82
Couric, Katie 152
courts 47, 83, 90–92, 135, 148. *See also* judges; Supreme Court
Cox, Ana Marie 155
Crazy 160
Creighton, Harriet 108
CREP (Committee to Reelect the President) 10
Crow, Sheryl 163
Cuban Missile Crisis 3
Cuevas, Maria ix
Curie, Marie 98
Cyrus, Miley 163
Cytoplasmic Genes ad Organelles (Sager) 110

D

"dame schools" viii
dance viii, 124–125
Danza, Tony 175
Davis, Caroline 79
Davis, Rebecca Harding 127
Death of Apartheid 119
de Beauvoir, Simone ix, 22
Dee, Sandra 32
DeLauro, Rosa 90
Democratic Party 2, 12, 31, 33, 78, 84, 86
    1968 convention demonstration 9
    Blue Dogs 90
    primaries 89
    pro-choice in 87
Dependent Care Tax Credit 143
DES (diethylstilbestrol) 49
DES Information Group 49
Destiny's Child 163
diaphragms 177
Diaz v. Pan American World Airways, Inc. 135
Dickey, James 127

Diemer, Emma Lou 124
diethylstilbestrol (DES) 49
Diggs, Taye 156
digital recorders 1
Dinner Party, The 121
disco music 160
Discovery Channel *103*
discrimination 4, 112. *See also* segregation; sex discrimination;
        sexual harassment
    barrier 98
    employment 78, 79
    gender 136
    Pregnancy Discrimination Act 148, 183
    workforce 134, *134*, 136
Diving into the Wreck (Rich) 128
divorce 17, 141
    children and 174
    family 171–174
    laws 6
Dixon, Shirley 85
Doctor's Case Against the Pill, The (Seaman) 44, 46
Dole, Elizabeth 5, 142
domestic abuse 80
Dooce 154
Douglas High School 69
doulas 176
Downer, Carol 47–48
drawing rooms viii
Dresselhaus, Mildred Spiewak 106
Duke, David 81
Dulbecco, Renato 105
Dworkin, Andrea 24
Dziech, Billie Wright 70

E
Ebadi, Shirin 31
education vii–viii, x, **59–75**. *See also* colleges; higher education;
        schools; Title IX
    advancement/obstacles 62–65
    choices in family 180–183
    future 73–75
    laws 65–66
    laying groundwork/creating doubts 59–62

mentoring 64
for nontraditional workforce 66
performance 73
science/medicine 99–103
single-sex schools 69
Supreme Court on 65–66
women's studies ix, 26, 71–73, 74
Edwards, Helen Thom 106
Edwards, Lena 45
EEOC. *See* Equal Employment Opportunity Commission (EEOC)
Ehrenreich, Barbara 45
Eisenhower, Dwight D. 5, 33, 84
Eisenstadt v. Baird 177
Elders, Minnie Joycelyn *107*, 109
elected women **85**
    campaigns 89
    congressional widows 88
    double shift 88
    House of Representatives 85–91
    open-seat races 88
    Senate 85–91
Elion, Gertrude B. 98, **102**
Ellet, Elizabeth Fries Lummis viii
embryonic stem cell 110
EMILY's list xi, 37, 87
Emory University 73
employment x, 65, 78, 79. *See also* career development; Equal Employment Opportunity Commission (EEOC); jobs; unemployment; workforce
Endeavour space shuttle *112*
English, Diane 159
Enovid 42
entertainment/sports 26, **151–166**. *See also specific sports*
    athletes 163–166
    film 155–158
    minorities 166
    music 159–163
    news media 151–155
    television 158–159
    Title IX and 66–68
entrepreneurs 144, 146
environmentalists x, 1
En Vogue 163

EPA (Equal Pay Act) 27, 79, 135, 136
Equal Credit Opportunity Act 141, 146
Equal Employment Opportunity Commission (EEOC) 66, 79
    establishment 6, 136
    NOW and 136
equal opportunity 66, 142
    goal of, in art 130
    measuring 68
Equal Pay Act (EPA) 27, 79, 135–136
Equal Rights Amendment (ERA) 24, 77, 92–93, 154
    Capitol March *79*
    defeating 82
    opposition 33–34
    protesters *82*
    ratification blocked 34
    supporters *2*, 33
equity feminists 36
ERA. *See* Equal Rights Amendment (ERA)
Erdrich, Louise 129
Erin Brockovich 157
Estefan, Gloria 161
ethnicity ix, 26, 71–74, 148
Evans, Mart 110
Evert, Chris 164
Every Woman's Bookstore, Los Angeles 47
Executive Order #11246 66

F

fake orgasms 48
Falletta, JoAnn 123
Faludi, Susan xi, 35, 61–62
family 8, 14, 69, 148, **169–183**
    career development and 35
    children and 179–180
    demographics 170–171
    divorce 171–174
    dual-earner 182
    education choices 180–183
    marriage 171–174
    motherhood 169, 174–179
    planning 139
    redefining 183
    shrinking 17

wages 63
whites 75
Family and Medical Leave Act (FMLA) **8**, 14, 35, 148, 177
Family Planning Services and Population Act 139
Family Protection Act 69
Fawcett, Joy 162
FDA (Food and Drug Administration) 42–44, 53
Fear of Flying (Jong) 6
Federal and Medical Leave Act (FMLA) **8**
Federation of Teachers 24
female anatomy 45
female child brides 54
"female occupations" 140
Feminine Mystique, , The (Friedan) x, 6, 21, 59, 71, 79, 115, 126–127, 137, 158, 175
femininity 32, 36
feminism 6, 24, 73. *See also* second wave feminism
    third wave 21, 35–37
    whites and 36
feminist activism x–xi
feminist art movement 117, 121, 126
feminists 26, 34, 51, 71, 82. *See also specific feminists*
    African American 23
    black 37
    bourgeois 29
    Christian 30
    equity 36
    Jewish 30
    "Lavender menace" 29
    liberal 25, 71–72
    Muslim 28, 30–31
    power 36
    radical 24
    scholars 35
    socialist 25
    turning into 48
Feminist Theory from Margin to Center (hooks) 71
Feminist Women's Health Centers 51
feminization of poverty 77, 180, *181*, **181**
Ferebee, Dorothy 45
Ferraro, Geraldine xi, 87
Field, Sally 155, 156
Fifteenth Amendment 15

film **156**. *See also* Hollywood; *specific films*
  career development 158
  entertainment/sports 155–158
Firestone, Shulamith 25, 48
First Amendment 15
"First Side Ever I Saw Your Face, The" 160
Flack, Audrey 120, 121
Flack, Roberta 160
Fleming, Renee 124
flex time 147–148
Flockhart, Calista 159
Florida *2*, 15, *22*, 44, *51*, *79*, *80*, *143*, 172
Flowers, Gennifer 14
Flowers, Vonetta *165*
Flying Nun, The 155
FMLA (Family and Medical Leave Act) **8**, 14, 35, 148, 177
Fonda, Henry 155
Fonda, Jane 155
Food and Drug Administration (FDA) 42–44, 53
food industry 137
food stamp program 181
Forbes billionaires list 138
Ford, Betty *152*
Ford, Gerald 5, 10, *152*
Ford, Henry 63
Forrest Gump 156
Fortune 500 list 137, 143, 145
Fortune 1000 list 142
Fossey, Dian 110
Foster, Jodie 157–158
Foudy, Julie 162
Fowler, Joanna *104*, 105–106
Franklin, Aretha 159
Franklin, Barbara H. 5
Franklin, Bonnie 175
Franklin v. Gwinnett Public Schools 68, 70
free love 7, 172
Friedan, Betty x, 21, 59, 79, 115, *116*, 126–127, 137, 158, 175
  bourgeois feminist 29
  liberal feminist 71–72
  NOW co-founder 6
Furies 83

G

Gage, Matilda Joslyn vii
gag rule 52, 54
Garner, Margaret 118
Garvan Prize 98, 102
Gay Liberation movement 29
gays 1, 29, 72, 183. *See also* lesbian rights; lesbians
    marriage 174
    rights 6–7
    studies 72
gender 63, 69
    barriers viii
    class and 26, 71–72
    equality 54
    race and 3, 26, 71–74
gender bias in classrooms **63**
Gender Equity in Education Act 69
gender gap 86, 91
    coining 84
    in elections 84, 86
    in science 63
    women conductors bridging 123
Genetics Society of America 108
genital mutilation 54
Georgia 10, 87, 90, 162
German measles x
Gidget 155
Gilead (Robinson, M.) 129
Gilman, Charlotte Perkins 127
Ginsburg, Ruth Bader 33, 91
Gioia, Dana *122*
Giovanni, Nikki 128
girl groups 161. *See also specific groups*
glasnost 12
Glaspell, Susan 127
glass ceiling xi, 6, 27–28, 91, 142–143, 152
Glass Ceiling Act 143
Glass Ceiling Initiative 142
Glen T. Seaborg Award for Radiochemistry 106
global warming 16
Go-Go's 161
Goldberg, Whoopi 155
golf 163–164

Goodman, Ellen 61
Goodman, John 175
Göpper-Mayer, Maria 98
Gorbachev, Mikhail 12
Gordon, Kim 161
Gordon, Linda 44, 48
Gore, Al 15
Gorilla, My Love (Bambara) 128
Gorillas in the Mist (Fossey) 110
Graduate, The 156
Graeme, Elizabeth viii
Graham, Katharine 137, 154
Grandma Moses 119
Grand Old Opry 160
Grant, Cary *157*
Grasso, Ella T. 33
Great American Novel 116
Great Society 4
"the great yogurt conspiracy" 48
Greenberg, Blu 28
Greene, Jeffrey B. 109
Greider, Carol W. 98
Griffin, Michael 52
Griffiths, Martha x, *62*, 65
Griswold v. Connecticut x, 31, 42–43, 82, 139, 177
Group, The (McCarthy) 116, 127
grunge 163
Guerilla Girls **126**
Guess Who's Coming to Dinner? 155
Gulf War xi, 15
Gunn, David 52
Guy-Sheftall, Beverly 71–72
gymnastics 165

H
Haener, Dorothy 79
Hamburger, Victor 105
Hamer, Fannie Lou x, 4
Hamm, Mia 162, 166
Hammett, Paula ix
Hammond, Harmony 119
Hancock, Kaziah *130*
Hanks, Tom 156

Hannah Montana 163
Harlem Renaissance 119
Harper, Ida Husted vii
HARPO Entertainment Group 138
Harris, Patricia 5
Harris v. Forklift Systems, Inc. 141
Harry, Deborah 161
Harvard University 61
Harvey, Mary 162
Hausknecht, Richard 42
Head Start *74*
health **41–55**, 87. *See also* breast cancer; women's health movement
    abortion x, xi, 34, 49–53
    birth control viii, x, 17, 41–44
    Boston Women's Health Collective 44–47
    Child Health Act 139
    Children's Health Insurance Program 15
    consciousness-raising meetings x, 25, 48
    DES action 49
    Feminist Women's Health Centers 51
    global movement 53–54
    National Black Women's Health Project 53
    national policy 53
    National Women's Health Network 44, 46, 53
    self-help movement 47–48
    Women's Health Conference 45
    women's health movement 44
health care x, 13, 41, *45*, 91
    African Americans and 44, 53
    debates 54–55
    federally funded 4, 17
    overhauling 13
    reform 15, 17, 55
    responsibility 90
    universal 14
Healthy Mothers, Healthy Babies poster *53*
heart disease 1, 46, 53
heavy metal 163
Hepburn, Audrey 155, *157*
Hepburn, Katharine 155
Heresies: A Feminist Publication on Art and Politics 121
Herman, Alexis 5
Hernandez, Ester *117*

higher education viii, 26, 61, 140
Hilbert, David 111
Hill, Anita 35–36
Hills, Carla Anderson 5
hip-hop 163
hippies 7, 159, 172, 173, *173*
Hispanic Business Magazine 142
Hispanics 74, *107*, 142, 148, 178, 180–181.
   See also Chicanos; Latinas
Hitchings, George 102
HIV/AIDS 17, 53
 research 109
 treatment 102
Hobby, Oveta Culp 5
Hochchild, Arlie 35
Ho Chi Minh 7
Hoffman, Darleane C. 104–105
Hoffman, Dustin 156
Hollywood 11
 ageism/sexism 156
 celebrity 155
 elite 152
home pregnancy tests *47*
home theater systems 1
hooks, bell 71–72
Horne, Marilyn 124
House of Representatives x, xi, 31
 congressional widows 88
 elected women 85–91
 speaker Pelosi 90
House on Mango Street, The (Cisneros) 128–129
housework 27, 78, 134, 176, 182
Houston, Whitney 161
Howard University 118
Howell, Mary Catherine *45*
How Schools Shortchange Girls 63
How Stella Got Her Groove Back 156
HPV vaccination 17
Huffington Post 155
Hufstedler, Shirley 5
human rights 10–11, 15, 91, 106, 181
human trafficking 73, 87
Hunt, Helen 159

Hunter College 102
Huntington, Anna Hyatt *120*
Hurston, Zora Neal 128
Hussein, Saddam 12
Hyde Amendment 52
Hynde, Chrissie 161

I

"I Am Woman" 160–161
I Have a Dream speech 4
I Know Why the Caged Bird Sings (Angelou) 128
imperialism 83
Indigo Girls 163
infidelity 173
inflation 12
International Ladies' Garment Workers Union *140*
International Reproductive Rights and Research Action Group 54
International Women's Brass Conference 124
Internet 1, 37, 53–55, 154–155
intrauterine devices 177
inventions 97
in vitro fertilization (IVF) 177
Iran-Contra scandal 12
Iraq War 16, 152
It's Complicated 156
It Takes a Village, and Other Lessons Children Teach Us (Clinton, H.) 13
IVF (in vitro fertilization) 177
I Will Survive 160

J

Jackson, Janet 161
Jackson, Laura 123
Jackson, Lisa P. 5
Jane underground abortion network 49–50
Janeway, Elizabeth 116
Jemison, Mae *112*
Jen, Gish 129
Jett, Joan 161, 166
Jewish feminists 30
Jewish Orthodox Feminist Alliance 28
Jews 28, 30, 105. *See also* Judaism

jobs x, 25, 27, 97. *See also* employment; unemployment
    changing 136
    expansion 137
    full-time 181
    getting fired 148
    government 73
    lower-wage 147
    low-paying 134
    men's/women's 134, 140
    part-time 176
    qualifying for 66
    scientific 60
    top-level management 142
Johnson, Lady Bird *74*
Johnson, Lyndon 9, 65
    administration 3–4, 6
    Executive Order #11246 66
Jong, Erica 6
Joplin, Janis 159, 166
Jordan, Barbara xi, 85
Journal of Developmental Entrepreneurship 146
Joyce Chen Cook Book (Chen) 137
Joyce Chen Cooks 137
Joy Luck Club, The (Tan) 128
Judaism 28–30. *See also* Jewish feminists; Jews
judges 60, 90–92. *See also* courts
Jury of Her Peers, A (Glaspell) 127

K

Kallosh, Renata 106–107
Kansas 53
Karle, Isabella Lugowski 103–104
Katzenbach, Nicholas *61*
Kaufman, Matthew 110
Kennedy, Caroline x
Kennedy, Florynce *82*
Kennedy, Jacqueline x, 32
Kennedy, John F. x, *3*, 22, *25*, 65, 78, 115
    administration 2–3
    assassination 3
    election 2
Kennedy, John F., Jr. x
Kennedy, Robert 9

Kent State University tragedy 9
Khomeini, Ayatollah 11
"Killing Me Softly" 160
King, Billie Jean xi, 164
King, Martin Luther, Jr. 4, 7, 9, *135*
Kingston, Maxine Hong 128
Kirkpatrick, Jeane 5
Klute 155
Koedt, Ann 48
Komen, Susan G. 50
Koop, C. Everett *107*
Koppel, Ted 15
Kraft Foods 145
Kramer, Larry 109
Kramer v. Kramer 157
Krasner, Lee 117
Krelle, Karma *100*
Kreps, Juanita 5
Kübler-Ross, Elisabeth 97, 107
Kushner, Rose 50

L

Lachance, Janice 5
Lady's Book viii
Lafrance, Noemie 125
Landrieu, Mary 89
Landrieu, Maurice ("Moon") 89
Latifah, Queen 162
Latinas 33, *55*, 129. *See also* Chicanos; Hispanics
Laubenstein, Linda 109
Lauder, Estée *139*
Lauper, Cindi 161
"Lavender menace" 29
laws 148. *See also specific laws*
  abortion 80
  American Law Institute 51
  anti-birth control 41–42
  anti-pornography 24
  divorce 6
  education 65–66
  rape 6
Leakey, Louis 110
Ledbetter Fair Pay Act (2009) 147

Lee Harper x
Leland, Ted 67
Lerner, Gerda ix, 116
lesbian rights 6–7, **29**, 81, 183. *See also* gays
lesbians 23, 119, 127
    activists 183
    studies 72
Leslie, Lisa 165
Less Than Zero 157
Levertov, Denise 127
Levi, Giuseppe 105
Levi-Montalcini, Rita **105**
Lewinsky, Monica 14
liberal feminists 25, 71–72
Life in the Iron Mills (Davis) 127
life sciences 109–111
life span 1
Light, Judith 175
"Like a Virgin" 161
Lilith Fair 163
Lilly, Kristine 162
Lion in Winter, The 155
literacy viii
Little Man Tate 158
Liu, Carol 91
Liz Claiborne, Inc. 140–141
Lobo, Rebecca 165
Look magazine *157*
Lopez, Nancy 163, *164*
Lorde, Audre 23, *23*, 50
Loren, Sophia 32
Love, Courtney 163
Love Medicine (Erdrich) 129
Luria, Salvador 105
Lyles, Latifa 81
Lynn, Loretta 159
Lyon, Phyllis 7
Lyte, MC 162
Lytton Galleries of Contemporary Art 120

M

MacArthur Fellowship 111
MacArthur Foundation 108

MacGregor, Molly Murphy ix
Mackinnon, Catharine 24
Maclachlan, Sarah 163
Macmillan, Shannon 162
Mad About You 159
Maddow, Rachel 152
Madonna 161
male privilege *72*
Malkin, Michelle 155
Malko International Conductors Competition 123
Malone, Vivian *61*
Mama Mia! 156
Mandela, Nelson 138
Manhattan Project 103
Manji, Irshad 31
Mankiller, Wilma 6
marble ceiling 90
march on Washington, D.C. (1963) 4, 6, *65*
Marrack, Philippa 110–111
marriage 2, 6. *See also* weddings
　family 171–174
　gays 174
Marshall, Paule 128
Marshall, Thurgood 36
Martin, Agnes 121
Martin, Del 7
Martin, Gail R. 110
Martin, Lynn 5
Martin, Steve 156
Mary Kay Cosmetics 137
mathematics 111
Matijasevich, Yuri 111
Mattel 32
May-Treanor, Missy 166
McCarthy, Mary 116, 127
McClintock, Barbara 98, **108**, 109, *110*
McCormack, Ellen *34*
McCormick, Katherine 42
McCorvey, Norma 53
McFadden, Cynthia 155
McLaughlin, Ann Dore 5
Mead, Margaret 97, *111*
"Me and Bobby McGee" 159

mentoring 64
"Mercedes Benz" 159
Mercy, A (Morrison, T.) 118
Meritor Savings Bank v. Vinson 70, 141
Mexican Americans 6
Miami Sound Machine 161
MichelleMalkin.com 155
middle-class ix, 71, 178
    counterculture from 7
    educated 86
    needs 36
    problems 59
    weddings and 171
midwives 47, 176
Mikulski, Barbara 89
Milbrett, Tiffeny 162
military service x
Millett, Kate x, 25, 60
miniskirts 60
Mink, Patsy T. 66, *68*
minorities 6, 65, 70–72, 136. *See also specific minorities*
    in art 126
    ethnic 75
    legal support 66, 148
    opportunities 148
    rights 65
minyan 29
"Mississippi appendectomies" 44
Missouri *69*
Mitchell, Joan 121
Mitchell, Joni 166
molecular biology 108
mommy-track 147
mommy wars **178**
Monroe, Marilyn 32
Monroy, Jenna *103*
Moore, Demi 157
Morawetz, Cathleen Synge 111
Morgan, Bette ix
Morgan, Robin x, 24, 25, 29
Morrisette, Alanis 163
Morrison, Harold 118
Morrison, Toni 23, 116, **118**, 128, 129

motherhood. *See also* childbirth; mothers; supermoms
   changing patterns 174–179
   defined 169
mothers 2, 47, 53, 112, 147, *170*. *See also* motherhood; supermoms; working mothers
   nursing 180
   single 180
   stay-at-home 178, 182
   welfare 177
Mount Holyoke viii
mp3 players 1
Ms. Magazine 24, 71–73
MTV 161
Mulcahy, Anne 145
Muriel Siebert & Company 138
Murphy Brown 159
music. *See also* conductors; opera; orchestrating; specific music types
   arts/literature 122–124
   blind auditions 124
   entertainment/sports 159–163
Muslim feminists 28, 30–31
Mussolini, Benito 105
My Best Friend's Wedding 157
My Fair Lady 155
Myth of the Vaginal Orgasm, The 48

N

NAFTA (North American Free Trade Agreement) 14
Napolitano, Janet A. 5
NARAL (National Association for Repeal of Abortion Laws) 80
National Abortion Rights Action League 80
National Academy of Sciences 105, 106, 108
National Association for Repeal of Abortion Laws (NARAL) 80. *See also* National Abortion Rights Action League
National Association of Women Artists 129, 130
National Association of Women Business Owners 145
National Black Women's Health Project 53
National Book Award 129–130
National Book Critics Award 118, 129
National Breast Cancer Foundation 50
National Coalition for Women and Girls in Education 63–64
National Council on the Arts 118

National Farm Workers Association 6
National Federation of Republican Women 87
National Foundation for Women Business Owners 145
National Institutes of Health (NIH) 53
National Medal of Science 104, 105
National Museum of Women in the Arts 122
National Organization for Women (NOW) x, 6, 7, 22, 29, **81**, 84, 111
    annual meetings 47
    EEOC and 136
    issues 81
    launching 79
    lobbying by 33
    members 37, 81
    New Left 80
    political clout 81
    pressure from 136
    sexual harassment and 80
National Science Foundation (NSF) 100, 103
National Women's Business Council 145
National Women's Hall of Fame 142
National Women's Health Network 44, 46, 53
National Women's History Project (NWHP) ix
National Women's Political Caucus 9, 87
Native Americans 1, 6, 23, 129
Navratilova, Martina 164
Naylor, Gloria 118
needlework vii, viii
Neel, Alice 121
Nelson, Gaylord 44
Neuberger, Maurine B. 31, *31*
New Left 80, **83**
news media 151–155
Newsweek 118
New York Radical Feminists 82
New York Radical Women 48
New York Stock Exchange (NYSE) 138
New York Times 46, 59, 116, 118
New York Times Book Review 128, 129
New York University 102
Nicaragua Sandinistas 12
NIH (National Institutes of Health) 53
Nineteenth Amendment viii, 71
Nixon, Richard 5, 9, 10

Nobel Prize 31, 98, 99, 102, 105, 106, 108, 118
No Child Left Behind 69
Nooyi, Indra 145
Noriega, Manuel 12
Normal Heart, The 109
Norma Rae 155
North, Oliver 12
North American Free Trade Agreement (NAFTA) 14
Norton, Gale 5
Novello, Antonia Coello 107, *107*, 109
NOW. *See* National Organization for Women (NOW)
NSF (National Science Foundation) 100
nuclear arms race 10
Nuclear Nonproliferation Treaty 10
NWHP (National Women's History Project) ix
NYSE (New York Stock Exchange) 138

O

O: The Oprah Magazine 138
Oak Ridge National Laboratory 104
Obama, Barack xi, 5, 13, 33, 54–55, 87
    administration 77
    woman appointments 16–17
Obie Award 128
O'Connor, Flannery 129
O'Connor, Sandra Day xi, 33, 91
Office of Women Business Ownership 145
La Ofrenda II 117
O'Keefe, Georgia 121
Oklahoma 85
O'Leary, Hazel 5
Olympic Games 162, *165*, 165–166
On Death and Dying (Kübler-Ross) 107
One Day at a Time 175
O'Neill, Terry 81
On Golden Pond 155
opera 124–125
Operation Rescue 52–53
Oprah Winfrey Show, The 138
orchestrating 122–124
organ transplants 17
Oswald, Lee Harvey 3
"the Other" ix, 22

Our Bodies, Ourselves 45, 47, 53
Outer Circle Critics Award 128
Ova II *47*
Overbeck, Caria 162

P

PACs (political action committees) 81
Pagoda 172
Paige, Rod 68
Palin, Sarah x–xi, 16, 87, *89*
Panama Canal Treaty of 1977 10
Parks, Rosa 4, 22
Parlow, Cindy 162
Partial Birth Abortion Ban 52
Parton, Dolly 160, *161*
patriarchy 24–25, 30, 72, 128
Patsy T. Mink Equal Opportunity in Education Act 66
Paul, Alice 33
PCSW. *See* President's Commission on the Status of Women
Peace Corps 2
Pearce, Diana 181
Pelosi, Nancy xi, *90*, **90**
PEN/Faulkner award 130
Pennsylvania 84, 87
People's Temple mass suicide 172
PepsiCo 145
perestroika 12
Perkins, Francis 5
Persian Gulf War 12, 152
personal is political 31–35, 78
Personal Responsibility and Work Reconciliation Act 181
Peters, Mary 5
Peterson, Esther 22, 24
Petigny, Alan 44
Phillips, Layli 73
Phillips v. Martin Marietta Corporation 135, 183
physics 98, 106–107
Pincus, Gregory *42*, 42–43
pink ribbons 50
Pizer, Elizabeth Hayden 124
Places in the Heart 155
Planned Parenthood 41
Planned Parenthood of Southeastern Pennsylvania v. Casey 84

Plath, Sylvia 116, 127
political action committees (PACs) 81
political lesbianism 29
politics vii, x, **77–92**, 81, 121
    abortion 77
    backlash 177
    career development 88
    elected women 85–91
    gender gap 84, 86, 91
    lesbianism 29
    National Women's Political Caucus 9, 87
    personal is political 31–35, 78
    post Watergate 10–13
    rebirth/controversy 77–84
    road to power 84–87
    transforming 92
    transgender 37
    women in power 87–91
Pollock, Jackson 117
Poor People's Campaign (1968) 7
pop music 163
Postcards (Proulx) 130
post-colonialism 37
poverty 43, 138, *179*
    feminization of 77, 180, *181*, **181**
    rates 170
    War on Poverty 4, *74*
power feminists 36
Pregnancy Discrimination Act 148, 183
Premarin 46
President's Commission on the Status of Women (PCSW) x, 115
    appointment of 78–79
    workforce documentation 136
Pretenders 161
Pretty Woman 157
Price, Deborah A. 67
Price, Leontyne *122*, 124
Pries, Sally 28
Priestly Medal 104
Prince of Tides, The 158
pro-choice xi, 30, 37, 77, 84
    advocates 84

in Democratic Party 87
demonstration *34*
lobby 80
movement 51
Professional Women: Vital Statistics 27, 62
progress without parity **85**
pro-life
　activists 1, 52, 77, *80*, 91
　Republican Party and 90
Proulx, Annie 129–130
Pulitzer Prize x, 124, 129, 130
Punchline 156
punk rock 161, 163

Q

Quayle, Dan 159, 180
queer theory 37
quilting vii

R

race ix–x, 118, 135, 180
　ageism and 152
　employment and 65
　ethnicity and 148
　gender and 3, 26, 71–74
　mothering and 178
　Mussolini and 105
　religion and 89, 136, 141
　riots 9
race and women's rights **23**
"race card" 36
racism 23, 82, 128, 149
Radar Programs 32
Radicalesbians 29
radical feminists **24**
Rait, Bonnie 166
rap 161
rape 24, 82, 83, 116
　laws 6
　victims 92
Rape Speak Out 83
Rashad, Phylicia 175
Rawalt, Marguerite 79

Reagan, Ronald xi, 1, 5, 54, 84
   administration 86, 181
   election 11
   Reaganomics 11–12
Reddy, Helen 160–161
Redstockings 25, 83
religion
   race and 89, 136, 141
   Religious Right 82
   society 28–31
   women and 28–31
reproductive rights x, 6, 21, 34, 54
Republican Party x–xi, 9, 11, 31, 33, 84, 86
   National Federation of Republican Women 87
   primaries 89
   pro-life and 90
   Republican Revolution 87
   sexual harassment and 90
Rescue America 52
Resier, Paul 159
Respect 159
Retton, Mary Lou 165, 166
Reyna, Janie *16*
Reynolds, Bert 155
Rhodes, Marcus 109
Rice, Condoleezza 5, *15*, 91
Rice, Susan 5
Rice-Wray, Edris 43
Rich, Adrienne 127, 128
Richards, Anne 90
Ride, Sally 97, *98*
Riggs, Bobby xi, 164
rights. *See also* Civil Rights Act (1964); Civil Rights Act (1991); Civil Rights Movement; lesbian rights; reproductive rights
   civil 4
   gays 6–7
   minorities 65
   National Abortion Rights Action League 80
   race and women's rights 23
   voting 6
   Voting Rights Act (1965) 6
   women's viii–ix
   women's debate x

Ringgold, Faith 119, *119*
Ringwald, Molly 157
Rio Piedras trials **43**
riots 9, 29
Rivlin, Alice 5
Roberts, Julia 157
Roberts, Patricia *4*
Roberts, Tiffany 162
Robinson, Julia Bowman 111
Robinson, Marilynne 116, 129
Rock, John 42–43
Roe v. Wade xi, 31, 34, 51–53, 80, 82, 84, 139, 179
roles
    care-taking 101
    changing 35
    conventional 137
    evolution in 133
    reexamination 26
    society 17, 21
Romer, Christina 5
Ronstadt, Linda 160
Roosevelt, Eleanor 24, *25*
Roosevelt, Franklin D. 5, 33
Roseanne 175
Rosen, Ruth 48
Rosenfeld, Irene 145
Ross, Diana 160
Rothman, Lorraine 47
Rust v. Sullivan 52
Rutgers University 73
Ruthsdotter, Mary ix
Ryan, Francis 110

S

Saar, Betye 120
Sadler, Barbara *182*
Sadler, Nicole *182*
Sager, Ruth 109–110
salons viii, *125*
SALT I (Strategic Arms Limitation Treaty) 10
Salt n' Pepa 162
San Diego University 71
Sanger, Margaret viii–ix, 42

San Jose State University 70
Sarachik, Myriam P. 106
Sarah Lawrence College ix
satellite television 1
Sawyer, Diane 152, 166
Schakowsky, Jan 86, 87
Schapiro, Miriam 119
Schlafly, Phyllis 33, *82*
Schonthal, Ruth 124
schools 63, 69
   charter/private/public 180
   "dame schools" viii
   school year 182–183
   segregation 66
   single-sex 69
   Title IX and 67
Schwab, Susan 5
Schwarzkopf, Norman 12
science, technology, engineering, and mathematics (STEM) 64–65, 97
science/medicine 64–65, **97–112**
   career development 99–103
   degrees earned 100–101
   discrimination barrier 98
   education 99–103
   gender gap 63
   low-paying specialties 101
   women in chemistry 103–106
   women in life sciences 109–111
   women in mathematics 111
   women in medicine 107–108
   women in physics 106–107
Scurry, Briana 162
SDS (Students for a Democratic Society) 83
Seaman, Barbara 44, **46**
Sebelius, Kathleen 5
Second Sex, The (de Beauvoir) ix, 22
second wave feminism 54
   arts/literature 116–119
   society 22–25
Secret Life of Supermom, The (Buckworth) 175
security moms 86

segregation 4, 74. *See also* discrimination
    class 74
    school 66
    workforce index 136
Seles, Monica 164
self-help movement 47–48
Senate 35
    elected women 85–91
    Thomas hearings 36
Send in the Clowns 160
Seneca Falls Convention 71
September 11 terrorist attacks 15
Seventeen magazine *136*
sex x, 48
    sexual orientation ix
    sexual revolution 7
Sex and the City 127, 159
sex discrimination 21, 70
    defined 66
    Supreme Court on 135
sexism 16, 24, 79, 83, 156
Sexton, Anne 125–127
sexual harassment xi, 36, 64, **70**, 77, 80, 159.
       See also Thomas, Clarence
    classroom 63
    college campus 70, 73
    as commonplace 78
    continual 68
    defined 66
    NOW and 80
    Republican Party and 90
    Supreme Court on 64, 68, 141
    victims 73
    workplace 78, 141
Sexual Politics (Millett) x
sexual violence 80
Shah of Iran 11
Shalala, Donna 5
Shange, Ntosake 128
Sheedy, Ally 157
Shipping News, The (Proulx) 130
Sidel v. Abbott Laboratories 49
Siebert, Muriel 137–138

Sierra Club 81
Sigman, Jill 125
Silence of the Lambs 157
Silent Spring, The (Carson) x
Sills, Beverly 124
"simultaneity of oppression" 23
Sisterhood is Global Institute 24
sisters 72
Slaughter, Susan 124
Smeal, Eleanor *81*, 84
Smiley, Jane 129
Smith, Howard W. 27, 65
Smith, Liz 155
Smith, Margaret Chase 31
Smokey and the Bandit 155
Snowe, Olympia 86, *86*
soccer **162**, 165–166
socialist feminists 25
social mores 1, 128, 178
social norms 144–145
society vii, x, **21–37**
    personal is political 31–35
    reeducating 25–26
    religion 28–31
    roles 17, 21
    second-class status 136
    second wave feminism 22–25
    third wave feminism 21, 35–37
Solis, Hilda 5
Sommers, Christina Hoff 36, 73
Song of Solomon (Morrison, T.) 118
Sonic Youth 161
Sophie's Choice 157
Sorenstam, Annika 164
Sotomayor, Sonia 91
South Dakota 6
Southern Christian Leadership Conference 4
Soviet Union 3, 10
    dissolution 12
    as "evil empire" 12
"speak-outs" 25, 34, 51, 82
Spears, Britney 163, 166
Spellings, Margaret 5

spermicides 177
Spivak, Lawrence E. *4*
St. Elmo's Fire 157
St. Louis Symphony Orchestra 124
Stahl, Lesley 155
"stalled revolution" 35
"Stand by Your Man" 159
Stanton, Elizabeth Cady vii
stay-at-home fathers 182
stay-at-home mothers 178, 182
Steinem, Gloria x, 6, *33*, 34
STEM (science, technology, engineering, and mathematics) 64–65
sterilization 44, 54
Stern, Susan 83
Stevenson, Adlai 84
Stonewall riots 29
storied art 119–120
story quilts 119
Stowe, Harriet Beecher viii
Strategic Arms Limitation Treaty (SALT I) 10
Streep, Meryl 155–157, 166
Streisand, Barbra 158, *160*
Strug, Kerri 165
Students for a Democratic Society (SDS) 83
suffrage vii
Sula (Morrison, T.) 118
Summer, Donna 160
super heroines in comics **153**
supermoms **175**
Supreme Court x, xi, 31, 33–34, 49, 51–52, 84. *See also specific cases*
　on birth control 42–43
　on education 65–66
　on public funds 69
　on sex discrimination 135
　on sexual harassment 64, 68, 141
Supremes 160
Swenson, May 127
Swoopes, Sheryl 165
Sybil 155
Synge, J. L. 111
Szostak, Jack W. 98

T

Tamm, Igor 106
Tan, Amy 128
Tar Baby (Morrison, T.) 118
Taylor, Elizabeth 155, *158*
television. *See also* news media; *specific television shows*
    cable 1
    entertainment/sports 158–159
    MTV 161
    satellite 1
tennis 164–165
thalidomide x
Tharp, Twyla 124
That Girl 158
Their Eyes Were Watching God (Hurston) 128
Think 159
Third Life of Grange Copeland, The (Walker) 128
third wave feminism 21, 35–37
Third Wave Foundation 37
Thomas, Clarence 35–36, 70, 141, 159
Thomas, Danny 158
Thomas, Marlo 155, 158, 166
Thousand Acres, A (Smiley) 129
Time magazine 123, 124
Title II 143. *See also* Civil Rights Act (1991)
Title IX 26, 59–60, 63, **67**, 99, 140. *See also* Patsy T. Mink Equal Opportunity in Education Act
    implications/controversy 66–71
    schools and 67
    sports and 66–68
    at thirty 67–68
    three-prong test 66, 68
TLC 163
To Kill a Mockingbird (Lee, H.) x
transgender politics 37
Travelgate controversy 14
Trethewey, Natasha 130
Turner, Tina 161
Tyson, Laura D'Andrea 5

U

Uhlenbeck, Karen Keskulla 111
UN Interagency Network on Women and Gender Equality 54

Uncle Tom's Cabin (Stowe) viii
unemployment. *See also* employment; jobs
    high 6, 139, 141, 181
    inflation and 12
    low 137
United States history vii–ix
United States v. Virginia 69
University of Alabama *61*
University of Alaska *100*
University of Arkansas 109
University of California-Berkeley 70, 104
University of California-Los Angeles 73
University of Florida 44
University of Maryland 73
University of Michigan 60
University of Washington 73
U.S. Census 27, 64, *134*, 169, 173–174, 181
Use Your Life Award 138
utopia 83

V

Van de Vate, Nancy 124
Vassar College viii, 127
Veneman, Ann 5
Venturini, Tisha 162
video gaming 1
Vietnam War 152
    ending 9–10
    history 7, 9
violence against women xi, 24, 72, 77, 87, 92.
        See also rape; sexual violence
Violence Against Women Act 72
Virginia Symphony Orchestra 123
volleyball 166
voting 4, 6. *See also* elected women
    African American *92*
    shifting patterns 84
Voting Rights Act (1965) 6

W

wages 27, 92, 137
    differentials 2
    family 63

        lower-paying jobs 147
        wage gap 62, 64, 146–147
        women's declining 22
Walker, Alice 23, 37, 128
Walker, Rebecca 21, 36, *36*
"Walkin' After Midnight" 160
Wall Street Journal 142
Walsh, Kerri 166
Walters, Barbara 151–152, *152*, 166
WAR (Women Artists in Revolution) 121
war correspondents 152
War on Poverty 4, *74*
Warren, Mercy Otis viii
War Against Boys: How Misguided Feminism is Harming Our Young Men, The (Sommers) 73
Washington, Martha viii
Washington Post 10, 137, 154
Watergate scandal 10–13, 154
Webster v. Reproductive Health Services 84
weddings 171, *171*, 173
Weiner, Linda 70
welfare mothers 177
Wellesley College 63
WellPoint 145
Where the Girls Are 73
whites ix, 4, 23, 44
    African Americans compared to 71
    family 75
    feminism and 36
Whitewater controversy 14
Whitman, Christine Todd 5
Whitney Museum 117
Whitworth, Kathy 163
Who's Afraid of Virginia Woolf? 155
Who's the Boss 175
Wie, Michelle 164
Williams, Serena 164–165, 166
Williams, Venus 164–165, 166
Wilson, Ann 160
Wilson, Nancy 160
Wilson, Staci 162
WIN, Georgia 87
Winfrey, Oprah **138**

WITCH (Women's International Terrorist Conspiracy) 25
With the Weatherman (Stern) 83
WLM. *See* women's liberation movement (WLM)
WNBA (Women's National Basketball Association) 165
Woertz, Patricia 145
Wolf, Nomi 35
Wolfson, Alice 44
Wolfson, Howard 16
womanist 37
Woman Warrior, The (Kingston) 128
Women Artists 1550-1950 122
Women Artists in Revolution (WAR) 121
women-controlled clinics 48
women in presidential cabinets **5**
Women on the Web 155
Women Rap about Sex 48
Women's Action Alliance *33*
Women's Campaign Fund, Pennsylvania 87
Women's Education Act xi
Women's Forum, Beijing 53
Women's Global Network for Reproductive Rights 54
Women's Health Conference 45
Women's Health Initiative 53
women's health movement 44, 48, 50, 54–55
Women's History Month ix
Women's International Terrorist Conspiracy (WITCH) 25
women's liberation movement (WLM) x, 1, 6, 21
    second wave 22–25
    "whiteness" of 23
Women's National Basketball Association (WNBA) 165
Women's Philharmonic Orchestra 124
women's studies ix, 26, 71–73, 74
Women's Salon, The *125*
Women of the American Revolution, The (Ellet) viii
Women Under Thirty, Read This! 49
Wonkette 155
Woodward, Bob 10, 154
workforce
    discrimination 134, *134*, 136
    index of segregation 136
    married women in 133–134, 137, 139
    PCSW documentation 136
    women in 27, 34

working mothers 100, 147, *176*
   children and 34–35
   "stalled revolution" 35
Working Mothers 100 list 147
World War II ix
Wynette, Tammy 159

X

Xerox 145
X to the 12th Power 120

Y

Yale University 61
Yalow, Rosalyn 98
Yardley advertisement *136*
Yellen, Janet 5
Yellow Wallpaper, The (Gilman) 127
Young, Chic *174*

Z

Zovirax 102
Zwilich, Ellen Taafe 124

PHOTO CREDITS. Brookhaven National Laboratory: 104 right. Centers for Disease Control: 52. Department of Defense: 14, 16, 28, 130. Florida Archives: 2, 3, 9, 22, 26, 51, 60, 79, 80, 81, 143, 164, 173, 176. Franklin D. Roosevelt Presidential Library: 25. Gerald R. Ford Presidential Library: 152. iStockphoto.com: 47 right, 67, 72, 146, 148, 175. Library of Congress. 4, 7, 11, 23, 31, 33, 34, 42, 61, 62, 65, 68, 78, 82, 83 left, 83 right, 84, 85 left, 85 right, 92, 111, 116, 117, 119, 120, 125, 136, 139, 140, 154, 157, 158, 160, 172. Mattell: 98. Morguefile.com: 171. NASA: 98, 104 left, 112. National Archives: 55, 74, 135, 179, 181. National Endowment for the Arts: 122. National Institutes of Health and Food and Drug Administration: 47 left. National Library of Medicine: 45 left, 45 center, 45 right, 53, 107, 110. National Science Foundation: 103. Social Security Administration: 170. U.S. Air Force: 15, 89, 161. U.S. Census Bureau: 134, 145, 182. U.S. Department of State: 36, 88, 128. U.S. Navy: 165. U.S. Senate: 86 right, 91. U.S. House of Representatives: 86 left.

 A Golson Media Production

President and Editor	J. Geoffrey Golson
Director, Author Management	Susan Moskowitz
Layout and Copyeditor	Stephanie Larson
Proofreader	Mary La Rouge
Indexer	J S Editorial